A Bit of Delhi University

[Remembering a Bygone Era]

By

Dr. S.S. Rana
Former Dean of Colleges
(1988-2000)
University of Delhi

Originals
Delhi-110052

First Published 2016

ISBN 10: 81-8454-163-5
ISBN 13: 978-81-8454-163-2

Published By
Originals
A-6, Second Floor, Nimri Commercial Centre,
Ashok Vihar Phase-4, Delhi - 110 052 (India)
Tel.: +91 11 2730 2453 Fax: 011 4706 1936
website: www.Lppindia.com
e-mail: info@Lppindia.com

Printed At
D K Fine Art Press P Ltd.
Delhi-110052

PRINTED IN INDIA

With Love to
Bhavini, Devansh
and all the other Grand Children

Contents

Apologue

Lives of noble men or women become subjects for biographies or rather great biographies if penned by men of letters. Such works depict not only the times of their subjects but also take us through the extraordinary thoughts and deeds of these great persons. But at the same time there is enough left unsaid about a person due to inaccessible information, which is buried for ever with the subject. Never the less, such works transcend the spacio-temporal and inspire generations to come. The field of autobiography is proliferated by those written by the great and the not so great. Such works have the advantage of being first hand account of an individual's tryst with his or her times. But here also there is a good deal which though generally known to many personally about a subject, is held back in the name of personal privacy or for the reason of the fear of libel. Then there are authors, who invent episodes for the purpose of putting some meat into the narration depending on the trends of the times or to sensationalize the narrative for extraneous reasons. Such authors, though not many, are not entirely unknown to us in our own times. Travelogues and memoirs betray a similar syndrome. More over, readers in general have no interest in books of the above genre, unless either the subject/author was a rich, famous, or renowned person.

Being an ordinary person myself, therefore, the idea of writing an autobiography never crossed my mind. Similar were my views about writing memoirs or travelogues. This refrain was abiding with me, not withstanding the fact that my destiny, starting from humble origins in a non-descript village in Haryana, took me to the high echelons of Delhi University after placing me in the testing waters of shouldering the responsibility of the head of a college for over twelve years. The period of more than forty-five years spent by me in Delhi University system, first as student and then as teacher and administrator, brought forward opportunities and challenges of the kind I could not have imagined. My sincerity of purpose and fidelity to the institutional set up paid rich dividends and continued to infuse me with renewed confidence in myself and unflinching faith in those with whom I happened to work. That may also partly explain my getting appointed in repeated stints by three successive Vice-Chancellors as Dean of Colleges, which is a tenure post, co-terminus with that of the Vice-Chancellor.

As Dean of Colleges for about twelve years at a stretch, I normally observed extended hours of work in my office, a reasonable amount of which time I devoted to personal interaction with all those who wished to meet me for help or discussions regarding various matters. My visitors included teachers, students, non-teaching employees and persons known or unknown to me from outside the University and also persons whom the Vice-Chancellor would send to me for any help. I did not insist upon prior appointment and visitors were free to walk into my room. If there were any private or urgent discussions involved I would move to the side room. This pattern of working proved to be time saving, helped in forging healthy inter-personal relations and strengthened my information system, so vital in handling matters of administration. My accessibility and availability had become almost legend in the University circles, as some people would put it. I kept discreet distance from press persons who had a very active presence on the University campus, lured as they ever were by the teacher organizations quartered close by. I made no efforts to seek their assistance for enhancing my 'image', unlike some others; nor did I abhor their presence if they happened to call on me for any work. My curtseys did not allow me to be curt but I was successful in cutting short the forays of the very tricky tribe.

The long drawn out meetings of the Academic Council and the Executive Council threw up many incidents and episodes worth remembering. Very early in my career I had developed the habit of taking down notes of what I thought was interesting and important happening in the University Bodies and around me. When in the mid nineties our offices were computerized I was one of the pioneers in the administration to start using the electronic mode personally for administrative purposes, much to the surprise of my already trained office staff.

The anecdotal content of such input, by the by and bit by bit grew in volume with the passage of time. At the time of my leaving the University in August 2000 I transferred the data thus cumulated to my newly acquired personal computer. While going through the data by and by some time later I felt that it deserved to be supplemented with some more information. I also felt that the same could be shared with the University community. So the nebulous idea of publishing the material in a book form emerged. With some amount of hesitation in my mind, with regard to the possibility of adding biographical element, I started recalling my impressions and experiences during the early days of my life, spent in my village and in the rural schools that I attended. The narration thus added led to a sizable manuscript making me feel encouraged to share it at least with students of modern generation, especially those with roots in rural areas like me to see how times had changed in the interregnum and how independence and democracy have opened doors of extra-ordinary places for ordinary persons. And I believed that the urbane would also find here enough stuff to chew upon.

In this way the idea of a book rolled on. I started reviewing the data and supplementing it wherever possible or necessary. I added to it a small account of my travels abroad, though it was very routine in nature and undertaken mostly in connection with my academic or official work. The only exception being my private travel to the United States of America, in order to pay a visit to my daughter Nandini living there. Many other pre-occupations coupled with my desire to add some more to the narrative held up the completion of the press copy. But having realized that further delay may defeat the very purpose of writing this book, and thus contradicting myself I expedited the work on it, and I am happy to present it to the readers in its present form.

Since the book does not tell a story nor does it aim at treating a definite theme, it shows no loyalty to the unity of time or place. Almost every bit is a stand alone piece. Even then I have tried to put similar pieces together in a cluster. Following convention I have divided the book into chapters. The first chapter deals with snippets from my early days, spent in rural setting. The second chapter includes anecdotes from my experiences in examination and the selection system. The third chapter peeps into the working of the University system in general through my experiences. In the fourth chapter I have tried to briefly share my experiences during my foreign forays which I happened incidentally to undertake. The last chapter deals primarily with matters which concern with the disconnect between law and practice in the University as I perceived it and some other matters of procedures.

Since the book deals, in most parts, with men and matters of the Delhi University System I owe some explanation regarding certain things. I have tried to leave the facts as they came my way generally undisturbed except when giving them, where ever necessary, minor camouflage to guard the confidentiality of the system. It is not my intention here to blame any body for things going wrong any where and names have been given only if required by the context. As regards the interpretations given of various rules etc., I stand open to correction and claim no finality on the subject. My comments on the words and deeds of others may also be seen in this light. As I do not have full access to the latest rules and regulations of the University, it is possible that my comments on them may sound obsolete at places, and therefore, those may be construed accordingly.

I had the opportunity and privilege of working closely with four Vice-Chancellors. They figure in my narratives as per the context. Two of them, Professor Gurbux Singh and Professor Moonis Raza are no more in this world. While the Punjabi affectionate warmth and endearing frankness of Professor Gurbux Singh brought out the best in me, Professor Moonis Raza, for me turned out to be a loving patriarch of the University system from whom I learnt a good lot in management of higher academic administration. The Sufi saying, often quoted by him, still rings in my ears- *had tapae so aulia, behad tapae so peer, had behad donon tapae usko kahaen faqir.* I pay my deep felt homage to the sacred memory of the two.

Professor Upendra Baxi and Professor Vrajendra Raj Mehta are younger to me in age. But their towering intellectual stature in their respective field was enough to elicit my deep regard and admiration for each of them. I enjoyed their trust and warmth of feelings, rare commodities in this *kali* dominated age. I shall ever remain indebted to both of them for the consideration they gave to me personally and for valuing the advice I happened to render in various matters as an official. I had occasion to work for a very brief period of about three months with Professor Deepak Nayyar. I was impressed by his knack for focusing on development and capacity to take quick decisions after due consultation. Personally, I enjoyed working with him.

The gallery of Vice-Chancellors of my days in the University is, indeed, dotted with other greats like Professor G.S. Mahajani, Dr. C.D. Deshmukh, Professor B.N. Ganguly, Professor V.K.R.V. Rao, Professor K.N. Raj, Professor Sarup Singh and Professor R.C. Mehrotra. Delhi University deserved them all as they all deserved to be there. I was fortunate to have got the opportunity to work at such a place for quite a good number of years. It was my privilege to have loving and considerate colleagues in the Vice-Chancellor's team at different times. Professor K.D. Gangrade, Professor Abad Ahmad, Professor A.L Nagar. Professor G.K. Das and Professor Abhai Mansingh, all in their own way made me feel valuable to them. I cherish their association.

It would be an omission on my part if I do not mention here the names of my valued colleagues, Principals Mohan Lal, B.M. Bhatia, Rudra Datt, G. S. Randhawa, Raj Wadhwa, late Narinder Singh Pradhan, P. C.Verma, V. Krishnamurti, N.K Oberoi, D.S. Maan, T.S. Rukmini, R.K. Kadyan and A. Shankara Reddy with whose co-operation I was able to solve many a knotty problem in the University. Worth mentioning in this behalf are also the names of Principals of the following generation like P. C. Patanjali, Meenakshi Gopinath, Lakshmi Devi, R. M. Singh, K.P.Chhinda, B.N. Kansal, G.R Chopra, Sarla Chahal, B. S. Yadav, Ram Avtar Sharma, Sarjeet Kaur Jolly and S.K. Garg. I would not forget to express my sweet remembrance of the association I enjoyed with Professors Nirmala Jain, B. S. Sharma, A. S. Narag, A.K.Sinha, T.N. Bali, P. B. Mangla and B. S. Garg in several assignments at the

University. I must make a special mention of all my colleagues in Shivaji College and the department of Sanskrit from time to time, who were always kind and considerate to me.

I would also like to place on record my indebtedness to the four Registrars for their help and co-operation extended to me in the performance of my duties as Dean of Colleges. Shri Madan Mohan and Shri J.C. Kochar were old friends and took personal interest in my welfare. Professor Wasan and Dr. K.K. Panda were affectionate and caring. I thank them all. I feel happy to mention the willing and devoted co-operation of the members of the staff working with me in the office of the Dean of Colleges. Since the list is long I would thank them all by mentioning the names of Sarvashri N. N. Thusu, G.K. Chhokra, J. C. Sachdeva, B.B. Gupta, J.P. Khullar, G.K. Gulati, Jagmohan Singh, Chatur Singh, Chandan Singh and last but not the least my driver Kehar Singh.

I would not forget to place on record the anxious but affectionate and constructive interactions that I had the privilege to have with many activist teachers of the Delhi University Teachers' Association. Late S.S. Rathi, D.K.Sethi, N .K. Kakkar, M.M.P. Singh, Zahoor Siddique, R.R.Suresh, Badri Raina, I. M. Kapahi, Harmohinder Singh, Jaswinder Singh, Nandita Narayan and late S.K. Batra are some of the names that come to my mind.

It will not be possible for me to omit to mention here my dear friends Comdt. O.P. Rana, Narendra Sharma, and J.P Vidyalankar who would surely know something more about me from here than what they already know. Nityanand Sharma and Lt. Col. J.R. Rana, are no more in this world to-day, but their memories remain.

My wife, Chander Prabha proded and inspired me frequently to complete this work. She richly deserves my thanks for that and much more. My younger brother Raj Roop Rana has been a constant source of my inner strength. He evinced keen interest in my work and has always stood by me. He deserves my sincere blessings.

My daughters Nandini, Manjari and Monica have always been keenly co-operative in enabling me in completing this narration. They expected it to be completed much earlier. I am happy that they would now be able to read in print what they, at times, happened to glance through hurriedly in parts on my personal computer. I must thank them for the patience and interest they have shown in the progress of this account.

My son Abhinav ungrudgingly managed to fix my computer, whenever I got stuck in my work because of one or the other trouble arising (not infrequently!) in the machine. He has been keenly constructive in making many useful suggestions. He deserves a pat on the back and my hearty blessings. My daughter-in-law Anju Rani has earned my blessings by taking care of the comforts of the family along with her preoccupations with her studies and care of the two young children.

My youngest grand-daughter, Bhavini (nine years old now), who has already started looking at my books with an inquisitive eye can look forward to, at appropriate time, knowing more of me and my work through the pages of this book. She represents all my other grand children (Nikita, Udit, Mallika, Chhavi and Jai Veer) and accordingly, I assign this book to her and to the youngest member of my family, Devansh, my grandson, who has turned sufficiently smart six year young lad.

On this occasion I sadly miss my grand daughter Dakshina, who met with untimely death in the USA some time back. She had so fondly and thoroughly gone through most parts of the manuscript and had wished to see it in print.

I would like to close this part with enormous sense of thankfulness to Mr. Pradeep Mittal of M/S Originals, for shouldering the responsibility of publishing this book expeditiously.

In the end I crave the indulgence of discerning readers to overlook the flaws that might have occurred in not a fully coherent presentation like the present one.

New Delhi **Dr. S.S. Rana**
2 April 2016

I

The Beginning

Ancestry

I was born in village Saidpur in Sonepat district of Haryana, thirty kilometers north west of Delhi.. My date of birth is recorded in the school register as 2nd April 1936 but shown as 16th August 1935 in the book of registration of births and deaths maintained by the village *chaukidar* (watchman). My father, Indra Raj (spelt as Indraj) was an ordinary peasant, being the eldest of four brothers. The other three were -Devi Singh, Hari Singh and Ramkala. Their only sister was Nihali. My grand father Shiv Nath had died young, leaving my grandmother to bring up her five children. She bore the responsibility with dignity and aplomb. The earliest known ancestor of our family was Chood Singh whose known date from the records of the *pandas* of Garh Mukteshvara is Samvat 1827 (1770 A.D.). His son was Daulat (Singh/Ram?), whose son was Mansa Ram. Mansa Ram had three sons-Mohra, Sadasukh and Bahadur, the youngest. Bahadur's son was Udmi (*Udyami*), the father of my grandfather Shivnath. My grandmother Munni Devi was from village Sanaspur near Charkhi Dadri in Mahendergarh district of Haryana. My mother Saaraan Devi was from village Pahladpur in Delhi province. She was younger of the twins, the elder being her brother Gopal Singh by sequence of appearing first. I was the second child of my parents. The first, a daughter, Phoolpati had died in her infancy. After me, four children–Kitab Kaur, Raj Singh (later given the formal name Raj Roop), Narain, and Krishna - were born to my parents. Narain died an infant.

Early Loss

My father passed away in the summer of 1943 (8th of *Jyeshtha*) after suffering an attack of pneumonia, following a heavy workout in winnowing the huge stack of wheat harvest. He left behind him not only a widow carrying in her womb his last child yet to be born and three young children but also a crestfallen mother and completely shattered three younger brothers and a married sister. It took quite some time for the family to gather its bearings. However, the immense goodwill left behind by my father among the village community helped us in coming to terms with the inevitable. I was hardly nine at the time of my father's death. I knew what death was but its implications did not come clear to me immediately. My younger sister Kitab Kaur and younger brother Raj Singh were too young to understand what was happening around. But they did not fail to grasp the seriousness of the occasion manifest in the wailings of the ladies assembled at our house. I innocently watched the members of my family and relatives who were crying at the loss of not only the one whom they adored but also of a man of great possibilities. Ours was a joint family. I was the eldest child of the family in my generation. Filial affection was not confined to parents alone. It was a pool of relationships where every member had the benefit of sharing each other's happiness and sorrow.

Soul Console

While arrangements were being made for the funeral of my father I stood calm and composed in one corner of our *Poli* (a living-cum-sleeping hall for the male members of the family). Apprehending that I could suffer a shock some one among those gathered there suggested that I be made to weep to give vent to my pent up grief. Shri Ram Narain,(popularly called Gutti because of his short hight), an admirer of my father came forward, hugged me tightly and burst into bouts of wailing. I was deeply touched by the sentiments he expressed and soon a strange stirring took place inside me. I could not contain myself and wept bitterly crying Babu ho! Babu ho! Having done his job well Shri Gutti joined others in consoling me. Soliloquies of several present diverted my attention and I again composed myself. An elderly neighbour described the tragedy of my father's untimely death as God's will. Another said that God needed good people around him in the heaven and therefore, He had called my father back after only a short span of life in this world of suffering. Yet another was cursing the physician Jeet Ram of village Garhi, who had administered a wrong dose of medicine for treatment of my father's ailment. I also witnessed the customary cursing of my mother by some ladies arrived to mourn, attributing the death of my father to her ill luck. That was a strange way of consoling and getting consoled.

Last Rites

The implications of my father's death slowly started dawning on my mind. People in the village reminded me how I had to wear the mantle of my father. Suddenly I was placed into the role of an adult though still a child. My uncles transferred to me the love and regard they had held for my father. I had to rise to the occasion. Normally young children were not expected to be present at funerals. On the suggestion of Shri Chandgi Ram, a friend of my father from village Garhi, I was allowed to join the funeral procession and be present during the cremation. Clasping one hand of Shri Chandgi Ram I silently watched the last rites of my father.

My two uncles present at the time of my father's death were completely heart-broken. They just managed to hold together with the help of some people around. My third uncle, Shri Ramkala serving in the Police department in Delhi was yet to arrive. I was considered too tender to participate in the last rituals of cremation. Shri Sis Ram, a second-generation cousin of mine lit the pyre and also performed the rite of breaking the skull (*kapal kriya*) using a long bamboo stick to rule out the possibility of any *Tantric* taking away the same for nefarious purposes. I can still recall Sis Ram's figure with quivering hands and choked voice while he called out my father's name thrice before throwing the bamboo stick across the pyre as if giving up the last hope of some miracle happening in revival of the departed.Alas! Sis Ram too is not alive now.

My Father, Some Images

A few images of my life till the time my father was alive vividly come to my mind. At an early age of less than three years my father would make me learn and reproduce in style, before a fond audience of village elders, my personal bio-data including my name, father's name, the name of our village, the post office, the sub-division, the district and the province. He also trained me in learning the Hindi alphabets (popularly called *barahakhadi*) much before I was due to attend school. At school Hindi was introduced later in the fifth class as Urdu was the first language of study.

I recollect vividly the progress of the construction of the *pacca poli* which he accomplished during 1940-41 with great sense of satisfaction after precariously organizing internal resources without taking recourse to raising loan. I learnt later in life from my mother how she contributed in the endeavour by donating her golden locket (*kanthi*) besides rendering manual labour along with other members of the family. A brick kiln put up with internal resources yielded the required quantity of bricks. Some cash was raised from the sale of surplus bricks. I still remember the handicapped carpenter who did an excellent job of woodwork. Even after more than sixty years the woodwork stood sturdy and neat, a standing testimony to the artisan's craftsmanship. Undaunted by the handicap he crawled on his knees from the workshop to our house located in the farthest end of the narrow street for his daily meals, which formed part of his wages. I still remember how happy my father was when my uncle brought home a miniature cut out of Mahatma Gandhi to be placed on one of the walls in the newly constructed building. He did not grudge the placing of a cut out of the Viceroy, Lord Wavel alongside as my uncle, a government servant had brought along.

Gears Change

My father, like many others in the village in his days was a Congress man. The struggle for independence by the early forties had gathered momentum under Mahatma Gandhi's leadership. The Hyderabad *Satyagraha* and following it the quit India movement of 1942 were events of mass participation of people from the villages. My father had thrown himself fully into this movement. By that time I had started attending school in the nearby village, Ferozepur. My going to school was no special event. No one from my family had to accompany me to the school. A senior from my village, Shri Attar Singh one day took me along with others of my age like Jage Ram and Om Prakash to the school. The school master enrolled me in the first standard recording my date of birth as 2nd April 1936 without asking for any document as proof of age. Perhaps he knew better, as to what was the right age to enter in school records. My father had planned to send me to a residential *Gurukul* for studying Sanskrit after my passing the fourth standard, as in his days the language was taken as synonymous with nationalism or patriotism. After his death the plans changed and I was sent to a school at village Mandaura where English was taught as one of the subjects. It is a different matter that my father's plan for my education got translated in my pursuing study of Sanskrit, though not in the traditional system.

Umbrella Role

I recollect my father playing a willing host to the volunteers of the Congress party touring the villages during the freedom movement. These selfless men and women could be often seen keeping themselves busy in spinning *khadi* on the hand spindle. The image of a lady clad in white *Khadi*, a guest in our house gracefully standing at the gateway spinning with the spindle still lingers in my memory. My father had made it a habit with him to wear only hand woven *Khadi*. He would change into freshly washed and ironed *Khadi* clothes after attending to the agricultural operations including ploughing the fields. Though a man of modest means he maintained his sartorial standard reasonably well. The white khadi turban wrapped in layers of round pleats on his head with a frail body below gave him the appearance of an umbrella, which form he had assumed figuratively too for the benefit of the down trodden. With the services of the village washerman Kalwa he could demonstrate how one does not necessarily require costly clothes to be a well-dressed person. Similarly in matter of food my father could create an aroma of richness by a mere décor of the simple and frugal menu.

News Views

He had keen interest in keeping abreast with the current affairs. For this he subscribed to the Hindi daily Hindustan, which reached him by the evening bus plying between Delhi and the Auchandi border (our village two kilometers away was not connected by road then). Daily he used to read out the newspaper for the benefit of many other villagers gathered at our *Poli* after dinner every evening. Comments and discussions generally followed. The simple village folk had enough political sense to demonstrate. This food for thought was no less delectable. After my father's death, the assembling of people in our *poli* continued but *sans* the newspaper reading sessions. The accumulated back numbers of the newspaper served as the material for manufacturing paper mashie baskets used for keeping cattle feed, especially for milch cattle and bullocks. What a journey for the newspaper to cover- from a source of food for thought to a receptacle of cattle feed!

Aryan Ways

Some times my father would borrow a gramophone with discs of patriotic songs from his friend, Shri Chandgi Ram, superintendent of Jail in Delhi and play it to provide entertainment to the gathering of the villagers. He was a neo-literate but had picked up the Sanskrit language rather well. He was a practicing *Aryasamajist* and performed *havan* on auspicious days. He along with his friends Sardar Singh and Lachman Singh performed *havan* in almost all naming ceremonies of the new born babies in the village. I have preserved his personal copy of the book *sanskaravidhi* written by Swami Dayanand, which I consider one of my valued possessions today. But the most important legacy of my father is the family image, which he had built by setting example of personal character marked by truthfulness, integrity and liberal humanism and by a strong advocacy of the cause of the poor and the downtrodden. He stood in opposition to the policy of domination of the upper castes over the lower castes especially the *harijans* (the word scheduled caste came later in the constitution of republican India). One of his close friends was a *harijan mahashayaji* from village Katewara near our village, who stood by our family and visited us often to console the family after my father's death. It is said that one day my father had brought this friend of his for meals at our house. My grandmother was very hospitable and served the guest the best meal she could prepare. After the guest had left, my father divulged to my grandmother that his friend belonged to the *harijan* community (*chamar*). She was highly surprised at my father's 'audacity' in inviting a *harijan* for meals in the inner quarters of the house. She told my father to take away the utensils used by the guest and hand them over to him as the same had been 'contaminated' by his touch. My father's reply was that in that case he also had been contaminated by his friend's touch and as such she should also hand him over to the guest. My grandmother had only echoed the general attitude of treating *Dalits* as untouchables current in the village. Personally she was very liberal and well disposed towards the members of the lower castes. In fact she had many women friends from among them. She immediately realised her mistake and retracted indulgently saying "who would win against your logic." She indeed felt proud of her son's attitude to life and things. The gentleman in question continued to be an honoured guest in our house for years even after the death of my father.

Modest Leader

My father's penetrating logic and debating skills earned for him the position of a much sought after speaker at *panchayat* meetings at various levels. His simple life style and humility contributed towards his wide spread popularity. Several of his contemporaries have later recalled and narrated for my benefit several incidents about his ways and stances. Certain year he was slated to be one of the speakers at a *panchayat sabha*. He reached the venue and quietly occupied a seat on the foot side (*paitana*) of a cot. While the speeches were c going on an elderly person sitting on the head side of the same cot remarked that he had come to the *panchayat* only to listen Indraj (my father) and wanted to know from my father if he knew Indraj and whether he was around. My father replied in the affirmative to both of his questions. With his face lit up the elderly person asked further, "Where is he, can you show me?" My father innocently replied, "I am Indraj, sitting beside you, uncle!" The elderly person stood to admire my father all the more for his humility suspending his disbelief.

A Repeat

I found myself in a some what similar situation at a function organized at Lady Irwin College to bid farewell to Sardar Mohinder Singh on his retirement as Dean of Colleges in October 1988.

Among other officials of the University I was also invited to the function. Shri Sushil Kumar Chaudhary sitting next to me, himself a member of the Executive Council engaged me into a conversation. Without getting introduced to each other we talked about several issues, especially the role played by Sardar Mohinder Singh during his tenure as Dean of Colleges. As the function progressed he asked me if the new Dean of Colleges had been invited on the occasion. I instantly said, "Yes, of course!" Shri Chaudhary enquired a little excitedly, "Do you recognize him? Can you show me where he is sitting? I have never met him earlier!" My subdued response was, "I am Dr. S. S. Rana, and happen to be the new Dean of Colleges." Though it turned out to be an anti-climax of sorts for Shri Chaudhary, he promptly gave me a warm handshake and wished me good luck in my new responsibility. During his tenure as member of the Executive Council I found Shri Chaudhary extremely polite and constructive in approach.

Primary Education

A couple of months after the death of my father I was diagnosed of enlarged spleen. I shifted to my maternal uncle's home in village Pahladpur where I received treatment from a local *hakim* Chandu Lal. The treatment was through Ayurvedic medicines. I was cured of the ailment within three months. I made up the three months' interruption in my studies for the third standard by putting in extra work during the remaining part of the academic session. My years of primary education were literally so in the true sense of the term primary. Our class was under the charge of a very dedicated headmaster, Shri Bakhtawar Singh who introduced us not only to elementary education but also to the ways of exploring life and innovating according to the environment around us. He taught us how one can turn a disadvantage into an opportunity. Fear was another name of ignorance he explained to us. Every winter he would arrange night classes to supplement the study hours. Students were made to sit around an oil lamp placed precariously on the back of an earthen pot put upside down. The headmaster personally supervised the programme of study, which largely included memorizing and revision work. Some times we stayed on in the school overnight and at other times we used to return to our village in a group. Such forays helped us in exploring nature and negotiating difficult situations. The sky at night during the dark fortnights used to be temptingly inviting for learning the rudiments of astronomy. The *dhruva* (pole star), the *saptarshis* (seven seers), the *harini*, the *Arundhati* and the *Rohini* remaining ever close to the moon are some of the well-known constellations which I could easily recognize in the clear night sky. The Milky Way, which is called the *Akasha-ganga* spread across the sky, as if dividing it half way, was an inviting sight. The bright fortnights presented a procession of lights led by the luminous moon surrounded by twinkling stars. With the increase in pollution levels in astronomical proportions and the dazzle of artificial lights I miss the panorama of the night sky of my childhood days. Watching a show at the Birla Planetarium at Calcutta later in 1969 I felt transported to the night sky of my child hood days.

The Huddle

Life in the village had charm of its own and the natural surroundings and clean air was a major factor contributing to the healthy growth of children. The joint family system was a strong bonding institution where sharing and caring for each other not only among the members of a family but also among the members of the neighborhood or the village community as a whole was a general norm assuring emotional stability. But the system had attached encumbrances as well. In it there was little room for private personal life. Personal hygiene and cleanliness got a back seat and some kind of messiness prevailed in the matter of daily living. It was this area that our teachers addressed almost daily hammering into our minds the importance and methods of keeping personal cleanliness both of the body and clothes which covered it. It was explained to us how a daily bath could keep us fresh and alert throughout the day. The limited sets of clothes that we could afford were kept clean by a daily wash of one set in the evening to be ready for use the next day. Our teachers helped us in developing an attitude, which was important.

Inventive Innocence

On occasions some of my friends in the village and I formed a group experimenting with life in several ways. Sometimes we managed to smuggle out rations and utensils from our respective homes for a session of cooking and enjoying food in the midst of our crop fields. This was apart from the normal practice of relishing roasted grams (*holas*) prepared by putting into fire of straws a few bunches of ripe plants pulled out from the crop or handfuls roasted grains of millet obtained from pounding between palms the torn grain shields baked on top of tinder fire or even not roasted when quite raw.

It was thrilling experience sometimes to catch hold of the goats grazing in the jungle unattended and take milk directly from their udders after tearing off the protective bands (*cheeri*) put up by their owners. On our way back from the school the minor canal running between our village and Ferozepur was our favourite rendezvous for a refreshing bath in the summer afternoons. The thick clusters of salvadora (*jaal*) trees laden with fruits did not fail to engage us in daily exercise of filling our small caskets (*sindoris* and *bohanis* made of straws) with the pearl like ripe *peelu* fruits of various hues. A feature that never failed to attract us was the majestic banyan tree with its widely spread branches and the entrenched air-roots hanging down embedded in the mud heap around it serving as pillars of strength providing shade and shelter from the scorching sun to men, animals and birds alike. A feast of its fruits (*barmata*) was equally rewarding only if one could make distinction between the good and the bad ones by opening each apart for a check on the worms inside before eating. I still remember the couplet the younger children unable to climb a tree used to chant entreating parrots to drop down a piece or two- parrot! O parrot! Be kind and drop down a fruit. I promise to share half of it with you. The whole would be mine in case you happen to die (*tote! tote! barmata ger de, adha mera adha tera, tu marjaa to sara mera*. What a wish, though an innocent one ! The tall and stout *neem* tree with its leafy branches stood nearby adding its own aroma and coolness to the surroundings. Alas both the banyan and the *neem* trees are no longer there.

The young and old met the challenge of heat of the noon during summer with longish sessions of swimming and diving in the village pond. The *keekar* tree standing on the bank of the pond served as the diving board. Each one of the young children could climb the tree at the height of one's choice and take a diving jump in the pond down below. Those less enterprising would ride the back of a buffalo making it crisscross the pond for a joy ride. As side show one could see children assembled in clusters under some shady tree engaged in sculpting figurines of domestic animals and household ware from fine clay scooped out from the wet and soft ends of the rampart of the pond. That reminds me of figurines of terracotta discovered from the Indus Valley sites of Harappa and Mohenjo-Daro. Children in villages are no more seen engaging themselves in such activities. They have now sleek plastic products easily available.

The late afternoons in summer saw us tending our domestic buffalos taken out for grazing in the green pastures. We formed small groups where each one took turn for looking after the cattle to enable the others to do their homework given at school. Some milch cattle were given a special privilege of being escorted to have a feast of dark green grass in the inner recesses of the standing crops. While on such duty each one of us used to carry our own empty jute sack to serve the purpose of a mat and also to be worn like a hood to save at least the upper parts of our bodies when it rained. To get the maximum protection we had only to bend down wards. The end of the rainy season was marked by the spectacle of leisurely moving cotton white clouds heading for some unknown destination, perhaps to render account of the residual stock after showering the bulk of it down on vast tracts of the earth. I recall how we young children lying under the shade of trees watched this procession figuring out different images therein, fancied and most favoured. Later as a student of Sanskrit literature I had chance to read a graphic description of the white clouds as bales of cotton in Shudraka's Sanskrit play Mrichchhakatika. I could very well relate to this scenario from above the clouds several times while traveling by air later in life. One such occasion I vividly remember was my air journey from Chennai to Delhi.

I was to be initiated into lessons on horse riding a little later in life. However, nothing prevented our youngsters' group from trying a hand or two in managing a joy ride on the back of donkeys harnessed from amongst the many straying in the outskirts of the village. I had learnt from experience that a donkey or for that matter a horse had to be handled from its front. Any activity behind its back in most cases invited a violent kick back from the animal. The rugged and sturdy way of life was an experience in those days, rarely available to the modern generation. The foundations laid during these earlier years stood me in good stead in erecting the edifice of my life and career. I fondly remember how along with my friend Jage Ram I cherished the ambition to possess a small car, just enough for seating two and pliable on the ramparts (*jeh*) of the *chaupal* (community hall) from where our school functioned. God has been kind enough in giving us all that and much more.

Relevant learning

After passing the primary level from Lower Middle School, Ferozepur I shifted to the middle school at Mandaura where I opted for English as one of my subjects, a facility not available at most of the rural schools in our area. Summer being severe arrangement was made for my stay in the boarding house for part of the year. During the period of my stay in the hostel I learnt lessons in community living and followed a disciplined schedule. I still remember the daily evening prayer assembly where attendance was compulsory for all the hostel students. Agricultural Science was one of the compulsory subjects in the school. We were taken daily to the school farm for practical work which we all enjoyed doing. A small well fitted with a light duty Persian Wheel was there to serve the needs of irrigation of crops in the small farm. It was drawn by batches of students turn by turn. For most of us it was work with play and fun. The experiment demonstrating that water on the same surface keeps its level uniform put up by our agriculture teacher Shri Jogi Ram is still fresh in my memory. I recall having seen some time earlier Chaudhary Chhotu Ram, minister in the Punjab cabinet addressing the students at a school function at Mandaura. Short and stalky he had an impressive personality enhanced by a white turban neatly tied in round pleats. I very well remember the names of two of my very distinguished teachers- Shri Prem Raj Sharma, the headmaster who taught us mathematics and Pandit Bhoop Singh, our social science teacher. They left on my mind an imprint of their competence and concern for their students. The teacher of English shri Prithvi Singh, a fresh graduate was equally painstaking and impressive.

While we were at school a Dakota aircraft had force-landed in one of the crop fields of village Jatola nearby. Along with some other schoolmates I visited the site on our way back from school. Luckily there was no casualty among the occupants of the aero plane and neither any one working in the fields down under was hurt. However, many fields full of lush green wheat crop became casualty under the trampling feet of milling curious crowds descending at the site of the mishap. For them it was a rare experience to see and even touch an aero plane from close quarter. Some early birds considered them selves lucky for having managed to get a feel of the cushioned seats inside before proper arrangements for guarding the plane were made and restrictions imposed. Presumably no villager had claimed damages for the loss of crops in the mishap. Today it might be a different story.

Kundal School

My stay in the school at Mandaura was for a year only. Thereafter I migrated to the middle school at Kundal where English had been introduced as a subject in the sixth class. For me it turned out to be a revision course in some part as I had already covered the syllabus of English in the fifth class. The new school was at a distance of nearly two kilometers from my village. So it was convenient to commute the distance by walking to and from the school. I found myself again in the company of my old classmates whom I had left at Ferozepur. Several of them had migrated to the school at Kundal to have the benefit of studying English. The three years in school at Kundal were years of sound academic grounding. I was again under the charge of Headmaster Bakhtawar Singh who took personal interest in the progress of our class. He had got himself transferred as also his son Rai Singh (who later rose to be genetics scientist of distinction and retired as Director of the Bureau of Genetic Resources, New Delhi) to the school at Kundal. He took up the programme of night study with greater regularity and gave it more depth. A kerosene lamp fitted with chimney was arranged and we literally burnt midnight oil (kerosene is also called a sort of oil) to pursue our target. The chant of Vedic prayer which our class sang each evening without fully understanding the meanings of the mantras still resounds in my ears.

There were hilarious moments too in an otherwise serious program of study at night. The well-meaning headmaster used to reach the school premises in the early morning at about four o'clock and give us a wake up call. Some times fatigued by the rigorous routine we fled to the temple nearby with the pretext of going out for a morning walk and relished long bouts of stolen sleep. I recall how one evening some one from our class presumably tired of the evening studies programme quietly took away and threw the chimney lamp in a well behind the school. Normal search having proved futile the headmaster devised a plan of voluntary disclosure of the misdeed without the culprit having to reveal his identity. Students were asked to go into an enclosure one by one and leave the clue if any in a box placed there. At the end of the exercise what turned out was a prank played by some mischievous element. A piece of paper with a drawing of sexual overtones was all that was retrieved from the 'clue box'. Since the headmaster was the first to eye the drawing there was no chance for any of us to save the situation. We could only hang our heads in shame. Most of us saw the needle of suspicion pointing towards one of our classmates, Hoshiar Singh (who was the opposite of *hoshiyar* in studies). But nothing could be said without proof. The episode, however, ended with a positive note the next day when the lamp was retrieved from a well near the school with the help of a multipronged jumbled iron hook (*bilai*) obviously after clue from some quarter.

On India becoming free in 1947 the first language Urdu gave way to Hindi. So our first language for the board examination for eighth class was also Hindi. The level of the syllabus was quite high seen from the angle of students who were accustomed to study Urdu till the seventh class. However, the difficulty was not insurmountable, as most of us in our class had started studying Sanskrit since the sixth class. Hindi was also the mother tongue in our area. My knowledge of Sanskrit came handy in making speedy progress in Hindi. We had a common teacher for both Hindi and Sanskrit. He was a hard taskmaster who ensured that nothing was amiss in our efforts to excel in both the subjects. He believed in the adage 'spare the rod and spoil the child' and did not hesitate to make use of the instrument, though sparingly as if to justify his role in shaping our future. I remember having been the lucky recipient of such of his blessing at least on one occasion when I was in the eighth class.

Innocent Ventures

Commuting daily to and from the school on sandy paths along with other schoolmates from my village I becam,e as others, some kind of an expert in map reading and also developed the faculty of recognizing and deciphering the footprints or shoe marks left behind on the sand by any of the members of our group. The journey between our village and the school was utilized in discussing matters of common interest, exchanging local news gathered individually and story telling among the members of the group. Sometimes the traveling time was utilized in eating late breakfast or early lunch, which we used to invariably carry, wrapped and tied in ghee soaked cotton napkins (*chhaalana*) every day. At other times the delicacies of each one were pooled and relished by all present. The innocent intrusions by school children into the cash crops and gardens looking for eatables like sweet corn, peas, water-nuts (*singharas*), watermelon, cucumber, guwava, prommagnates etc. was taken as a normal privilege of students. We helped ourselves to the delicacies available without devastating the crops or inflicting any damage on them. Remnants of the harvested mustard crop fell to the lot of young enterprising children fetching them cash enough to buy *murmuras* (small sweet balls of parched rice mixed in molasses), though custom bestowed this privilege to the members of the lower castes. The community took these 'enterprises' of the young students rather sportingly. The students in reciprocation always protected the vital interests of the former. Those of us in the village who went to school and did well in studies were a little pampered lot. But it did not turn our heads stiff. I recall our humility always scored endearing us to the elders of the village.

Growing Up

As I grew up with the tide of time human emotions of love and hatred, fellow feeling and jealousy, charity and niggardliness, happiness and sorrow, friendship and enmity, piety and cruelness and spirit of healthy competitiveness touched my life directly or indirectly in varying measure. To bear with the situation when bullied and to prop up the morale of the cowardly were the sentiments which contributed to the growth of my inner strength. I tried to learn from the mistakes of others and always felt impressed with the golden middle path, the rudiments of which were explained to us by our teachers both by precept and example. We received moral education through the personal example of our teachers and also through exposure to extra-mural lectures by pious men invited to the school now and then and through relevant literature made available to us as supplementary reading. I remember one Panchayat Officer Shri Fateh Singh taking keen interest in making available good books for the benefit of the students.

Fairs and Frays

The biannual fair on Shivaratri held at village Kundal was slowly loosing its lusture due to the increasing contacts of rural folk with the towns and cities. In my younger days it still lingered to have some of the old charm with multitudes of people from different places in their colourful new clothes thronging the venue. I remember the youngsters receiving as their pocket money of two annas (1/8th of a rupee), which was however, enough for buying little bits of wares like toys or for stimulating the taste buds of the tongue with a feast at the *chaat* stall. Some kind of voluntary (not forced by any code) apartheid could be noticed at the fair. The members of the *Harijan* community by convention attended the fair towards the concluding hours when wares started selling at throw away prices.

By this time most of the upper caste members would have left for their homes or made it to the arena *(dangal)* to witness the wrestling bouts invariably organized on such occasions. People were hailed to the venue with the beating of drums. The umpire not only conducted the bouts in accordance with norms announced in advance but also enforced discipline among the crowd gathered around the arena in clusters supporting one or the other fighter through specially appointed volunteers The bouts were conducted on a specially prepared pit filled with soft earth. An unwritten protocol of wrestlers was scrupulously observed by all participants. A spirit of sportsmanship and fair play prevailed throughout the events. A peculiarity of the *dangals* was that it used to be an all male affair. Women folk were not supposed to be there even as spectators. It was not for the reasons of male chauvinism but a discreet step to save women from the spectacle of little clad muscular bodies of the contestants. Segregation of sexes in any case was a general norm in the villages those days. More over the concept of the brave knights winning the fairies did not touch Indian life. Here we subscribed to the idea of *Veerabhogya vasundhara* (the brave rule the earth). The fair held annually on the compound of the religious seat of the *Saadhs* in village Nahri used to be a bigger draw. One of the scions of the Saadh family Joginder Singh was my schoolmate at the District Board. High School at the same village. He is now known to have donned the cap of the chief priest of the religious order.

Hukka Hot

An interesting feature of the fair at village Kundal was the holding of *hukka* (Hubble-bubble) fair a day before the fair proper. Potters from far and wide participated in this unique fair offering their earthen *hukkas* of various designs and sizes for sale at reasonable rates. The village folk fully utilized this opportunity and made purchases of stocks enough to last till the time of the next fair. Villagers interested in acquiring metal *hukkas* (*pharsi*>*parsi*>persian) of a more fancy design had to visit the market in the towns or the cities.

Hukka was no mere contraption for smoking tobacco. It represented a culture and served as a symbol of communal bonding and close fraternity. It was shared among the members of the community of equals and offered as a means of hospitality to a visitor. Before joining a smoking party a stranger would invariably ascertain the communal identity of the group. Denial of the privilege of sharing a *hukka* was among the major measures of social sanctions imposed against a person as punishment for violating a social code. The material, size and design of the *hukka* indicated the standing of the owner in his community. The higher the gathering in a smoking parlour the higher the popularity it indicated in respect of the owner. Proper up keep of the *hukka* was no less important. The aroma would wane out unless the *hukka* was intermittently overhauled by replacing the stale water with fresh one and the waste deposits removed from the interiors of its various tubes with the help of a pull through. A fine and smooth gurgling sound when put into operation was indicative of the desired level of performance of the contraption.

Out in the crop fields the farmers carried their personal mini *hukkas* called *huktis*. A midi *hukka* used by a smaller group or an individual was called *kalai* (perhaps for its pot being made of nickel plated metal). *Narial* would be the name of a still smaller *hukti* if the pot was made of coconut shell (and by extension of meaning to any small (*hukti of such shape*) Farmers working in close proximity in the fields relaxed the caste restrictions in sharing the *hukti*. However, the relaxation in case of the members of the harijan community was limited only to the sharing of the earthen top fire-pot (*chillum*). Tobacco under a round lid (*thekari*) was placed atop an earthen ball trapped on the hole in the middle of the fire pot fixed on the smaller stump of the *hukka*. Continued supply of tobacco and fire tinder, were the main ingredients for keeping the smoking sessions go on and on.

Tobacco supply was hardly a problem as most of the participants kept their own stock of locally grown home made tobacco in small pouches (*kothalis*) safely tucked in the pleats of the waist band (*adbund*) of their *dhoti*. Fire tinder could be obtained from the reserved stock kept ready simmering in an ash covered fire pit called *poor* (hearth). The tinder was replenished by an additional supply of pieces of cow dung cakes buried in the ash pit placed in a queue, one touching another ahead. In case of emergency the fire places of the households in the same street were sought after but not before discreet enquiry made from the concerned housewife was answered in the affirmative. When all other sources of fire tinder were exhausted the stock invariably intact under the earthen milk pots of households became a target. Some enterprising young man would help himself by laying hand on the pot for a lump of creamy crust as a bonus. As a general norm cross street attempts to get fire tinder were not countenanced. It was however, pass if a youngster ventured out on such a mission. Showing deference to the privacy of the women folk was the main consideration behind such self-imposed restrictions.

The first few pulls at the recharged *hukka* following the customary inaugural one by the senior most present were to be made by a junior member of the smoking party for warming up (*sulgaana*), especially if the instrument had been lying idle for quite some time. He also had the responsibility to manipulate the instrument holding it from the calf region (*gatta pakarna*) and offer it to the other members gathered turn-by-turn starting with the senior most among those present. If per chance the protocol (determined on the basis of seniority in clan relationship and age) of the persons concerned turned out to be at par each one would push the mouthpiece (*nay*) of the *hukka* forward to the next man in the manner of passing a buck. Similar was the norm when the group engaged in smoking comprised only a father-in-law and a son-in-law. Here the seniority in age came into clash with sociologically higher status of a son- in- law, hence the compromise.

Food and Drinks

In my younger days village life was as a whole integrated with the environment in all its aspects. Food was based on local agricultural products. The *rabi* crops yielded the major grains of wheat and gram as the mainstay of the food items round the year and also providing some surplus for marketing. The *kharif* crop was short lived and yielded grains just sufficient enough for change of taste for a couple of months in winter. *Chapaties* made of millet flour eaten with vegetable prepared from the tender leafy stalks of mustard plants with lumps of fresh white butter on top used to be real treat. *Khichdi* made from pounded bits of millet laced with a rich serving of clarified butter was a favourite dish in every household of the village at dinner time during winter. In summer the morning breakfast constituted of *chapaties* made of wheat flour with a sprinkling of gram flour. Butter milk in abundance was available for topping up according to the needs and liking of an individual. Onion was common at any meal time as it was generally home grown.

Lunch time menu included *chapaties* made of wheat flour with some vegetable or dahl, generally of local product. In summer *rabari* (wheat flour soaked in yogurt cooked after fermentation) was a hot favourit, especially the overnight saved scruff mixed with yogurt to be savored the next morning. In case of the vegetable items there used to be great amount of give and take between close neighbours. The universal potato was easily available and stood in good stead in cases of emergency. During their spare time on sunny days in the rainy season women folk used to prepare *seviaan* from clods of thick paste of fine wheat flour placed on top of earthen pots turned upside down. Dinner time was *dahlia* (porridge) time. It was cooked from pounded bits of wheat painstakingly obtained through a long process- soaking the grains in water for some time, placing the same on a cloth spread on a cot till it dried half, pounding gently to let the crust shed off, then winnowing it to obtain fine grain, and finally vigorously pounding with a heavy wooden staff (*musal*) the grains placed in a deep cylindrical stone container (*ukhal*) to get a ready to cook stuff. The preparation was on different days by rotation sweet-mixed with jaggery, salty or just plain to be left to the choice of the individual member of the family to have it sweet or salty.

Festival time saw ladies preparing dainty dishes of *halwa purie and kheer* and the added specialties were *gulgule* and *poodey* if it happened to be rainy season. *Suhalies* were deep fried small cakes prepared from a hard thick paste of wheat flour mixed with jaggery solution. This preparation lasted months and therefore was prepared in large quantities. Youngsters would tuck a piece or two in their pockets when going out for playing to savour the same in case they felt hungry. *Laapsi* was the fat free version of *halwa* with jaggery replacing sugar as sweetener. It could be called a poor man's *halwa.*

Today village is no more cut off from the ways of life in the cities and towns. Only the sophistication is lacking, the polish is not there. Means of communication and transport have bridged the gap substantially. Proximity with Delhi has opened avenues of employment in government and private sectors to many a people in the villages. Most of them being daily commuters to and from the city serve as carriers of the latest trends in food habits from the city to the village. At marriage parties also the menu is usually a carbon copy of what one finds in the city though *laddoo* and zalebi continue to rule the roost. Of course *guldana* has almost disappeared from the table and similar is the fate of vegetable made of kaddu along with the delectable *chatni* of *kalonji* so painstakingly prepared by the local *halwai*. The aroma of smell of leaf plates and cups is missing as these have given place to the exotic items of crockery linked with status. Similarly the buffet system has taken away the sweet side of hospitality oozed at the guests by bands of young men serving entreatingly the different items of the menu at the feasts. The event today has turned impersonal and the guests hardly have a chance to relate to the hosts. The aura of getting served entreatingly is missing in marriage feasts these days. Water was the main drink. It was served sweet mixed with country made sugar. In summer some enterprising hosts arranged for ice from the nearby towns. The modern beverages had not reached the village. Consumption of liquor was rare and was discreetly kept a private and personal affair in a manner that those who did not indulge in it, hardly got a smell of it.

Marriages and Merriment

A marriage in the family or in the neighborhood or anywhere else in the village was a celebration time for all. The ceremonies and festivities were eloberate and marked by community participation and co-operation in a big way at all stages. The post-harvesting season extending from May to July was generally preferred for solemnizing marriages. The betrothal (*sagai*) ceremony preceding marriage by about a year's time used to be a simple affair but made impressive by the presence of the village elders and relatives and friends of the prospective groom. All present earned the sweets in the form of five *batashas* (small cakes of sugar) each and also a one rupee coin as a token of respect. But before deciding to go for the relationship it was ascertained that the restrictions of marrying out side the three *gotras* (viz. that of the father, the mother, the father's mother) were complied with. In the nineteenth century the mother's mother's gotra also fell in the prohibited category but had been dropped with the passage of time though no khap panchayat is believed to hsve sanctioned the practice. In the same way in the new third millennium in several places the gotra of the father's mother also has been taken out of the list.

The date of marriage was fixed with mutual consultations of the two families and confirmed by the girl's parents through a written letter called the *peeli chitthi* sent sufficiently in advance of normally three to four weeks followed by another similar letter called *lagna* some eleven or seven days in advance. Festivities at the bridegroom's place started seven to eleven days in advance of the date of marriage whereas at the bride's place the period ranged from five to seven days. This was called the period of *baans* during which the extended families and friends offered hospitality by treating at lunch all the members of the groom's and the bride's family, as the case may be, including guests if any at their respective places. It meant no cooking at lunch time for the concerned family - a substantial relief in summer, especially when the guests started arriving several days in advance of the date pf marriage. On the other hand the increased manpower helped in taking care of the additional work relating to the preparations for the marriage- community solution to individual problems !

During this period the bridegroom and the bride got the treatment generally extended to very important persons. Both at their respective places were put to a daily regimen of application of paste made by mixing gram flour with turmeric (*ubtan/batna*) and mustard oil followed by a bath amid a ritual accompanied with singing of traditional songs by the women folk of the family and the neighbourhood. All this was geared to give a sense of well-being and physical fitness to the young couple to-be. The application of *ubtan* was supposed to enhance the fairness of the skin, an indication of the preference for the fair colour of the partner. Amulets were tied on the wrist and the ankle of the groom and the bride to serve as marks of distinction and impending bonding and also signifying the medicinal efficacy of the contents in the amulets. The bridegroom, in addition carried an iron rod (*gaj*) shaped into a fancy walking stick with a tingling ring trapped at the lower end, supposedly to ward off evil. But I suppose it was meant to serve as a handy weapon in case of any emergency, say against a menacing dog or something.

Feasting Flavour

The penultimate day was a day of community feast at the house of the bridegroom. The number of invitees depended on the social connections of the groom's family. However, beyond a limit the feast was no free lunch as the system of *nyota nithar* (reciprocal contribution in cash) was in place. Under this system which still continues, financial contributions were made by the invitees on a calibrated basis to be recorded for future reciprocation. The details of receipts and payments on this account were kept in a special type of long folded book with a red cover called *bahi* and inscribed in the *mundi ior modi* script by the village *mahajan* (trader). There was no confusion regarding the number of persons to be feasted at the party. Oral lists were drawn and passed on to the village barber (*Nai*) who acted as the go-between and messenger at all stages of the marriage ceremony. He faithfully carried out the instructions regarding invitations specifying the number of persons to be invited from a family. As a general rule in most cases only one person from a family was expected to turn up at the feast. However, if any child accompanied an elder of the family clasping the latter's index finger no objection was made to the additional member. Self imposed discipline in such matters was taken for granted. Some times niggardly hosts made a physical check to ensure the adherence to the number expected at the feast. There were also some liberal hosts who left everything to the skies oblivious of any pilferage taking place under their nose with the connivance of the very persons who had been marshaled to protect his interest. The feasts comprised a very simple menu. At the bridegroom's place the main dish was *laddoos* (sweet balls) followed by puries served with some vegetable, usually of pumpkin. At the brideplace *zalebi* was an additional dish. With the access to cities becoming easier more delectable dishes started appearing at the marriage feasts. Counts (like *satpakwani* etc.) done of the items served gave an idea of the level of the celebrations. But progressively the difference between menus served in marriage feasts in the villages and the cities or towns has gradually disappeared.

On the March

The march of the marriage party was preceded by the important ceremony of *Ghurcharhi*. The bridegroom mounting a mare followed by a procession of singing womenfolk went round the village stopping at a temple or Bhumia seeking blessing and good luck. A musical band accompanied playing contemporary tunes provoking some young friends of the bride groom to break into improvised dancing. The marriage party aiming to reach the bride's place early on the day of marriage invariably started the journey the previous night. The Procession formed a caravan of bullock carts – large and small. Occasionally a horseman or two joined the party. At the center stage used to be the decorated chariot (*ratha*) of the bridegroom having two compartments- one meant for the bride and her attendant and the other for the groom. The driver of the vehicle had a separate seat ahead. Such vehicles were not common. They wee kept by selected families and were hired out during the marriage seasons at good price. A medium level verson of the chariot was the *majholi or bahli having only one compartment and with a lower height than that of the ratha.*

Merry making and fun and frolic continued throughout the journey. The occasion also witnessed some kind of competition in cart racing along mostly *kachcha* tracks. The winner earned a prize in the form of sweets. A modest band formed an integral part of the marriage party. The members of the band invariably belonged to the *chuhara* caste. The band playing choicest tunes would lead the marriage party at all outings for different ceremonies at the bride's place. The marriage party was housed in the village *chaupal* (an open door community hall also used for holding meetings of the village *panchayat*). However, some members voluntarily opted for staying with some relatives of their own in the village concerned. But they were kept abreast of all the events in the ceremonies of marriage and were supposed to join the same. The bullocks yoked in the vehicles of the marriage party and horses if any received due attention at the bride's place. Their owners got a scaled ration of grain and fodder for their maintenance and comfortable stay.

Ceremonies Galore

The bridegroom was received at the door head of the house of the bride by an assembly of women where the elder married sister or sister- in-law performed the welcome ritual by doing *arata* (*arati*) of the bride groom. It was known by the name *barauthi* (*dvara-stha*). Marriage was solemnized during late afternoon (*godhuli*- when the cattle came home raising dust through hoofs in their strides). The ceremony was *havan* centric, accompanied with vedic mantras irrespective of the denomination- *aryasamaji* or *sanatani*. *Agni Pradakshina* (going round the fire alter), *lajahom* (offering roasted rice into the fire), *ashmarohan* (toeing a rock), *dhruvadarshan* (sighting the pole star) and *saptapadi* (walking seven steps together) were essential parts of the ritual. The ritual progressed amid singing of songs of the occasion by the ladies of the side of the bride. Some of these songs contained material deriding the members of the groom's party. The latter no doubt enjoyed the stuff as it all was said in jest. With the abolition of child marriage *patrapher* (exchanging seats taking the bride to the left of the groom) slowly came to be a general rule serving as a replacement of the ceremony of *muklawa or gauna*.

Immediately after the marriage ritual was over the bride and the groom were conducted to the inner quarters of the bride's house where impressions of their palms soaked in *mehndi* and *ghee* alternatively were put on a specially prepared panel on one of the walls of the house. This practice along with several others served as a document of proof of marriage and continues to be followed though today we have better and enduring and legal tools to be used as documents attesting a marriage. Custom has its own charm and flavour even if redundant today. The crown mounted on the turban of the bride groom was retained by the bride's family and hoisted prominently on the wall of the main room of the house as if to announce to visitors of the event of marriage of a daughter having taken place in the family.

Send off Honours

The next and final day was the day of relaxation and preparation for journey back to home. Lunch on the second day was a decentralized affair. The marriage party broke into small groups, each to be feasted by a householder close to the family of the bride. The menu used to be simple though not without a rich dose of *ghee* (clarified butter) and *boora* (refined sugar). *Vida* (send off) ceremony was the major event in the afternoon. The bride's family offered gifts and cash to the groom and his family. The members of the marriage party received a rupee each as token of respect. Gradually with the passage of time a brass tumbler was added. The bridegroom gradually graduated to the entitlement to a golden ring, a watch and a bicycle. If the above three items included the gifts the marriage was ranked as the best possible settlement. These days we witness cars and many more expensive gifts finding easy passage to the quarters of the groom. After all, the pie of the cake of progress must be shared.

The side of the bride groom did not fail to play host on this occasion. Any body present there having married in the gotra/ village of the bride groom was offered rupee one as token of honour. Any son of the above was similarly treated. The ladies of such families were separately honoured by the bride groom going round the village during the evening getting sumptuously feasted with hot sweet milk.

Brother is there

Another important ceremony was the contribution of *bhaat* by the brother of the mother of the bride or bridegroom as the case may be. It included clothes for the bridegroom/ bride, the respective mother and near relatives and also some cash meant to offset part of the expenditure incurred on the marriage. Early morning hours, before daybreak next day was the time for the bride's departure for her new home. An elder of the groom's family came forward to receive on his chest the seal of recognition in the form of an impression of the *mehndi* dipped palm of the bride's mother proudly disregarding the consequence of his white shirt getting soiled by the paste of *mehndi*. Sometimes innocent pranks were played on such occasions. The bridegroom received farewell gifts in the form of modest amounts of cash from the ladies of the bride's family (*jawahari*). The amount thus collected was perhaps meant for the couple to meet any contingencies arising immediately after the marriage.

Tearful Adieu

The send off scene became poignant with almost every one in the bride's family sobbing with tears and the bride crying as if she was being carried to a sacrificial alter (are'nt we familiar with unending stories of bride burning and wife beating and dowry deaths!). There are stories of even the groom sobbing amid tears at such occasions. The ladies, especially the young girls from the circle of friends of the bride would burst into tears to the singing of the familiar song – *saathan chaal padi he mere dab dab bhar aaye nain*- our friend is leaving us, my eyes are overwhelmed with tears. Which heart would not melt at the sight of display of such tender emotions! Even the legendry *sanyasi babaji* squatting on the outskirts of a village could not abide by the contract to control his emotions on one such occasion regardless of the prize that awaited him otherwise. Even a rock would melt or the core of stone would fall asunder at such poignant moments as Bhavabhuti, the great Sanskrit playwright has aptly said-*api grv roditi api dalati vajrasya hridayam.*

Members of the marriage party (*baratis*) on the other hand. feeling proud and pampered, ready with their respective vehicles, would start their journey back to home committing themselves to a sort of competition for reaching the groom's place first would use all their navigating skills for a win. The front runners, however, were from among those who came in the rank of a brother- in- law of the bride. The winner would come and sit at the feet of the bride and utter the words "my sister- in -law shall get a son and I earn two sweetmeat balls"(*Bhabi ne beta , manne do laddoo*). Such scenes are rare these days.

These days ceremonies are cut short. Short cuts for covering distances are available. Two day's ceremonies are compressed to be completed the same day. Fast and easy availability of means of transport is responsible for the change- for the better or the worse is difficult to say.

New Home

Arriving at her new home the bride got ceremonial welcome accompanied with household rituals indicating the importance that was attached to the new member of the family. All efforts were made to make her feel comfortable at her new home by organizing some fun filled games. Feasts were organized in her honour by friends of the family. She was hardly left alone to think of her parents' home and family. A youngster of her family or a maid (a female of the Barbar's family) accompanied her as a mate. In cases of child marriages the role of the maid was very crucial, especially in protecting the virginity of the child bride till she returned to her parents' home. Some member of the bride's family, usually a brother arrived the next day to take her back a day after. The induction in the new family was made through a gradual process of frequent visits to her parental home.

In the days of child marriage the ceremony of *muklawa* was in vogue. Till this ceremony was performed a married girl living in the family of her father continued to wear a specially designed scarf (*doriya*), which indicated her marital status and the fact that she was under the protection of one more family –her in-laws. Her honour was sacred trust to the whole of the village community. Marriage was supposed to be consummated only after this ceremony. Till it happened the bride and the groom were not allowed to see each other intimately. By this time the bride as well as the groom acquired the appropriate age for cohabitation. The period between marriage and muklawa could therefore be described as the time of courtship in absentia and the time for fostering conjugal fidelity. *Muklawa* was followed by *Doosar* (second coming) when the newly wed bride brought the first and the major installment of clothes for herself and presents for near relatives, both male and female. The bride groom's sister was entitled to pick up at ill any of the garments from the box of clothes brought by the bride. Some times it became a Hobson's choice for an innocent sister- in –law of the bride. Elderly ladies of the house were always around to help in the matter. Women of the village, young and old were invited to come and see the bride and the ware that she had brought from her parental home. The visitors (only ladies) came in small clusters singing songs as they wended their way through the village s alleys leading to the house of the host. Some elderly ladies of the neighbourhood paid modest amounts as a token of having seen the face of the bride (*Munh dikhai*). The bride on her part would offer reciprocal amount as recipient of blessings from the touch of elderly lady's feet (*Pair padai*). The visitors got a modest sweet meat or a handful of boiled gram as a token of thanks.

Entertainment Train

Growing up in the village environment I got an opportunity to understand the sociology of folk entertainment. Marriages and festivals were the major occasions to provide opportunities for getting entertainment. *Saang* and *Ramlila* were the two main platforms for the purpose. The electronic media had not appeared on the scene ye,t and radio was either inaccessible or unaffordable. *Saang*, an open air folk theatre was not patronized by the discreet, particularly those who had come under the influence of the *Aryasamaj*. The medium had male characters for playing female roles. They had no compunction in presenting lewd fare. Unmarried girls were not expected to visit such venues. Women folk stole a glance of these performances either from their house tops or if they lived close by, from behind the doors open 60 degrees ajar. Even the great performer of this genre, Pt. Lakhmi Chand of village Jaanti failed to draw the puritans to his shows. The voyeuristic overtones in his *raginis* continued to bog the vedantic and other philosophical contents of his presentations. Though an intellectual giant of his days he could not occupy a reverential niche in the hearts of majority of the rural community.

The bards playing on their *saarangis* (a kind of guitar) roamed about the villages entertaining the folks with ballads sung to the tunes of their instruments slinged round the left shoulder. The ballads of Alaah and Udal were very popular items with them. Some individuals perfected the art of playing the flute. But the instrument remained restricted to personal enjoyment rather than a means of public entertainment. Conventions held frequently by the *Aryasamaj* in different villages provided opportunity for getting entertainment along with lessons in social and political awareness. The *bhajanopadeshaks* at these conventions used to be big draw. One famous name was that of Prithvi Singh '*Bedhadak*. Almost every village staged *Ramlila* on a modest scale every year during the *Dussehra* celebrations. The big Ramlila at the near by town Kharkhauda used to attract large crowds from the villages around.

The person playing the role of Ravan at this venue had become a legend. But alas! these features of rural life have almost disappeared from the scene giving place to the urban elements of entertainment, which ironically has led to alienation of the villagers from traditional moorings and folk culture without intrinsically impressing them.

Games and Sports

Games and sports were simple and did not require any equipment or specially made play fields. Girls played hide and seek and *adda badda, kolada samai* etc. Boys were interested mostly in outdoor games like *khattam khatta* (the fielding team collects the ball sent to the farthest distance through a hit by a member of opposite party standing inside a small circle) , *geend khali* (a sort of free style hockey match played between two teams, where the ball was made of rag tags stitched together in layers and the sticks were made out of tree twigs with one end crooked), *kaan- danka* (A group of players to be reached and touched by one member of the opposite party by rotation playing the chaser, who had first to reach out to a club-*danka* thrown at considerable distance from under one leg by one of the players) *gulli- danda,* , *peethu* (where a pile of bits of bricks erected by placing one upon another by one team was hit with a soft ball by a member of the opposite team in the manner of a bowler in a game of cricket leaving minimum time for the playing team to rearrange the pile. The team was out if the fielding team collected the ball and hit any one member of the playing team with it. Wrestling and *kabaddi* were vigorous games where only the physically strong ventured out to play.

Harvest Time

Participation in the agricultural operations according to one's capacity was both a responsibility and an opportunity to learn the skills, which would stand in good stead in later life. Work here was a way of life rather than a burden. Leisure and entertainment was integral to the way of life and socializing took place as a matter of routine without people making much effort. Though there was broad division of roles, especially among the male and female members of a family there were some operations, which needed the joint and concerted participation of all members–young or old. At several stages additional help was procured by hiring labour from the non-agricultural lower castes not engaged in any independent economic activity. Harvesting was one such occasion. Wages to the labour force were given in kind on the basis of a percentage of the total output of the concerned worker. In addition food for mid-day meal served at the site formed part of the wages. Such arrangements took care of the escalation in prices of grain. To work out the percentage a unit roster was used. For example, at a percentage of 8.33 every twelfth sheaf of the crop harvested would go to the labourer concerned. Continued vigil was required to ensure that no labourer indulged in the malpractice of making every twelfth bundle of the harvest unduly heavier and bulky in comparison to the other bundles. If any such practice was noticed the proprietor farmer had the right to replace the concerned bundle by any other in the lot.

Wages Won

After harvesting the wheat crop the small bundles were heaped in a rectangular stack (*chhaur/chhauri*) to be later transported to the thrashing floors (*paer*) in the outskirts of the village. In case of the bundles of gram no such stacking was done at this stage. After waiting for some time for the bundles to dry the same were picked one by one and put into a moving cart and then taken to be stacked in a heap at the thrashing floors. This method was resorted to in order to avert loss of grains in frequent handling of the fragile grain buds. In subsequent operations it became easier to sift the grain from the chaff in case of the gram crop Wheat crop however, entailed a more elaborate process to get the final yield. In case of both types of the crop the final stages saw the harnessing of several bullocks and buffalos intertwined in an array going in rounds pounding the stock. Men standing on a tripod would pour down contents of bucketfuls sent up by the supporting members. The gently blowing wind would carry the chaff away leaving the grain to heap below just in front of the tripod. A senior member of the family, usually a lady would be promptly and neatly keep the grain mound free from chaff using a broom of fine stalks (*manjan‹marjni*). The accumulated mound of grain (raas‹*raashi*) would be measured by using a standard large earthen pot (*map*).

The artisans like the black smith, carpenter, the barber, the potter, the bangle man as also the representatives of castes providing services like scavenging got their share on the spot before the grain was carted to the farmer's house. This constituted part of the barter system-'payments in kind, receipts in kind'. These days thrashers and other machines have made the job quite easy and quick and cash transactions have replaced payment in kind. But the old system re-emerges in the form of welfare measures like food for work programmes and the institutionalized system of supplying free ration to certain cadres of the armed forces as relief in contemporary times.

Agriculture and animal husbandry were two sides of the same coin viz. the village economy. Similarly grain and chaff both had equal importance. While the former was basic need for the human population, the latter was necessary for the subsistence of the cattle. Another component of the agricultural produce was the waste, which served as instant fuel, fodder, manure or raw material for several other products. Timely and abundant rains were a normal feature almost every year. Water table remained within easy reach. Sinking of wells either for the purpose of irrigation or for drinking water was not a costly affair. Greenery around the village was in plenty. Summer or winter or be it rainy season life in the village was free from tension though full of activities. All this has undergone a sea change due to the degradation of environment, resulting from hectic urbanization and industrialisation. Development has its rewards and the accompanying liabilities too.

Sugarcane Crushers

With improved irrigation facilities and adequate rainfall the farmers in our village as else where preferred to go for sugarcane crop, which yielded a rich harvest. Sugar mills being small in number and not easily accessible the farmers of the village formed their own co-operative ventures street-vise to process the crop for obtaining jaggery etc. The new cast iron Kohlu had already replaced the outmoded wooden version, which was proving quite expensive as it needed frequent repairs and replacements. The new metal machine was patented by Thomson and Myine and was lent on hire. It had three heavy rollers with gears on top and varying in size with the main roller moving with a long wooden bar (pait) fitted into a hub at its top operated for crushing sugarcane. The Kohlu was rolled by harnessing a pair of bullocks at the extreme end of the wooden bar to move round the Kohlu anti clockwise. An attentive fellow called *Muthia* would put the sugarcanes into the mouth piece of the Kohlu. A tin canister with a capacity of fifteen-kilolitres was Placed in a small pit below the out let flow of the juice and formed one unit for the purpose of determining shares of each member. A family could opt for contributing a certain number of units in one round of roster of the members. The product obtained was divided in accordance with the proportion of the units a member held. The members mutually shared the expenditure incurred on the operations.

All accounting work was orally done with striking precision and authenticity. Some times, to make the process more intensive, the system was modified so as to tackle the crop of th members turn by turn (*Bari lagana*). These small manual sugar mills were a feature on the outskirts of every village. The winter sun added charm to their otherwise hospitable milieu. The partners in a venture stacked their stocks of sugarcane in earmarked individual enclosures forming a semi circle. Thatched walls were raised behind each enclosure securing the sugarcane stack from pilferage or damage by wayward animals. Some people made cosy beds in their enclosures by spreading layers of begasse (*khohi*) and the soft dry leaves (*paatti*) of sugarcane. They were focal points of socializing among the village people joining in long drawn out sessions of smoking *hukka*. I remember having often utilized the cosy corner of such enclosures for doing my homework.

On the opposite side was located the Gurgoi (the station for preparing Gur (jaggery). The collected juice was placed in a large iron pan (primary) fixed along with another (secondary) atop a two holed cavity deep enough to hold sufficient fuel for boiling the juice. One side of the cavity was covered with a wall with a narrow hole left for intake of fuel. The other end of the cavity took the shape of a tunnel for serving as an exhaust chimney for the smoke and excess energy. The hot earthen smoke tunnel (*dhoondala*) used to be a favourite rendezvous spot where young and old thronged to beat the shivering cold. It was here that an elderly member of the co-operative *Kohlu* distributed fresh hot jaggery in lumps of small measures to all present every evening. The pigs reared by the *chuharas* got their share of the press mud (*maili*) discarded in the process of clarifying the boiling sugarcane juice with the sap of stalks of the bhindi plant used as catalyict agent to obtain neat jaggery. Carrots fixed in hooked iron rods were dipped in the boiling pan to obtain delectable delicacies. These co-operative ventures have almost disappeared with the mushrooming of large sugar mills in the nearby towns on the one hand and the scantiness of the sugarcane crops in many villages on the other. Their old world charm was not lost even to a contingent of British troops on their way to Delhi whom I recall having halted on a sunny day at one of these venues in my village way back in 1944 to relish a treat of chewing sugarcane. The crop of sugarcane is slowly vanishing from our village because of paucity of irrigation facilities.

Habitation Code

Habitation in the villages was generally in a circular form. Families having common closer kinship settled in clusters of houses located on either side of the same street, which usually closed at its convergence at the center where other streets converged with their last houses meeting back to back. Security and privacy were the main consideration for adopting such a pattern of habitation. An outer circle provided inter-street access. A person of one street entered another street only if there was any specific valid reason. Aimless intruders were not welcome in the privacy of the streets where women folk of the neighbourhood could freely meet and chat. Elderly persons of the street for whom womenfolk of the neighbourhood observed purdah announced their entry to the inner parts of the street by coughing feigned for the occasion.

Minimal Animals

The street dogs observed the street code by forging their loyalties and association with a particular street. The cats however, were more cosmopolitan and exhibited a propensity to traverse over several streets in search of their cherished food, the rats. Dogs of a street were not welcome to the dogs of another street. Fierce fights ensued if any indiscreet animate violated the well-established code. The mating season however, threw open the option to bitches to go out in search of a mate across the street. But they undertook such enterprise after moving to a common area in the outskirts of the village as if to save the householders from the awkward scenes. Younger children of innocent age had all the fun. The street urchins did not have to wait for more than a couple of months for the fun transforming into a fond celebration when the mother bitch delivered a litter of young lovely pups. From feeding the mother bitch with food gathered by alms obtained from various households (*malhotta maangana*) to providing nursing care to the young ones, they put in their best efforts. Sometimes even humans fail to receive such care from fellow beings. In spite of the efforts of the children the survival rate of the pups was not high. Thus every delivery of a bitch would add to the canine population only marginally. Hasn't nature taken care in its own strange ways to ensure the perpetuation of all species? Isn't Malthusian theory of population working among the canines too?

Street Rights

The street dogs observed their own code at meal times. They divided themselves into small groups and waited at the doorsteps of different households broadly allocated between them. They would religiously maintain a safe distance from the dining area as if observing a *lakshmana rekha*. One could learn a lesson or two from them in keeping hope and patience. No household would ignore and disappoint them. Different members of a household parceled out food portions to the animals in accordance with their propensities in such matters. Also the left over food fell to the lot of the dogs' squad waiting patiently outside the door of the house. There were occasional cases of loaf snatching from the hands of children, of course without causing any physical hurt to them. At harvest times the dogs followed their patrons to the scene of their activities in the fields. They knew well that food would be available there only. It is a different matter that as the saying goes a dog patronized by a washer man sometimes ended up missing its share of food by oscillating between homestead and the venue of washing clothes (*dhobi ka kutta na ghar ka na ghat ka*). Some dogs by their individual merit received the exclusive patronage of a family, which took full care of such animals and gave them personal names.

Late evening sessions of barking bouts was a common phenomenon of village life.. Such events sometimes got prolonged, especially when the dogs of different streets arrayed in groups against each other. Sometimes these face-offs ended only with the intervention from a member of the neighbourhood. The positive aspect of these events was the clue provided of a habitation to wayward travelers during night. At night the dogs posted themselves strategically at the entry points of the village, thus serving as watch and ward staff to apprehend any intruder during late hours. The adage 'barking dogs seldom bite' was truly demonstrated in the behaviour of the street dogs. In a rare case when an indiscreet dog ventured to take a bite at some one's leg (usually at the region of calf) the well-known antidote of red whole chilies soaked in heated mustard oil was applied on the wound. Any street dog committing the misdemeanour was isolated event and put under observation till it showed any signs of infection of rabies. In case of positive result the animal was awsarded capital punishment, which was invariably executed by a sturdy young man of the scavenger community by giving *lathi* blows to the hapless creature.

Canny Cats

Cats had a special privilege of access to the inner apartments of houses as they ensured freedom from the menace of rats. The bottom scratching of the earthen milk pot was normally their share. Some times these shrewd animals helped themselves to the unsecured milk-pots or containers of food falling in their reach. The falling down of hanging food containers is attributed to the good fortune of a cat (*billi ke bhagya se chheeka tootana*).

Cattle Care

Among the cattle, bullocks took the top position as far as diet and care was concerned. They were the mainstay of the village economy. A pair of bullocks in the family served almost all needs of power, be it ploughing the fields, pulling the multipurpose cart, drawing water from wells by various technologies like the persian wheel (*rahat*) and the pulley and for operation of several machines like sugarcane crushers, seed crushers for obtaining oil, fodder cutting units, grinding etc. Supplementary food was given to the bullocks during peak season of *rabi* (October-November) sowing. The bullocks were rested once in a month on the new moon day (*amavasya*). Special attention was paid to their hygiene. They got daily brushing massage for removal of dust from their bodies. They were made free from the menace of parasitic worms by patient plucking by their owners.

The farmers usually took *advantage* of the bright fortnights of summer months to harness the bullocks for various operations at night, thus saving the animals from the heat of scorching sun. During winter their stead was made as cosy as possible by laying a thick carpet of millet husk (*boomle*) and rubbish of begasse (*khohi*). Specially designed quilt coats were hung on their backs to protect them from extreme cold. Some times fancy silken or ornamental cotton coats adorned the bullocks harnessed in lightweight cart (*rehroo*) on occasions like a marriage procession or a joyride to a fair. Their urinations were held in specially made contraption of an earthen pot tied to a Y shaped sturdy long wooden pole (*otana*). The dung, as soon it fell from their behind was removed with the help of a specially designed shovel made of wood. The farmer did not mind getting up even in the mid of night to perform such jobs. Old animals were not assigned the asylums (*goshalas*) but were given proper care which they amply deserved after silently and faithfully working for their owners. However, there was always a distinction made between the gentle 'holy' cow and the quarrelsome and treacherous buffalo.

Deepaavali time was a celebration for the cattle also, especially the bullocks, which were laid off from work. People fondly decorated them by stamping their back and flanks with marks of orange coloured solution (of *agru* or *geru*) and by hanging around their necks ornamental necklaces (*gaandalies*) made from strips of stalks of peacock feathers artistically woven around a string with bunches of multi coloured cloth waste procured from the obliging village tailor. To make things more musical *tallies* (jingle bells) of conical shape, bunches of *ghungroos* (round hollow balls of brass with a slit at the bottom and a bead of iron placed inside) and *chaurasis* (about two inches wide leather bands with several strings of small bells fixed thereon) were also tied around their neck. The bullocks indeed deserved such attention and pampering. The female specie of the cattle was decorated with *patias* (necklaces made from stems of peacock feathers) and *ghantaalies*. Some people fondly painted the horns of their cows red. The jingle bells in their case were cylindrical as different from those meant for bullocks which were made of brass in conical shape. The holiness of the cow, the giver of the progeny and milk has been justifiably celebrated since time immemorial in our country and has been a swear word among the rural communities. *Govardhana* (Cattle wealth) or Gobardhana (cow dung wealth) Puja was a pointer to the usefulness of the cattle.

But alas! the cow is a much neglected specie today. The buffalo which superseded the cow as a milch cattle is itself on the wane of its one time prominence. The machine age has led to the decrease in the utility of the cattle power and hence to its neglect. There were times when the number of cows in the village ran into several hundred. Every neighbourhood of the village required the services of a cowherd called *paali* (‹*gopalaka* i.e. cowboy) assisted by several young boys as his apprentices. The *Paali* received a fee in cash (*beet or veet*) in respect of each animal put under his charge for the day. Each herd developed its own identity and loyalty by the operation of the law of association. Buffalos and cows during their milk giving seasons were not placed in these herds called *lenhdas* as the owners could not risk the loss of the day's milk to their enterprising calves if let loose. Further, the rough and tumble of the life in the herd would tell upon the health of the milk yielding cattle. The female calves grew up as a bonus without much effort on the part of their owners.The male calves (*katras*) of buffalos either died young for want of nourishment or headed for the butcher's flock to be beheaded in due course of time for serving the needs of food for the non-vegetarian communities elsewhere or in the best cases to be exported to areas where such animal stock was used in ploughing the fields and pulling the load carts. But the bull calf (*bachhra*) of a cow had a different destiny for the reason of its value in the agricultural economy. It got the best fodder nourishment and care till it showed a prominent hump as one of the signs of attaining youthful vigour. Its induction as an animal of draft was made after getting it castrated. In the initial stages it was treated with indulgence and given lighter work, its senior partner sharing the major load. The yolk of a plough or a cart was so oriented as to pass only the desired amount of load (through *naad*) to the young partner called *Naria*. It slowly grew into a youthful *Naara*, then *Baihada* and matured as *Bulad* (ox) to be labeled as *Dhaanda* in the evening of its life.

The bullocks of each household did not fail to receive their respective names. The names were based on either colour (*dhaula, leela, laakha* etc.) or after some part of the body (*seengla, bheenda, jhoonga, khoonda, laanda, teekala* etc.). There were cases, though rare, of aggressive bullocks which were kept tied when not harnessed to a plough or a cart. Such cattle were handled only by senior members of the family carrying a stick in hand as a warning to the animal against any menace. The buffalo stock too had its classification. It was *kaatadi* at very early stage. As a grown up adolescent it took the label of *katia andpassing through the state of a Jhotadi graduated into a jhoti* (buffalo heifer) ready to mate for the propagation of her specie and gradually landed into the mainstream class of *bhains* or *mhains› mahish›mahishi* of Sanskrit. In old age it was given the name *of kholan* to finally earn the sobriquet of *dhaank*, not a flattering one. A *roondhi* (having acutely curly horns close to either temple) buffalo was considered better than the *bheendi* (with its horns hanging downwards, each forming a simple curl at the end) one. The normal yield of milk from a buffalo was about ten kilolitres per day (milched twice). In exceptional cases it could be more than twelve kilograms with a yield of nearly 800 grams of ghee (clarified butter). A buffalo would be classified as *Baakhadi* when it yielded very little milk (which, of course, had greater fat content).Beating of oxen was not seen favourably by the community and anybody indulging in such an act was frowned upon. The bullocks were kept neat and clean and were cared well by applying *khurera* (steel scrub) and brush.

Keeping a horse was a luxury, which only a few families could afford. Our family was one of the three in our village which possessed a horse each. I do not recollect when and how I started riding it. I certainly remember how I fell from the back of the galloping horse when one day it suddenly halted to avoid bumping into a bunch of women going ahead of it carrying loads of water pitchers on their heads. I received only superficial injury as I glided slowly on to the ground over the mane of the horse. There was another accidental fall from the back of the same horse. My eldest uncle Shri Devi Singh nursed an injury for months as he had fallen from the back of the running horse one day while negotiating a sharp turn on the way. The family replaced the horse with a docile mare, which served the needs of conveyance for most of the male members of the family. Even small children felt comfortable with the mare. Our family had to handle frequent requests from other villagers for landing the mare hire free for their joining a marriage party in style. With the passage of time the aging mare gave place to a bicycle to serve the needs of conveyance. And with it I moved to Delhi to join college.

The village *banias* falling in the traditional *vaishya varna* restricted their occupation to trading. agriculture and animal husbandry described as their vocations in the ancient *varna* system were nowhere near them. They were suppliers of the non-agricultural products to the villagers and were economically well off to buy grain and milk products for their needs from the farmers. Pickle, especially mango pickle was a common item with enormous volume of sale carried through barter system in cash starved village. Money lending also fetched good returns to the *banias*. In rare cases they reared a cow or a buffalo to be comfortable in their needs of milk and its products. With the increasing trend of urbanization the village *banias* started migrating to the cities and towns for taking advantage of opportunities for greater business enterprises. Delhi has sucked into its vortex many a migrants from this class from far and wide. A very few of this community now live in the village. Their place has been taken by other communities, especially the Jat youth who could not make progress in education and were compelled by circumstances to adopt the new profession to beat unemployment.

Beast of Burden

The members of the potter's community reared donkeys, which served the needs of their occupation best i.e. transporting large volumes of good earth excavated from specially identified spots in the outskirts of the village for the purpose of making pottery. It was less costly to maintain donkeys. They were beasts of burden and could tread on precarious paths where carts could not be easily taken. Clods of earth extracted from the beds of dried ponds were better brought out by employing the services of donkeys. They could also be used to carry small quantities of load for which a cart would not be economical or desirable. They could ply equally well on all kinds of track or even on rugged passages. Sometimes I heard the stories of enterprising businessmen hiring donkeys for the purpose of smuggling grain or other prohibited wares across the countryside avoiding normal roads or tracks to dodge the intercepting officials.

Hand in Hand

Among the *harijans* the *chamars* reared cows or buffaloes depending on their financial position. In most cases they took responsibility of rearing a female calf (*katia*) of some farmer against fifty percent share of the value realized from the sale or repatriation on turning a milk-giving cattle. Apart from disposal of the dead cattle, skinning them and making hides for footwear they collaborated with the farmers in the intensive agricultural operations. In some cases a member of this community would enter into partnership of twenty percent of the produce by undertaking all the responsibility of a ploughman of the land owning family. I recall Bharatu *chamar* having worked in this capacity for our family for some time after the death of my father.

Scavenging Scourge

The *chuhras(now harijans)* specialized in rearing pigs, goats, sheep and chicken in addition to their basic work of scavenging and disposal of animal dung by making cakes to be used as fuel when dry by their patrons (*jajman* – a reminder of *yajaman* in relation to the *purohit*). The dried dung cakes were stored in mounds (*bitoda*) of different shapes and size. These mounds were secured from rain by application of thick layer of dung plaster on the outer surface and covered with a specially designed thatch made from agricultural waste. A small opening was made in the mound for taking out dung cakes for daily use of the household. An unusually wide opening showing signs of removal of substantial quantity in an emergent manner indicated the stock having been used as fuel for cremation of a person who might have died in the family.

As the villagers were strictly vegetarian in their food habits the *chuhras* took their poultry and piggry products to Delhi, which had a huge consumption of such products. A number of chicken were put in two separate netted containers slinged on either side of a bamboo pole to be carried on the shoulder of the entrepreneur heading to the market. Pigs and hen thrived on the food available on the dunghills of the farmers heaped on the periphery of the habitation. The pigs in addition feasted on the night soil scattered all over the out skirts day after day. A unique way of scavenging indeed! A scene of cock crowing well on his own dunghill was not a mere cliché as I could see it actually happening often. The shepherds took their sheep and goat herds out in the village jungle where enough green vegetation was available for meeting their needs. With the passage of time all these things have disappeared from the village scene. The *chuhras* (scavengers) indeed have made very little progress in spite of the programmes frequently announced by the state for amelioration of their lot. Many of them have migrated to the cities in pursuit of menial jobs. But even in the cities they continue to live in poor conditions, still deprived of a fair share in the wealth of the nation. They are passive recipients of occasional favours showered at the time of elections.

Fodder Feed

The household cattle received a fair share of care and attention of their masters for the reason of their vital role in the economy. Proper arrangements for animal fodder were invariably made in time and appropriate supplementary diet was given wherever required. Green fodder was kept at hand as far as possible throughout the year. Dry fodder was made delectable by moistening and adding a dose of gram flour or a solution of *khali* (the remnant of mustard seeds after taking out oil). During the sowing season bullocks received additional diet containing lots of fat administered down their throat through a *naal.* Slabs of *saindhava* salt were placed in the fodder trays of the bullocks to enable them to make up for the loss of salt and water through perspiration during intensive cultivation in summer. They were taken to the water bodies as frequently as required for quenching their thirst. The buffalos were bathed and cleaned followed by a sumptuous splash in the village pond normally twice a day. In summer time the buffaloes lingered on submerged in water for hours with their necks afloat intermittently for breathing. A milk giving buffalo received the supplementary nourishment in the form of boiled cotton-seeds and grams mixed in the fodder. Such diet went to increase the fat content in the milk that they yielded. I recall having associated myself with all the activities connected with the rearing and keeping of cattle. Whenever free from school I shared the responsibility of fetching loads of bundles of animal fodder from the fields and participated in the process of cutting the same in small bits through the manually operated hexing machine. Rainy season offered a bonus in the form of green grass (*loonjha*) ready for use as animal fodder, especially for the buffalos. One could see armies of females returning from green pastures with heavy loads of grass on their heads.

Wild animals gradually disappeared from the environs of the village where very little forest land was left. An odd hyena or leopard could be sighted far away in the wastelands. With the conservation of forest land for agricultural purposes wild animals became a thing of the past. Fox and Jackal lingered to live in the thin jungle of the village for some more time to ultimately seek new pastures. The same happened in the case of deer. Their flocks of the early forties either fell prey to the hunters' guns or found their habitat in zoos in the cities. I recall having seen British troops passing by our village near about the days of the end of the Second World War. The villagers felt bad when the British guests went hunting for the innocent flocks of deer out in the crop fields.

Birds Flutter

Birds formed an important part of the ecological system of the village. Though forestland was being progressively conserved for cultivation there were enough trees and vegetation in addition to the crops to attract and offer shelter to different types of birds. Several water bodies around the village and in its outskirts with shady trees standing on their banks invited large number of birds for resting and nesting. Small mango groves here or there in the fields witnessed the cooing and wooing of birds of all kinds. Vultures flying high in search of their favourite food – the corpses of cattle abandoned by cobblers after skinning could be often sighted. The kites and crows in search of worms presented a menace especially to the children. Other smaller birds with their sweet chirping provided music like fare to the ears. It was only when the crops showed signs of grains in their buds that these small birds turned to be pests.

As the time of ripening of the crops neared farmers made special arrangements to ward off the pests. Platforms were raised in the middle of the crop area with wooden props from where a watch could be kept by some member of the family, usually a grown up child or an elderly person not required to participate in intensive physical work elsewhere. Two types of sling like contraption made from strings with one end getting thinner and thinner were used to facilitate the efficient performance of this duty. One was a simple whip like thing (*taat*), which produced a sound of a cracker when played with a jerk. The sound scared the birds away from the crop. The second (*gophia*) was a combination of the first type with provision of a container weaved in the middle of the whip to serve as launch pad for the missiles in the form of dried small clay balls. This contraption was used to throw at a designated target the clay balls creating at the same time a sound of a cracker to scare away swarms of sparrows and other birds, intent on devouring the crop. The job combined fun with fulfillment of duty. Parrots were abounding in the groves of fruit trees like mango, guava and apricot. The chilies crop was another favourite target of parrots. It required continued vigil to protect this crop from the menace of parrots which were very fond of plucking away the green chilies and throwing away the same after taking a few bites safely perched on the top of some tree nearby. I remember having attended to such duty of warding off the parrots in my younger days quite often. This crop has slowly disappeared from the scene in our village and others in the neighbouring area. The scene of vast spreads of red chilies on the vast tracts out side the agro markets of Narela and Sonepat is a thing of the past now.

Pests and Pets

On several occasions in the late forties I was witness to the devastation brought on standing crops by the swarms of locusts descending like dark clouds on the crops. Villagers used to flock to their fields with whatever implements they could lay their hands on to ward off the menacing pests. Mercifully this phenomenon no more recurs. The dove, the quail and pigeon continued to prosper in the village. As vegetarianism did not give rise to hunting, there was little threat to their life. An attack on pigeons by a cat in their unguarded moments was an exceptional happening. The cats were content with their favourite diet - the rats, which were available indoors on the floors of houses in sufficient quantity. Further milk being in plenty the cats had their share of the drink-both patiently earned and stealthily managed. Moreover the delicacy of the partially burned creamy crust (*khurchan*) retrieved from the core of the earthen pot placed on simmering fire tinder for boiling milk (*kadhawani*) legitimately belonged to the cats. Peacocks were in plenty and were zealously protected by the village folk, perhaps in continuity of the tradition set by the Maurya king Ashoka, who had progressively prohibited the slaughter of the bird even for the purpose of preparing delicacies in the royal kitchen. Peacock is our national bird, the herald of the rains with its sweet pea-hoo notes and majestic dance. Autumn was the season for peacocks to cast away their matured feathers from their tufts. Occasionally I used to go into the fields in the early mornings with my friends in search of this much sought after commodity. Of these the *chhad* was a bit longish piece with a small circular tail end, while the *chanda* was somewhat shorter with a round shaped tail end beautifully crafted by nature to look like a multi coloured moon whence it derives its name. It has the honour of adorning the crown of Shri Krishna especially when he is depicted in his *Balakrishna* or *Gopikrishna* attire. Apart from their religious and decorative use these feathers are known to have medicinal properties. Application of pounded ash obtained from burning these feathers is believed to cure external head injuries speedily. Another bird associated with rain time was the sandpiper (*titihari› tittiri*). It is believed that a hen-sandpiper having laid her eggs on dried bed of a water body would frantically fly hovering over the spot making shrill sounds on sensing rain. Her notes were taken as a panic call for saving her eggs from being inundated by rain water- a good omen for the farmers awaiting the onset of rains. Some birds like herons, cranes, ducks and drakes preferred to settle at water bodies away from the village in the pasture lands. With the disappearance of these water bodies one hardly comes across the above species of birds these days in the village environs rendering them not only colourless but also barren and lifeless.

Freedom and Partition

I was studying in seventh class when India got independence in 1947. India was divided into two countries-India and Pakistan. Panjab was partitioned as Muslim and Hindu (including Sikhs) Panjab. Memories of the news of celebrations and misery brought by communal riots on both sides still conjure mixed feelings of joy and sorrow. Horror stories emanating from across the border reached our part of the country with the worst distortions creating a climate of hatred between the two communities who together had fought many a battles against their common foe, the British. Iqbal's famous national song of *Hindustan Hamara* was sold for a song of communal divide. Human life was at its lowest value. Even animals were not slaughtered in the manner of the genocide that took place in the name of religion.

Carnage Caravan

Accompanied by a few friends grazing our cattle on the bank of the nearby canal one day I saw for the first time a dead body floating in the water going for some unknown destination down the stream. It did not take long for such bodies to accumulate and get clogged on the head of a lowly bridge. It was a scene of horror for us. We called our seniors and managed to get the dead bodies pass under the bridge. Later I learnt that the dead bodies were a result of revenge killings of some Muslim residents of the nearby town while they were negotiating the canal to reach another habitation considered to be safe for Muslims. I vividly remember the euphoria and frenzy prevailing in the rural areas seeking to eliminate the Muslim population in the towns close by. The provocation was the sordid tales of killings and molestation of Hindu women by the Muslim diehards in Pakistan. News of train loads of Hindu dead bodies reaching Indian territory had spread far and wide. All kinds of weapons were being locally manufactured and put on trial runs. Almost every able-bodied youth managed to acquire a weapon of offence and join the surging crowds, laying seize of the Muslim town of Kharkhaudah a few miles away. It is a pity that the *jagirdar* of Kharkhauda, Meharban Ali and other members of his family could not be saved in spite of the pleadings of some kind souls in the crowd.

The only redeeming feature was the protection given to the members of the Muslim families of our village under the cover of converting them to Hinduism. Kalwa *dhobi* (washerman) and the family of Baru *Teli* (oilman) were among them. However, the 'converted' Muslims opted to leave for Pakistan as soon as the government provided them safe passage. I remember Major Maan Singh (father of my friend Om Prakash Rana) of our village escorting one of the transport vehicles on this mission. It is a different matter that these migrants to Pakistan did not get a dignified life in their new country as could be gathered from communications from them received in our village some time later.

On the Indian side it did not take very long for the refugees from Pakistan to attain a dignified status in society. They made an impact on the economic, social and cultural life of the country by their grit and determination. I was to learn a lot from this component of society later during my educational and professional career. The label 'refugee' did not stick to them much longer which unfortunately still continues to cling to the Muslims of Indian side who chose to flock to Pakistan. Even today they are contemptuously addressed as *muhajirs* (refugees). The tragic event of Mahatma Gandhi's assassination took place on 30th January 1948 at the hands of Nathuram Godse, a fanatic Hindu from Maharashtra. I could not fathom the depth of the tragedy at that time. Communication in the village was slow. There was hardly any media access. The tragic news reached our school through verbal distortions. But by the by our teachers explained what loss the country had suffered in the death of Gandhi ji. He laid down his life for the cause of communal harmony especially Hindu Muslim amity.

Under the Open Sky

Our board examination for the eighth standard had concluded by the end of April 1949. Till the results were declared I as other friends of the same class got immersed in the family work of agriculture and animal husbandry. But the new feature of life during the couple of summer months was staying in the agricultural fields during nights. After having early dinner most of the young boys settled in their respective fields to guard the crops from stray cattle and animals like deer and others. The herds of deer used to descend on the newly sprouted crop of sugarcane. So we were required to keep a strict and close vigil on the fields. During the early part of the evening the boys of the neighborhood would come together for socializing through singing, story telling and having fun through various games. Some seniors would always be there to inspire and guide the gathering. Such night outs instilled in me a sense of fearlessness and love of nature. During day also most of our time was spent in the fields. We used to fathom the depth of the wells around by jumping from their parapets and reach their bottoms to retrieve certain items previously thrown in. Remaining afloat in a deep well for considerable time was our favorite sport. The youngsters meticulously managed the water drawn through the Persian wheel for irrigating the crops combining work with fun and frolic. Discovering and plugging rat holes in the water channels was an exciting endeavour. The tak tak sound coming from the languish landing of the brake lever on the gullies of the rotating smaller wheel turn by turn could be heard from a distance indicating that the wheel was in operation. The buckets in the chain mounted on the larger wheel emptied in the tray below one after another resulting in a gushing flow of water which fell in a deep reservoir from where it was directed to a desired channel for irrigation. The fresh water thus obtained was cool in summer and warm in winter responding to the needs of the environment in conformity with nature's law. Such scenes are not common these days. Pumping sets, operated with electric power or diesel have taken the place of the Persian wheels. The synergy between man and animal power is missing. The community character of the facility is no more witnessed. Water table having gone down considerably, tube wells fail to deliver the goods in some places. Danger of vast tracts turning into waste land is looming large.

High School Nahri

The results of the middle school examination (1949) were declared in due course of time. I passed the examination with quite high marks in the first division. Search started for a good high school for admission to the ninth class as Kundal School was only up to eighth class level. I had heard about the reputation of D.B. High School Nahri situate a couple of miles away from my village. Some seniors also advised me to join the Nahri School. Master Shri Chand of our village was a teacher in the same school. So I along with my friend Jage Ram joined the Nahri School. Our teachers were among the best in the area. Master Gurmukh Singh laid for us solid foundations in Mathematics. Master Charan Singh with his amiable manners and pleasant countenance was a past master in turning Social Science teaching into a pleasant discourse The Sanskrit teacher Beg Raj Shastri was a picture of sturdy scholarship with soft speech. The Hindi teacher Kapil Dev Shastri (elected to the Lok Sabha in 1977) was erudite but very demanding. At times he could be harsh beyond imagination if the students failed to come up to his expectations. His idea of discipline transcended to the area of dress code and hair style. I had to pass through a trying time for some period in keeping my hair free from application of oil to hoodwink his code. The Head Master, Shri Shiv Lal was a caring and affectionate teacher. Having noted the academic profile of some of the students of my class he arranged to lodge a couple of us in his residential quarters, which he had not chosen to occupy. This provided us an environment for serious study as compared to the conditions in the large dormitory where we were initially lodged. The food in the hostel was simple but wholesome. Use of *desi ghee* on the scale of a minimum of two seers per month was a normal thing for almost every one of us.. The students residing in the hostel supplied wheat flour as per the consumption quantity determined per student. Normally the students took their meals in the kitchen sitting in a semi circle around the fire place in front of the cook, who would toss and pass on to the students turn by turn chapattis fresh and hot from the furnace. The weekly sweet dish usually served on Sundays included *kheer* prepared by cooking rice in buffalo milk with full cream. As a supplement I purchased every day half a seer of milk from a village household. Morning walk, light exercise, participation in games kept me in reasonably good health. Along with other friends I visited my village on Saturdays to return on Mondays. During rainy season these visits meant wading through waist deep water for parts of our journey. On such occasions we carried spare clothes safely tucked on our heads. These days there are no rains of the magnitude of rains in olden times. During the two years in school at Nahri I made good progress in my studies. The two of us, Jage Ram and I living in a common cubicle had a healthy competition and got inspiration and help from each other. Both of us have maintained the same spirit till this day.

The center for our matriculation examination was fixed at Sonepat. Our class was lodged in the premises of Jat School. My uncle had got a new dress made for me to wear on the occasion. I visited Delhi to collect the dress from him. It was during this visit (March 1951) that I boarded a train for the first time. The dress included a pantaloon of Khaki drill and a blue poplin shirt and a pair of oxfordblack leather shoes. The examination was a smooth affair and I did well in all the subjects. It was during my stay at Sonepat that I happened to notice for the first time the coloured ice-cream bars hawked by young boys from the refugee camps. I do not remember having tasted any at that time.

Second Stage

There was a long break before the result could be declared. The prospect of future was nebulous. Joining the family in the agricultural work was the normal alternative for the time being. As I was born and grew up in the same environment nothing was unusual or strange. Boredom would not settle as there was always something to be done. Age wise I had entered the sixteenth year. Talk of my marriage started coming to my ears through my younger aunt. By that time I had gathered sense enough to think of marriage only after completing my education and taking up a career. When I learnt of a party visiting my family to explore the chances of a matrimonial alliance I conveyed my views to my uncles in no uncertain terms. All the members of my family respected my views and the subject did not crop up again until I was prepared for it.

Destined to Delhi

I passed the matriculation examination (1951) in the first division. My uncle had decided that I get admitted to Punjab University Camp College in New Delhi, which functioned during evening from 5.30 to 9.00. Studying there I could do a job during the day if required. Along with my friend Jage Ram I came to Delhi in the New Police Lines where my uncle was working as Law Instructor for the new recruits. He deputed a staff member of his to accompany us to the Punjab University (Camp) College located at Mandir Marg (then called Reading Road after Lord Reading, one time Viceroy of India). We all travelled in a police bus up to the Central Secretariat from where we walked the distance on foot. The admission counter of the College was open. The clerk at the counter checked our documents and offered the combination of History and Civics instead of Economics and Mathematics desired by us. Since there was no choice we accepted what was offered and paid our dues. We were happy to become collegiate with any combination of subjects.

A room built of mud bricks with a thatched roof was rented for the two of us in village Malikpur near New Police lines. There was not a single *pakka* house in the village, nor a *pakka* street, nor an electric connection. We fetched water from a community tap nearby. All this was however, nothing unfamiliar to us. We had lived in such conditions or still worse in our own village. We made our own arrangements for cooking our food. At times my uncle with a friend or two would join us and help in our newly acquired vocation. Himself not satisfied with the arrangement my uncle hired a room for us in a new colony, Jawahar Nagar. It had electric and water connections and was located on the main road dividing the area from Kamla Nagar. Jage Ram and I commuted to the College on one bicycle. One day a traffic constable on duty at the junction of Panchkunyan Road and Reading Road (now Mandir Marg) stopped us and deflated the tyres of our bicycle as a punishment for violating the rule prohibiting double riding. We had to walk only a few yards for getting air pumped in the tyres at a roadside vender's point. As almost every student commuted by bicycle there was always a scramble for finding parking space at the College premises. Size of the class rooms being smaller in comparison to the number of students we had to jostle with each other for a seat. Attendance was almost hundred percent and motivation level of students high. Teachers were competent, experienced and prompt. Many of them had migrated from Pakistan after the partition. Sardar Niranjan Singh was the Principal. Among my teachers were- Ramji Lal, D.D. Gupta , Kishan Singh, Mago and Durga Das in English, Devraj Chanana, K.N. Bhatnagar, Raghu Nath Safaya, Manohar Lal Chaudhary and B.K.Wali in Sanskrit, Randhir Singh, R.K.Bhatia, M.C. Mehta and Kul Bhushan in Political Science, R.R.Sethi, Balraj Madhok and B.R.Grover in History.

Green Scene

After a couple of weeks of the start of the session Jage Ram chose to migrate to CRA College Sonepat. I was left to live alone in the room hired at Jawahar Nagar. I cooked my own food and organized my time to concentrate on my studies. The medium of instruction for subjects other than languages was English. I developed the habit of making notes from good books on all subjects. My stay at Jawahar Nagar did not last long. My uncle was transferred to the Police Station on Tughlak Road where a staff quarter was allotted to him. I shifted to the staff quarter along with my uncle. It was entirely a different kind of place. There was no humdrum of a market place. The green and serene surroundings added to the charm of the area. Long walks in the mornings and evenings along the wide and clean roads filled me with an invigorating feeling. I discovered the beautiful Lodi Gardens during one of my exploratory walks in the neighborhood. I used to go to the Garden occasionally to study under the bright sun in winters and under the shady trees in summer. What is a posh colony Jorbagh now was open ground and venue for the burning of the effigies of Ravana and his kinsmen on Dussehara. During my walks along the green vistas I would fondly read the name plates of the dignitaries living in Lutyen's city.

My studies progressed quite well. I passed the intermediate examination (1953) in the first division. My friend Jage Ram and other classmates of school days did not fare as well as their academic caliber was. Jage Ram passed the examination in the second division and others either managed to just pass the examination or simply failed to pass the same. My performance in the intermediate examination was the talk of the town (as they say) in my village and elsewhere in the area. I got an opportunity for selection for a job in the Imperial Bank (now State Bank of India) on the basis of a competitive examination, which I had taken a couple of months earlier. By the time the result of this examination was declared I had taken admission in the B.A.Honours (Sanskrit) course. My uncle also favoured my continued foray with education. He took pride in my excellent performance throughout and supported me ungrudgingly in spite of the financial burden he had to bear. His happiness knew no bounds when he learnt about my result in the graduation examination. I had passed in the first division obtaining second position in the University in the honours stream in my subject Sanskrit.

In Delhi University

My uncle and I were quite clear that I should continue to pursue postgraduate studies. It was also decided that I should move to Delhi University. To begin with I sought admission in M.A. history in St.Stephen's College. I was selected for the course. But when I went to submit my marks sheet the admission in-charge Dr. P.L. Bhatnagar (later Vice-Chancellor of Rajasthan University), having noted my level of achievement in Sanskrit Honours, took me to the Principal, Dr. Raja Ram. Dr. Raja Ram persuaded me to change to Sanskrit M.A. His argument was that I was bound to do very well in Sanskrit and that there were better opportunities for the bright students in Sanskrit. Feeling convinced I opted for the change as advised.

Around this time I came into contact with Shri Ram Sarup of village Jharauda in Delhi State. Shri Ram Sarup introduced me to Dr. Sarup Singh, then Vice-Principal of Kirori Mal College. Though his wife Shrimati Sushiela was distantly related to my mother's family I had never met him before. The meeting with Dr. Sarup Singh turned out to be very cordial and inspiring. He showed keen interest in my educational programme and advised me to change to M.A. History as he did not see any future for me in Sanskrit. He even offered to help me to get admission in his college in case there was any difficulty in getting the same done at St.Stephen's College. I came back pepped up by the conversation I had with such a sympathetic senior academician. I pondered over his suggestion but decided to continue in St.Stephen's College with Sanskrit as my subject. The choice of college dominated over the choice of subject. Kirori Mal College was yet to gain the reputation, which it acquired later under the leadership of Dr. Sarup Singh. Thereafter I did not meet Dr. Sarup Singh before he spotted and accosted me in the verandah in front of my classroom in the Arts Faculty building one day. I was apologetic for not having met him regarding the change of college and course. Smiling at my discomfiture he said that he knew why I had decided not to change the college. After all St. Stephen's was a college where any student would like to go. He blessed me to do well wherever I was and encouraged me to be in touch with him for any help or guidance.

At St. Stephen's

My days at St.Stephen's College were not eventful. As M.A. classes were held in the Arts Faculty building there was very little interaction with other students of the College except in the moral lesson classes during the first year. However, I had the opportunity of meeting several students during my participation in sports and visiting the library. Omprakash Rana, Dalel Singh Mann and Ran Singh Mann were at St. Stephen's in my days. I won the College cycling championship and represented St.Stehen's in the inter-college championship in 1955. I missed the winning slot after leading till the last lap in the National Stadium as a result of slip of my foot from the paddle of the bicycle. I was awarded the Ground Colour by the College. Vijay Kapoor, Pushkar Johari, Vinod Dikshit, Raghubar Dayal, Vivek Sagar Minocha, Satish Chawla,K. R.G.Nair, Virbhadra Singh, Jai Pal Singh, Balbir Singh and Harsh Kumar were some of my other contemporaries. Satya Bhushan Yogi and Vedgya Arya were my teachers. Both gave personal attention to my academic growth. Yogi ji trained me in making the best use of the library. He also taught me interpretative skills. His emphasis was on developing the faculty of independent thinking. I still remember how he spread the pearls of wisdom in teaching Yaska's Nrukta not withstanding his predilection for reeling out etymologies of umpteen number of English words from Sanskrit originals. I can not forget the debt I owe to him for getting me on his own account any number of books that I needed from the College library. Arya Sahib was friendly and thorough in his teaching. His brevity and preciseness always impressed me. He was equally erudite but did not wear his scholarship on his sleeves.

Arts Faculty

Life at Arts Faculty was quite fulfilling. I had the opportunity of studying in a co-education class for the first time. We in a class of twenty were divided equally into male and female students and represented as many as seven colleges. Nityanand, Jai Pal, Narendra Kumar and Pritam lal Aneja were among my classmates. Among the girl students were Yajnaseni Sahai, Prabha Mathur and Ayodhya Gupta. Shanta Mohan, the daughter-in-law of Daulat Ram Gupta discontinued midway as did Rita Langar and Madhuri Iyer. Our Head of the Department was Dr. N.N. Choudhuri, a loving and soft-spoken patriarch. The other teachers drawn from different colleges included S.N.Shastri and Ramashraya Sharma (Hindu), Ganga Ram (Ramjas), Satya Bhushan Yogi (St.Stephen's), Sadhu Ram (Kirori Mal), Ram Gopal and Satya Vrat (Hansraj), S.N.Nigam (Delhi/Zakir Hussain), Sushila Ambike and Sita Bhat (IP). Our batch of students brought about a more homogeneous atmosphere in the department. College loyalties dividing the students gave place to homogenizing departmental loyalty. Staff and students went out on a picnic together for the first time in the annals of the department. The lorry(bus) of Miranda House was hired to take the picnic party to Okhla barrage. Several cultural functions were successfully organised. Boys and girls mixed freely inside the classroom and outside. All students co-operated in making inter-college functions arranged by any of the colleges successful. I remember having participated in a recitation competition at Indraprastha College. It was my first experience of the type.

Break in Journey

I was on my way to attend interview before the Service Selection Board (SSB) at Bangalore in November 1956. I was a student of M.A. at that time and had no inclination to join the army at that stage. However, I made preparations and set out on the journey to be present on the event. During my travel I made friends with one Mr. Ahuja who worked in the Employees State Insurance (ESI) office at Secundrabad. He was returning from Punjab along with his wife. He persuaded me to break journey at Hyderabad/Secundrabad and visit places there, especially the famous Shalarjung Museum. As I had a day spare I accepted the invitation. When the train stopped at the station it was early morning. A light drizzle added to the pleasantness of the weather. Some friends of Mr. Ahuja received us and took us to his office in Secundrabad in a car. I was given a room with attached bath in the office nearby. I quickly got ready and after breakfast set out on a trip of the Museum. After several hours of speedy viewing of the exhibits (missing many in the process) there I went to see the Usmania University. I found the Arts Faculty building quite impressive. On the Campus I also happened to meet a few groups of students who were quite friendly.

Lost and Found

Evening had descended and I thought it was time to return home. But which home! Where to go! I had forgotten to note down the address or even the name of the locality of Mr. Ahuja where I was staying. I had changed several buses during the trip of the city and could hardly trace the various routes I had taken during the day. It was getting literally dark and I was in real dark about my whereabouts. I was to catch the train next morning to proceed to Bangalore. The danger of missing the interview loomed large on me. I composed myself and headed straight to the railway station from where I thought I could figure out the route to the place we had been escorted to in the morning. I made progress in identifying a few features of the route but only for a short distance. As rain had frosted the windscreen during most of the morning journey I had not registered much of the features on the full route. I thought of reaching the nearest ESI office where I could inquire about Mr. Ahuja's address. I hired a cycle rickshaw and reached a factory. The owner there knew that one Mr. Ahuja was working in a ESI office at X place. Reaching X place I learnt that Mr. Ahuja had been transferred and was working at Y place at the moment. Happy with my progress in tracing Mr. Ahuja I took the rickshaw to the final destination of the day but only to be surprised once again. I found Mr. Ahuja's house locked. An elderly Mohammedan neighbour informed me that Mr. Ahuja had gone for dinner at a friend's house and would return home after watching the late night film show. The gentleman offered me his quarters to sleep for the night. Taking note of my hesitation in accepting his offer he guided me to reach the dispensary near by where the friend of Mr. Ahuja, a doctor could arrange things for me.

Another surprise awaited me. A peon who lived in the other twin city quite some distance away had taken away the key of the room where I was staying. The doctor made arrangement for my night stay in his examination room. Mr. Ahuja woke me up next morning. All arrangements for my onward journey had been made. After breakfast Mr. Ahuja escorted me to the railway station. I boarded the train well in time and reached Bangalore, my heart filled with gratitude for Mr. Ahuja.

Averse to Army

The candidates had hardly settled at the SSB venue when we were called to appear before the Board for personal interview. After a few preliminaries the Board President asked me what I wanted to be in life. Without waiting for a moment I replied that I wanted to be a professor in a University. This invited the natural question from the President that in that case why I was there to attend the interview. I innocently remarked that the free travel warrant had prompted me to undertake the journey and make a tour of that part of the country. The president had a hearty laugh. The other members of the Board joined him. What followed was a brief but cordial conversation with the President about my subject and my other interests. He also wished me to fare well in the tests that were to follow in the coming couple of days. I realized that I had burnt my boats but still I did not spare any effort on my part to do well in the tests. The result was a foregone conclusion. I returned to Delhi after halting at a couple of places including Mysore, Bombay and Gwalior. It was clear to me that I had to concentrate on my studies to do well in the examination to be able to get into the teaching career.

I passed the M.A. examination (1957) in the first division and joined teaching in S.G.T.B. Khalsa College in January 1958. In between I had attended a training camp in field archaeology at Ujjain. I served in the Institute of Post Graduate (Evening) Studies and Hindu College briefly before settling in a permanent post in Shivaji College in 1961.

NCC Training

As a lecturer of Shivaji College I was trained and commissioned as Lieutenant at NCC academy Purandhar in January 1963. Shortly after I had joined the three month course external emergency was declared in the wake of the Chinese attack on India. I had done very well in all areas of training except firing arm. My performance in firing came low as I had not got my eye sight corrected by wearing spectacles. My close association with a group from Punjab, who got unpopular with the authorities for some unknown reason was also responsible for my getting lower scores in personal assessment by some officers. In spite of the above handicap I was ranked at number twelve in the order of merit of one hundred and four officer cadets. Teaching is universally accepted as a noble profession. But it is equally true that noble people are found in all professions. We do not expect military men to behave the same way as civilians do if the assignment is teaching.

I recollect an incident during the period of my training as NCC officer. Irritated at the slow progress of many of the officer cadets an officer of the rank of Captain punished several of them by giving them a run with their rifles lifted above their heads. It did not end here. He herded all the trainees at one place and gave homilies using such phrases as- I will chase you from pillar to post-I could not care less etc. Officer cadets were visibly disturbed. At a hurriedly convened meeting it was decided to boycott dinner. The Chief Instructor, Major Sable got a wind of the decision. He immediately arranged a meeting of the Officer cadets and persuaded them to lift the boycott. In good humour he explained the diction in the military language. After every thing was settled the major took a long breath and said –you all are fools! Right in the soldier's language, of course ! Every one laughed and the episode ended with a happy note.

The Refresher

Later in 1966 I attended a refresher course at same Academy where I stood first in the course. I would like to recount here the exciting competitive overnight route march of about ten kilometers on the later occasion. Our course was divided into two companies. I was commanding one of them. Every one was in battle geared uniform and carrying the allotted personal rifles .I carried a sten gun. In addition each squad of ten or eleven trainees carried a light machine gun. The 'troops' marched out of the head quarters on the Purandhar hill top after break fast to reassemble at some distance from the foot hill for a break for lunch. Several aspects of military studies including map reading, recce, patrolling, laying ambush, mine clearing etc. were taught through demonstration. We reached the spot of our night halt well before sun set.

Immediately on our arrival there competition started for fixing our individual small tents all complete with making of beds and laying a snake trench around each. Rations had been supplied to all but cooking had to be done by different squads individually. This was also a competitive item. The referees were busy allotting marks to individuals and the formations separately at different stages. Discipline during night was also under assessment. Crucial stage was the last lap of the exercise next morning . Each squad was to leave after giving a time gap of ten minutes and reach a point at the head quarters on the hil top. Leaving a few kilometers of level fields the climb on the hill was steep. The winner squad was to be determined on the basis of time taken counted from its starting time till its last member makes it to the finishing point. It was an exercise in learning to pull together mutually helping each other. I inspired the members of my squad to go fast at a steady pace till the march was through the plain and climb the steep distance steadily with proper breathing rhythm. My squad was the last to leave. We marched ahead in a team, reached the foothill only a little behind lingering members of some squads. As the climb on the hill started I took charge of the rifles of two of my colleagues who were a little older and appeared to be vulnerable. This done I did a swift climb of the hill and reached the finishing line first of all. I realized soon that my reaching there alone would not suffice for a win. I rushed back to give a helping hand to other members of my squad and this way managed to take all my colleagues at the finishing line in a spectacular manner winning the first prize for the squad and a special award for myself. At the end of the course I was adjudged as the best officer. The Board of Honour maintained at the academy carried my name for record. A colleague of mine who attended a similar course at the Academy a couple of years later felt proud to read my name there.

Days with Army

In summer of 1967 I was attached with an army unit located near Poonchh in Jammu and Kashmir for a month. I got the opportunity to have a closer feel of the functioning of the army at the border. One month's stay with the army made me tougher and fit. It was exciting to climb high peaks where our forward posts were located. The training included firing of all arms. It was quite a thrilling experience to fire rockets and throw grenades on marked targets.

But let me not forget to mention the warm welcome which I received on reaching Poonchh. With me there were some twenty NCC cadets from colleges in Rajasthan. All of us were received at the Pathankot railway station by a young Sikh officer. A medium size army vehicle took us to our destination making stop over at Jammu, Rajourie etc. for breakfast and lunch respectively. It rained heavily as we traversed the last lag of our journey. Our host turned out to be 6 Garhwal Rifles, a valiant unit which had many battle honours to its credit. A young Major escorted me to the double fly tent which was to be my home for the coming thirty days. He straight away asked me what would I have for a drink-Whisky or Rum? He looked at me in disbelief when I replied that a hot cup of tea would be ideal for me. He did not argue and went back. In a few minutes a cup of steaming tea was served. A little later dinner was served in my tent. I had a sound sleep during the night. The next day started with a meeting with the Battalion Commander Colonel Quinn and other officers at breakfast.

I found Colonel Quinn and other officers very warm and hospitable. It took several days before they all got convinced that I was a teetotaler. Trough out my stay with the unit I got special treatment especially in matter of food and drink. My cadets were equally well looked after. I cherish the time spent with the army. During our one month's stay with the Army we got an opportunity to fire arms like Grenades and Rockets. We were taken to several pickets located on peaks with very high altitude. It was a rare experience to have climbed these at heights of up to nine thousand feet from the sea level.

After serving Shivaji College for eleven years I joined the department of Sanskrit in Delhi University as Reader in July 1972 only to return to Shivaji College in 1976 as its Principal. In 1988 I was appointed Dean of Colleges of the University where I continued with renewed appointments till August 2000 a couple of months after Professor Deepak Nayyar had taken over as the new Vice-Chancellor. Both of my stints – first as Principal of Shivaji College and then as Dean of Colleges of Delhi University- were quite exciting and fulfilling. I have recorded some of the episodes of those days later in this volume.

Matter of Heart

I had been keeping reasonably good health apart from occasional fever or cold in spite of the fact that I was more or less a workaholic through out my life. Even in my sixties I felt agile and carried out my duties with enthusiasm of a young fellow. I got the shock of my life when I was diagnosed of angina in May 2000 and was advised to go for bypass surgery. I had gone to Thiruananthapuram on 13 May 2000 as observer for the medical entrance test conducted by the Central Board of Secondary Education. I stayed at the Center for Development Studies. Next day I visited the designated examination center along with Professor Nagpal of the department of Slavic Studies. Both of us went round the various rooms on four different floors. I did not feel any difficulty in climbing the stairs in two different wings. After the examination was over and the records were sealed I made for the railway station to catch a train for Kanyakumari.

I had visited the place earlier in 1956. The scenic beauty of the dark green landscape made my journey to Kanyakumari enjoyable. The train passed through thick groves of coconut trees leaving the habitations on the sides. I stayed at the Vivekanand Ashram, a place having a serenity of its own. The community mess of the ashram offered simple and inexpensive food but I had to bear with the excessive dose of salt in all the dishes. The next morning I headed for the spot at the beach from where the rising sun could be watched. It did not take me long to reach there. I occupied a vantage point on a mound of rocks. The reward came soon. The sight of the sun like a golden ball emerging from the dark waters and spreading crimson colours on the horizon was bewitching. I took some photographs and then descended on the beach to have a feel of the waters of the mighty Indian Ocean stretching its arms, the Bay of Bengal and the Arabian Sea as if to welcome the tourists.

After paying my obeisance to the grandeur of nature I resumed my return walk to the Ashram. I had hardly covered a few hundred meters of distance when I felt fatigued and was sweating. Realising that the gradient was reverse I slowed my pace and also stopped intermittently for rest. A cool breeze blew helping me to cover the distance without much trouble. From the Ashram I took the shuttle bus and reached the point from where I could take a steamer to reach the Rock Memorial. There was a long queue winding its way in circles all over the market place. I joined the queue without any loss of time and saw it getting longer and longer every minute. Dr. Sarabhai and another teacher of Hindu College, Dr. Negi joined me. It did not take us long to graduate to a senior position in the long queue and reach the launching platform to ride the steamer. The Vivekanand Memorial was beautiful and a fit place for meditation. Its architecture merged with the rock at the base and integrated there above. The colossal black rock sculpture of Thiruvelur an icon of Tamil identity erected later gave company to the memorial breaking the monotony of isolation. We spent an hour at the memorial and then returned to make the journey to Thiruananthapuram.

Dr. Sarabhai and Dr. Negi went out for shopping. Having taken my breakfast I proceeded to the bus station. There was no vehicle in sight to take me there. Though the sun was hot I chose to walk to the place. But I felt tired and exhausted. There was some time left before the scheduled bus was to leave for Thiruananthapuram. I had a cup of coffee in the station canteen and relaxed there for some time. Dr. Sarabhai and Dr. Negi also arrived. We all took the bus for Thiruananthapuram.

A cool breeze was blowing. The large open windows of the speeding bus gave the passengers full advantage of the fine weather outside. I felt quite refreshed. On reaching Thiruananthapuram I did some shopping and had my delayed lunch before leaving for the Kovalam beach. I spent some time at the beach. Walking towards the bus stop a short distance away from the beach I felt pain in my chest. I stopped at a wayside stall for a cold drink. I got well and boarded the bus heading for the city. It was dark by the time I reached the city. Oblivious of my ailment I stopped on the way to do some shopping and reached the guesthouse to retire for the night Till morning next day I did not experience any discomfort

White pepper was the only item I had not been able to procure out of the list I had carrie from Delhi. So I decided to devote half of the next day available to buy the item from the market. I boarded a morning bus and reached the market place. After doing reconnaissance of the market for some time I spotted the right shop and bought white pepper. Happy with my enterprise I proceeded to return to the guest house when a signboard of a North Indian restaurant caught my eye. I entered the place and had my breakfast, which included oily preparations with liberal dose of salt. A short walk to the bus stop gave me chest pain, which subsided every time I stopped for breathing in a bout of fresh air. All the signals received so far did not deter me from my resolve to break journey at the state secretariat for some photography. I winded up my photography session quickly as the sun was very hot. I entered a telephone booth to ring up the new Vice-Chancellor to greet him on the day of his joining duty. My call materialized but the V.C. was not in his seat as he was in a meeting. However, my message reached him. In a few moments I experienced severe pain in my chest. I sat down and had some cold water. The pain subsided in a couple of minutes. But I got worried. I took a three-wheeler and went straight to my room in the guesthouse. I asked the driver to wait till I packed up my luggage.

Suspecting least of harbouring angina I reached the airport well in advance of the reporting time. The check in counter had not opened yet. I put my luggage in one corner and settled in a chair in the lounge. Unfortunately the air conditioning system was not working due to power failure. The vantage seats under the emergency fans had already been occupied. It was hot inside the lounge. I started having considerable pain in the chest once again. It persisted even after my taking cold water repeatedly. I wanted to believe it to be result of gas or something. Problem of heart was far from my thoughts. But I took discretion as better part of valour and called for a doctor's help. The airport doctor immediately attended me. She gave me solbitrate, disprin and a diuretic. The medicines had their effect and I started feeling better. In the mean time my other colleagues from Delhi including Dr. Sarabhai and Professor Nagpal and Mrs. Neelu Khanna arrived to take the same flight, which I was to catch. All of them felt concerned about my welfare and took good care of me till I reached home.

Facing Fact

On reaching home I took the episode lightly and was casual about it. But my wife and daughters to whom I narrated it the next day insisted that I should consult Dr. M.D. Gupta, a family friend in the first instance. I went to Dr. Gupta in Hindu Rao hospital. He advised me to get admitted immediately as he found abnormalcy in my ECG and my blood pressure was found higher than reasonable limits. My meeting with the new V.C. had been fixed for five p.m. the same day. Promising to Dr. Gupta for reporting to him for admission in the hospital the next morning I came back with prescription of some medicines to be started immediately. I had half an hour's meeting with the V.C. I did not say anything about my illness to him.

Next day I reached the hospital. Attendants were waiting with wheel chair for my arrival at the appointed time of 9.00 a.m. But I went up straight to the ICCU unit on the first floor and introduced myself to the doctor on duty. The doctor was surprised that the patient for whom a wheel chair was waiting on the ground floor has managed to climb the ramp to reach his unit. In any case I was immediately put into a bed in one of the cabins in the ICCU. Soon Dr. Gupta and the senior cardiologist Dr. Mittal also arrived. I was given the best possible medical care and was discharged from the hospital after three days with two week's package of medication and advice for complete bed rest. I was advised to visit the hospital after two weeks for a follow up check. I was still under the illusion of my being in perfect health. I did not adhere to the advice of the doctor to have complete bed rest for some days at least. The very next day I was in my office. In retrospect I must say it was fool hardy on my part to have ignored the advice of the doctor.

True Status

My son Abhinav, however, did not believe in experimenting with the matter of heart. The very next day he took me to Dr. S.K.Gupta, the eminent cardialogist of Apollo hospital for a check up. He got my Echocardiogram done which was followed up by angiography the next day. The result showed blockages of up to 90% in three different arteries and the advice was for bypass surgery. I was still not ready to face the reality. Promising to report later for surgery I got discharged from the hospital. Dr. Ashok Chauhan took me to Dr. Naresh Trehan in the Escorts Heart Institute for a second opinion. Dr. Trehan after examining the film of angiography done at Apollo also advised surgery. He even reserved June 1st as the date for surgery, which I could postpone as per convenience. I was looking for excuses to avoid surgery. I cited my daughter Monica's programme of going to Canada a couple of months later, which could run into uncertainty if I was sick and lying in bed.

Moreover, I was trying to convince myself of the availability of other therapies to reverse the blocking of my arteries. I took shelter under the claims made in this behalf in the writings of Dr. Dean Ornish and Dr. Vimal Chajjar. I also liked to believe in the powers of Yoga for dealing with the cardiac ailments. My consultations with the famous cardialogist, Dr. Khalil Ullah helped me to decide against surgery. But at the same time I did not get persuaded by him to go for angioplasty. A long and relaxed meeting with Dr. Gambhir of the G.B. Pant hospital was fruitful to me in understanding the implications of various therapies. His advice, though very feebly rendered, was in favour of going for surgery.

Fond Hope

Going by my instinct that I would pull through the problem with alternative means like dietary control and yogic practices I decided to abandon the option of surgery for the time being. Shri C.B. Singh of the Yoga Center of Gandhi Bhavan of the University initiated me in the technique of yoga. I also started performing *havan* daily with the chanting of *Mahamritunjaya* mantra. My tea was now made with the powder of dried bark of *arjuna* tree, which was available in the University garden in abundance. I started taking food devoid of fat and salt. Nine months of rigorous regimen of the new life style brought about tangible improvement in my condition. An echocardiogram done in March 2001 at Siddharth Diagnostic center of my former student R.P.Malik showed my EF as 45% from the 36% shown in the first check at Apollo hospital last May. I visited Pune for a week in connection with some UGC work. I felt quite agile and thought that I was out of the woods as far as my health was concerned.

Complacence took the place of caution and care. Dietary control was thrown to winds. Yogic exercise or even morning walk hardly found place in my routine now. In a couple of months I started feeling weak and exhausted even after mild exercise or brisk walk. Still I was hoping against hope expecting a miracle to happen to cure me of my ailment. The marriage of my youngest daughter Monica in November 2000 pepped me up temporarily. I felt like a debtor after paying off his debts. But the relief I felt turned out to be temporary. On 25 th December I attended Maharaja Surajmal martyrdom day function organized by Surajmal Memorial Education Society at the Samadhi of Maharaja Surajmal in east Delhi.As Secretary of the Society I devoted better part of the day in working in connection with the function On 26 th December I drove all the way to Faridabad to attend a seminar organized by Shri Sukhbir Singh Dalal, a former IAS officer from Haryana. I can now recall that I was stretching myself oblivious of the status of my health.

Signals Start

The call bell of my luck rang on 27th December. At three a.m. at night I woke up from sound sleep experiencing writhing pain in my chest. I immediately gulped a tablet of aspirin and managed to move to the room where my son was sleeping. I woke him up and told about my problem. He gave me a tablet of solbiterate, which I put under my tongue. He also called a doctor, who checked my blood pressure. It turned out to be on the higher side. I got relief from pain in half an hour's time. But it became clear to me that surgery was unavoidable and any more complacency could lead to serious consequences. I therefore decided to go for surgery immediately. My wife was away in Roorkie with her youngest sister Sulbha. I informed her on phone that I was going for a check up at the Escorts Heart Institute and there was no cause for panic. Co-incidentally she had already planned to return to Delhi the same day. I got admitted to the hospital on 27th December 2001. Angiography was done on 28th and open-heart surgery was performed on 29th of December by Dr. Jugal Mishra. Every thing went off well and I came home on the 10th of January 2002. My recovery was quite satisfactory and I gained normal health speedily.

My Uncle

My uncle Ram Kala passed away on 18 September 2003. He was brought to Jaipur Golden hospital on 16th after three days of ailment of severe headache initially accompanied with vomiting. CT scan and MRI revealed hemorrhage in the brain region. He was getting disoriented and restless. As there was no other way out he was operated upon on 17th.The doctors told us that the operation was successful. We waited the whole night. But my uncle did not gain consciousness. Another MRI test during the night revealed a fresh hemorrhage. The doctor opined that after the first operation not having helped another operation, to be much more complicated than the first one was not be advisable. Next morning he suggested that we could take the patient home. But all family members preferred to let the possible medical care continue at the hospital. However, putting the patient on a ventilator was ruled out. My son Abhinav and I had hardly returned home when we received a call from my cousin Devraj informing about the passing away of my uncle. Both of us with my wife rushed back to the hospital only to find my uncle a bundle wrapped in a white sheet and placed in the hospital van.

We took him to our village Saidpur, the place of his birth and his last station for over twenty years after retirement from Delhi

Police in 1983. Devraj drove his car ahead of the van to serve as an escort. Devender, grandson of my uncle, drove the car that followed the van as if it were a vanguard. I was with him in the car. The caravan passed through the route so familiar to my uncle. The last return journey from Delhi was different from the many he had undertaken during his long tryst with Delhi. Did he come to Delhi to pay goodbye to the city, I wondered! It was his last journey in this world. His mortal remains were consigned to fire at the time when the sun was retiring from its journey of the day. All men and women gathered to pay their last respects to my uncle felt his death was a personal loss to them. Though he had crossed the age of eighty years his agility and helpful nature had created for him a special place in the hearts of all who came into contact with him.

I personally felt orphaned for the second time. During the sixty years after the death of my father my uncle did all he could humanly do to make me forget that I had lost my father. The financial support he extended to me pales out in comparison to the love and care that he accorded to me throughout. The years, 1951 to1957 were the years of my educational growth when I was in his closest company. He kept me under his caring wings and inspired me to go from height to height. Communication with him was through the use of very few words. Most of the time, we would understand each other's mind through some mysterious channel. A part of my life has gone. I will miss him as long as I live.

Father Figure

Some images of my uncle's life come to my mind. He was 12 years older than I. My memory goes only up to the time he had already left school and joined police service. Perhaps he had hardly turned eighteen when he joined Delhi Police. By that time I had joined school. I remember him visiting home on short leave. Once or twice I saw him in uniform also. My mother used to feel highly scared of the police uniform even when her own brother-in-law donned the same. More than the Khaki it was the red herring on the turban, which was like a red rag to John Bull. I also remember how he was sought after by many in the village whenever in trouble at the hands of the highhanded ways of the police of the British days. He was on duty in Narela police station when my father expired. He rushed home immediately on receiving the terrible news. He started wailing on reaching the outskirts of the village. Several people joined to console and escort him to our house. Very soon he realized the tragedy was not restricted to him or the members of the family alone. It had affected the village community as a whole. In course of time he settled back in his duty and focused on helping the family.

I can recall his picture of fondly helping me wear new clothes - a light blue shirt and khaki shorts – and a new pair of oxford black leather shoes which he had bought for me when I was in the fifth standard. Every time he came home he showed interest in my progress in studies. I was a student of sixth class in 1946. My uncle took me to Delhi on the occasion of *Kartiki* for the holy dip in the Yamuna. I stayed with him overnight at the police station Kotwali in Chandni Chowk and joined other members of the family who had separately traveled in bullock carts up to Tripoli (near R.P.Bagh). At that time he was serving in the traffic department. I had the opportunity of having a ride in the buses of Gwalior Transport Company, the pre-partition ancestor of the Delhi Transport Corporation. Shri Tara chand (alas, he passed away in August 2013 at 91), a friend of my uncle from our village and an employee of the company escorted me. I still remember the first meal I had with my uncle in the police mess which by quite sumptuous one.

My uncle always impressed upon me the need to keep good health. When I started living in hostel in high school he arranged to send extra money for buying my daily milk. He got me a new dress of shirt and pantloon on the occasion of the annual examination for the 10 th class held at Sonepat. I had personally visited him at Delhi to collect the clothes. It was then that I traveled by train for the first time. Delhi presented a different scene this time. Large number of refugees had reached here from Pakistan struggling to settle down. Young children hawked their wares to earn their daily bread. The bazaars were abuzz. Anxious but enterprising faces thronged the hubs of the city. Colour had replaced drabness. Hope appeared to be heading for success. My uncle also took me to his rented room in Chandrawal (near Kamlanagar). On arrival there we discovered how a candle left burning the previous night on a table by default inside the room had consumed itself not before piercing a hole on the top. It was sheer luck that had saved the house and the neighbourhood from what could have been a conflagration.

The Migration

Back to Sonepat I found the town transforming into a new settlement of people undaunted by the adversity of being plundered in Pakistan. The natives were accommodating and helpful, though curious. With years gone things have changed beyond recognition. Sonepat is now a district city, largely of prospering Punjabis well integrated with the locals in speech and stance and in turn passing on to them several of their ways of life, especially food and dress. The Punjabi salwar and kameez have been willingly and fully adapted by Haryana women. The turban, formerly a common headgear among people of Haryana and Punjab has some vestiges among the former (restricted to mostly elderly rural folk, while the latter with the exception of Sikhs, of course, have completely abandoned the head gear. There are several other sartorial changes among the village youth, especially girls.

II

Testing Times

Strong Hold

Holding examinations on schedule and timely declaration of results has been one of the major strengths of Delhi University. The administration is expected to deliver 100 % efficiency and examination is taken as zero tolerance zone as far as mistakes and irregularities go. The administration has always tried to adhere to this goal and the teachers have generally co-operated to guard this reputation. Even the so called examination boycotts at different times have been observed more in form than in substance. Leakage of question papers has occurred in very exceptional cases and that too in predictable areas, especially where responsibility is diffused. The collegiate system of the University is very strong and well organized for the conduct of the annual examinations or entrance tests for admission to various professional courses. It was this image of the examination system of Delhi University, which proved a catalyst in my deciding to accept the responsibility of performing the duties of the Controller of Examinations as OSD in 1985.

Wall Collapse-

It was the time when the University was in the midst of a crisis of sorts. The wrong application of keys to some series of answer sheets in processing the results of the medical entrance test of 1984 brought about highly distorted results. Naturally it gave rise to a hue and cry on the part of students who were in disbelief of their unexpected result. The revised and corrected result failed to satisfy people. The Academic Council appointed a committee to under take directly under its supervision a manual checking of answer sheets. The manual checking generally confirmed the revised computerized result declared by the University. But a very unfortunate case of a patch implanted on the scores of a candidate came to surface during the manual checking. Through systemic scrutiny of records and checking of possible linkages the patch was traced to be the handiwork of the husband of the Programmer of the University Computer Center. The gentleman had managed entry into the computer center and had gained access to the records on the pretext of helping out his wife in the processing of the result. On this finding the Programmer was suspended and a report lodged with the police. Shri J.C. Kochar, the officiating Controller of Examinations requested the University to relieve him of the responsibility as he did not feel comfortable in handling examination work. The University, on the basis of its assessment of the working of the Deputy Controller (Shri S.N. Gupta) was not willing to hand over to him the charge of the post of Controller. The Deputy Registrar ,Shri M.K. Bhatnagar working in the secrecy section was appointed to officiate as Controller and the Deputy Controller being senior to him was given independent charge of the result section. This arrangement too did not work satisfactorily as controversies would erupt almost every day. The post of Controller of Examinations was advertised and interview date fixed. Before the interviews were to be held the Vice-Chancellor, Prof. Gurbakhsh Singh called me one day and asked if I could agree to accept the post. I politely declined saying that I would prefer to continue as Principal of Shivaji College. Though both the posts carried the same pay scale I considered the job of the head of college more challenging and academic in nature. I couldn't agree less with the V.C. that the Controller's position carried lot of power.

Prepared to Repair

Ultimately a suitable person, Shri S.C. Gupta of the CBSE was selected for the post of Controller of Examinations. But he was not in a position to join immediately and therefore requested for three month's time for joining duty, which was granted. The next annual examinations were drawing near. The term of the Vice-Chancellor was to end in a couple of months. In these circumstances the Vice-Chancellor called me again and desired that I take up the work of OSD examinations till the person selected for the post joined duty, which I was told would be within three months. He told me that he did not want to leave the University with the examination branch in a crisis and added in Punjabi-*'meri pag rakh le'* (please keep my honour). I could not say no to this plea of the V.C. and joined as OSD Examinations on 20th February 1985. The assignment as I had desired was in addition to my duties as Principal of Shivaji College. My experiences as OSD Examinations gave me insights in dealing with different kinds of situations full of challenges and risks. The period served as a fit ground for training in holding trust, confidentiality and achieving higher levels of efficiency in working. Some episodes pertaining to my association with examinations deserve to be recounted.

Leakage Proof

(i) To hold the MBBS entrance test in 1985 without a mishap was a major challenge before me in view of the circumstances leading to my appointment as OSD Examinations. My first task was to ensure complete secrecy of the question papers. To accomplish this I devised a foolproof system. Four different examiners were asked to prepare four different question-papers. Each of the papers was arranged in four sets, each set having different sequence of questions. The examiners were requested to give the sets in neatly typed format (so that the same could be printed through laser printing which did not involve the job of proof reading) and arranged and sealed in separate envelops in the manner described above. On receipt of all the four question papers I put the sets of each in a separate outer envelope bearing no mark of identity. One of the four identical sealed envelopes was picked through draw of lots arranged by witnesses present in my room. The whole process was recorded and signed by the witnesses. The remaining three sets were kept in a separate packet duly sealed for future reference.

My aim was to achieve secrecy through transparency. I also chose to change the old printing press and gave the assignment to a new printer in a metropolis far away from Delhi. I did not disclose the identity of the University or the examination to the new printer. I personally handed over the sealed cover containing the question paper and obtained a receipt describing the format of the seal. This way the responsibility for maintaining secrecy was confined solely to the printer. I also gave him packing instructions using codes throughout in a manner that each center of examination would receive a separate packet of question booklets with the original seal of the printer. I took delivery of the packets at the printing press and took them to the airport with my own transport arrangement and booked the consignment as stationery sufficiently in advance of my flight to Delhi. I was told that as cooling time was needed my cargo could be loaded only after the expiry of twenty four hours. I had no alternative but to accept the situation and take my scheduled flight back. My office staff received me at the airport at Delhi at the tentative time given by me. To my surprise my cargo had reached Palam airport by an earlier flight. I happened to recognize the consignment packets on my way to the main exit of the airport. I had not disclosed my destination or my precise travel schedule to any one at my office.

We took charge of the consignment and got it stored overnight in a strong room duly sealed. The sealed packets already arranged center wise were delivered in the morning of the date of examination to the respective colleges. It may be observed from the system followed that the OSD Examinations at no stage had access to the contents of the question paper. Luckily every thing went off smoothly, except a graceless allegation in one of the newspapers that questions were known in advance to some examinees. This paper could only manage to mention a few topics from the syllabus without even stating a single question in the format required and that too a day after the examination had been over. Obviously some elements were determined to pick holes where none was there.

Bundle Bungle

(ii) The system of central evaluation of answer scripts was introduced in 1987. Fictitious marking of scripts was done at the evaluation centers within the blocks of numbers allotted to each center for generating new numbers. Miranda House was one of these centers. During the processing of results it was discovered that awards for a certain paper in history in respect of thirty students had not been received in the examination branch. The

Deputy Controller reported that the answer scripts in respect of these students could not be located in the strong room and were presumably not sent in by the concerned college. The Principal of the College, Dr. T. S. Rukmini firmly maintained that all the answer scripts allotted to her college center had been duly forwarded to the University and that no answer script had been lost or left behind in the College. The University ordered a re-examination for the concerned candidates and also simultaneously asked me to inquire into the matter and fix responsibility for the loss of the answer scripts. The Deputy Controller who was in-charge of the strong room perceived the decision as a reflection on his working. But my hunch was that the answer scripts could have been mixed up in the strong room and that perhaps full efforts had not been made to locate them. The V.C. issued instructions that I should be given full access to the records in the strong room of the examination branch and that all required help and assistance should be rendered to me. I went about my work systematically. First I checked the area where the answer scripts in question were supposed to be stored. Not finding them at the designated place I started searching the adjacent stacks where scripts of political science had been stored. To my pleasant surprise the history scripts were found mixed up with political science scripts. The mix up had evidently happened at the time of rearranging and restacking of all the scripts received from the different evaluation centers.

The re-examination had already taken place. In the interest of the students it was decided that the better of the two performances would be taken into account. The responsibility for the mix up could be attributed at three points, viz. (a) the examiner, who submitted the evaluated answer scripts without transferring the marks obtained on the award list (b) the College administrative staff, who failed to tally the total awards list with the answer scripts before forwarding the same to the University and finally (c) the staff responsible for handling the answer scripts in the strong room in as much as they mixed the History answer sheets received from Miranda House with the Political Science answer sheets received from Daulat Ram College. The benefit of doubt could be given to the last named on the ground that the fictitious codes of history and political science scripts were in the range of close proximity and a mix up of the type that had happened was quit possible in a fresh exercise of rearranging of answer scripts.

Instant Justice

(iii) Another episode that occurred at the Shivaji College evaluation center needs to be related. As the person in-charge of the center I had made all arrangements to ensure secrecy and confidentiality of the total process. One day a teacher from a sister college and known to me personally brought another teacher of his college to me with a request for allotment of answer sheets for evaluation in a paper of third year instead of first year paper for which he had been appointed as evaluator. The reason given was that the teacher would be out of station during the period of evaluation of the first year paper. I took it as a normal request and in consultation with the head of the department concerned allowed the change. The same teacher again appeared when evaluation of answer scripts of first year commenced. I went up to him and asked as to what had happened to his plan of going out of town at that point of time. He fumbled and could not give a coherent reply. This raised suspicion in my mind regarding the motive behind his request for evaluation of scripts of third year. Working on certain clues gathered at the center I discovered that the daughter of the teacher who had earlier brought this teacher to me was a candidate for the third year examination.

I wanted to ensure that no undue favour had been shown to the concerned candidate. I therefore took the head examiner into confidence and showed him the answer book of the candidate to ascertain whether the evaluation was just. The head examiner was of the opinion that marking was on the higher side to the extent of 10 % and it would meet the ends of justice if the award was reduced by 5%. I called the concerned teacher and offered to take a lenient view if he told me the truth, otherwise an inquiry would be instituted and action taken as per findings of the inquiry. The teacher took no time in admitting his misdemeanour and begged of me to pardon him. I asked him to re-evaluate the answer script concerned impartially, which he did. The revised score turned out to be in the vicinity (a little lower) of what the head examiner had estimated. Since the ends of justice appeared to have been met and as there was no written complaint or written confession I thought it fit to let the matter lie there.

Through Curfew

(iv) The annual examinations of 1990 were in progress. The printing press entrusted with the printing of major question papers fell in the area of the city which was engulfed in serious communal tension. Curfew had been imposed to maintain law and order. As a result the supply of question papers was put into jeopardy. Though there was some advance supply the University could not afford to take the risk of being caught napping. Immediate action was required. The joint Controller, Shri M.K. Bhatnagar and I were given the mission to visit the place and get the maximum supply of question papers. Secrecy and safety were the primary concerns for us.We obtained from Delhi Police a letter addressed to their counter-parts in the city of our destination indicating that we were on important public duty and that we be given safe passage in the curfew bound area. We hired a vehicle without divulging our identity and headed for our destination. On reaching the outer police post of the city we showed to the staff posted there the letter from the Delhi Police. We received all co-operation and were advised to use a certain password wherever required and to reach the head quarters of the Police in the curfew bound area. After satisfying them selves the Police asked us to leave our vehicle in the police station and gave us a police vehicle with armed escorts. We completed our mission successfully and returned to the University thanking God that nothing untoward had happened.

Stakes at Shyam Lal

(v) In the year 1975 Shyam Lal College was going through turmoil. Teachers and students were divided on factional lines and a state of rampant indiscipline prevailed there. When the annual examinations of 1975 approached near the Principal, Dr. G. C. Ahuja wrote to the University saying that in the given circumstances he would not be in a position to conduct the examinations and therefore the students of his college be allotted a center elsewhere. The University however, thought that it would set a wrong precedent and therefore decided to retain the center at Shyam Lal College. Those days I was working as Reader in the department of Sanskrit. Dr. V. k..Ahluwalia, Reader in the department of Chemistry and I were deputed as observers to be present at Shyam Lal College and help in the smooth conduct of the examination. On the first day of examination I reached Shyam Lal College an hour before its commencement. I parked my new Fiat car in the front parking area of the College and went about surveying the campus. I could notice some suspicious looking elements moving all over the compound. Soon a police officer in plain clothes approached me. We got introduced to each other and turned out to be name shakes and originally from the same state, Haryana. He briefed me of the situation in the College and promised to render all help in the smooth and peaceful conduct of the examination.

To ensure safety of my car he arranged to get it parked in the compound of the police station nearby. Then both of us moved inside the building where the center was located. To my shock and dismay I noticed the Principal and some teachers standing as helpless onlookers in front of the staircase, which had been blocked with stacking of furniture by some miscreants. The blockade was total making it impossible for the examinees to reach the rooms on the first floor where the examination center was located. I immediately started removing the furniture from the stairs and called upon everybody present there to help.

My action proved infectious and every one present joined hands in clearing the stairs. The situation changed drastically and soon the examination started. The police officer, Mr. Sube Singh Yadav had done some very useful public relations work for me. He projected me as some kind of a superman commanding vast powers. My polite but firm and confident posture perhaps helped in forming of such an image. In any case this came handy to me in dealing with tricky situations, which at times looked like going out of hands. As Dr. Ahluwalia was to join me a couple of days later, I went solo and fell back upon whatever resources were available to achieve my objective. I managed to herd into a room, the students' union office to be precise, some apparently unwanted elements hovering all over the College compound, in order to engage them in a dialogue. I was told that some of them were former students who had arrived from outside Delhi to render help to their friends during the examination. I tried to convince them of the futility of their attempt if any made as I was duty bound to come in their way at all costs. My clarity of purpose and friendly demeanor appeared to be proving effective as undesirable elements were hardly seen around the college in the days to come.

But my native skills came handy when on another day a teacher (K.M. Singh) on invigilation duty signaled to me to reach his room. On my joining him he showed me a student who he said was copying from some unauthorised material. It came as a surprise to me that the teacher concerned had not thought it appropriate to challenge the student in the first instance but had instead wanted me to do the needful. As this conduct on the part of the student could not be condoned I went straight near him and asked him to hand over whatever books or notes he had on his person. After some initial resistance he gave up and surrendered all the books and other material he had concealed all over his body, of course bit by bit. I also took away his answer book and gave him a fresh one. To avert any more attempt on his part to use unfair means I shifted his seat to the examination office where he would be under the watchful eyes of several teachers on duty there. He sat there for a couple of minutes and then abruptly got up and went out leaving his answer book in the examination room. Then he took a chair and made himself seated in the verandah outside the examination halls and announced in a raised voice that he would ensure that no one used unfair means and that he himself would never do such a thing in future and would instead pass the examination if ever, without resorting to any dishonest practice. I went near him and persuaded him to leave the place and go home for introspection.

Tough Tact

The peace achieved proved to be deceptive. Minutes later the president of the student's union came out of his examination room and went to different rooms announcing that no one should care for the invigilators and every one was free to use any unauthorized material. Chaos spread to all the rooms. The invigilators appeared to be helpless. Accompanied by the Principal and some teachers I rushed to the spot of disturbance and brought about order with some police help and tough talk. Students responsible for creating disorder in different rooms were identified and it was decided to report cases of use of unfair means to the University. As no teacher was ready to come forward to sign individual reports a letter from the Principal containing the full details of the incident including the names of the concerned students and duly witnessed jointly by the teachers present was sent to the University. I also countersigned the letter.

The University took the required action in the matter as I came to know later. However, one of the steps taken immediately was the change of center for the concerned students from Shyam Lal College to Khalsa College and Arts Faculty building. Another step taken was the appointment of some senior members of the non-teaching staff of the University as additional invigilators for rest of the duration of the examination. There remained perfect order and discipline in the examination center for the future. For me the assignment proved to be an experience, quite instructive and rewarding.

High Court High

(vi) One of the important assignments that I was to handle after I joined as OSD examinations on 20th February1985 was to conduct the Entrance test for M.D./M.S. and Post-Doctoral super specialties (D.M. M.Ch.) for the Faculty of Medical Sciences. Professor Krishnaji Committee appointed by the EC in the case of the Medical Entrance test of 1984, had recommended the use of ink for marking answer sheets in multiple choice format and evaluating the same by using two separate optical mark readers. After getting trials done at a few places it was confirmed that reliable optical mark readers for reading answers marked with ink were not easily available. So it was decided to have marking of answers in ink but evaluation was to be done manually through data entry process in two sets to be compared and mismatched for ruling out any possible error. The work was assigned to a Government undertaking handling such type of work. A Xerox copy of each answer sheet was retained in sealed cover to be kept in the custody of the Secrecy Officer to serve as a back up document in case of a doubt or any mishap during processing of the original sheets. After the declaration of the result, re-checking was done in case of those candidates who applied for the same. During the course of rechecking done under the joint supervision of the secrecy officer and myself it was discovered that one of the answer sheets had been evaluated by application the key of a different set by mistake. The only choice before me was to get the mistake rectified. As a result of the rectification the candidate's marks increased by twenty. There were some minor variations in case of a few more candidates arising from oversight in reading the markings. These were also rectified as per the interpretation of the marking scheme. After rechecking the revised result of the candidates concerned was notified.

Major revision in the result of one candidate and marginal in several others as stated above gave rise to speculation in some sections of the candidates regarding the authenticity of the revised result. A couple of candidates presumably inspired by some vested interests filed a writ petition in the Delhi High Court asking for the quashing of the test and for ordering a fresh test. Even as the proceedings were on the University on a suggestion of the Court agreed to undertake a manual evaluation of all the answer sheets directly under its supervision. The work was entrusted to senior teachers from different subjects. The Secrecy Officer Prof. T.N. Bali and I myself supervised and verified the manual evaluation. On satisfying ourselves of the accuracy of the evaluation we packed the answer sheets and the result in separate sealed covers and reported the progress at the next hearing in the Court. The Registrar, Shri Madan Mohan and I myself were present in the Court along with our Senior Counsel Shri P. P. Rao when the matter came up for hearing.

The learned judges J. Satish Chandra and J. Natarajan after hearing the case for some time asked both the parties along with the respective counsels to come in their chamber. All of us reached there along with the sealed covers containing the results and the answer sheets. I handed over to the leaned judges the sealed result sheets for their perusal and examination. When asked I explained procedure of evaluation adopted by the University. Then the judges gave me a few roll numbers one by one taken out at random from the result sheets. I evaluated the corresponding answer sheets and gave out the respective scores. All the scores tallied with the confidential result earlier handed over to the Court. The lawyer of the petitioners being a witness of what was demonstrated in his presence was amply satisfied and said that the petitioners had not properly guided him with regard to the procedure of evaluation. The petition was subsequently dismissed in the resumed sitting of the Court the same day. The Court made a special mention of the assistance rendered by me in the proper understanding of the case.

A sidelight during the hearing of the case was a strong rebuff given by Justice Satish Chandra to Dr. Govind Rai Chaudhary who repeatedly attempted to intervene in the case. At one stage the court had asked for the Court Marshals to do the needful to contain him. Mercifully Dr. Chaudhary made voluntary exit and the show down was averted.

Transparent Trump

(vii) A sequel to the above Court case regarding Entrance Test for M.D./M.S. etc. was a bunch of petitions, which cropped up subsequent to the declaration of the result of M.B.B.S. Entrance Test held in June 1985. Having got wiser from the experience gained in conducting the M.D./M.S. Entrance Test I obtained written clearance from Prof. Krishnaji for the use of pencil instead of ink for marking the answers so as to get the result processed through Optical Mark Reader rather than a manual processing. Apart from computerized processing in two sets a back up of manual scoring was employed in respect of the top one thousand answer sheets in the computerized result. Random checking was also done for 5 % of the answer sheets. I was quite confident of the accuracy of the result. So when the hearing of the petitions started I instructed the University's Senior Counsel to straight away offer the inspection of the answer sheets, which we had kept ready along with the keys of answers. The Court asked the petitioners to assemble in the lawyers' common room where the University would arrange the inspection.

Eminent Jurist Soli Sorabji was the Counsel for the petitioners apart from a few more senior lawyers. After personal examination and evaluation of the answer sheets by the petitioners themselves no doubt was left in any one's mind with regard to the accuracy and transparency of evaluation system adopted by the University in the examination concerned. Mr. Soli Sorabji was candid in remarking in our presence that the University, by adopting the transparency strategy had taken the wind out of the sails of the petitioners. On resumption of the hearing in the Court the petitions were dismissed.

A corollary to the above case turned out to be a tribute to the working of the examination system of the University and a great source of happiness for me. A few days after the High Court had dismissed the bunch of writ petitions, yet another writ was filed. On the very first hearing for admission of the writ Chief Justice Prakash Narain observed that the court had seen in earlier cases brought before it that the University had done a good job that year in processing the result. When the petitioner's lawyer persisted in arguing further the Chief Justice remarked that either the petitioner withdrew the petition or else the Court was going to reject it without notice to the responding University. The petition was withdrawn. The court ruled the petition dismissed as withdrawn without notice to the University. The University's lawyer Mr. Mariarputtam was present in the Court at that time. He immediately rang me up on telephone and gave the news complimenting me for what he considered to be my contribution in building up a system of transparency and efficiency in processing the results.

Credibility Credit

(viii) The Medical Entrance Test was held in 1995 a couple of months after Prof. V.R. Mehta had taken over as Vice-Chancellor of the University. Not satisfied with the results of their wards several influential persons known to Prof. Mehta met him and expressed their serious doubts about the accuracy of the results at least in respect of their wards. As the number of such persons was substantial he felt alarmed and also worried. He asked for my advice in the matter. I explained to him how a foolproof system had been developed in processing the result and that the University could demonstrate to any one that there was no flaw. On my suggestion the Vice-Chancellor took written representations from the concerned persons and asked them to meet him in his office on a date and time fixed for the purpose. The secrecy officer Prof. B.S. Garg and my self were present at the time. Both of us then proceeded to demonstrate the evaluation of the answer sheets of the students concerned one by one. The outcome of evaluation in each case tallied with the result already declared. Half way through this exercise some of the parents started saying that the system of the University was flawless. Finding every result in order they went back saying that it was the case of the survival of the fittest. In fact one parent was gracious enough to acknowledge it in a letter to the V.C. The V.C. was happy that the highly placed persons went back fully satisfied with a greater credibility of the University examination system registered in their minds.

Benefit of Doubt

(ix) There was a unique case of alleged use of unfair means in the L.L.B. examination of 1989. Dr. Krishna Bal, the Principal of Ram Lal Anand College, New Delhi was reportedly found in possession of unauthorized material while taking his examination for L.L.B. as a student of Evening Law Center-II, Dhaula Kuan. As soon as the case was reported the news spread all over the University like wild fire. Some teacher activists went to the V.C. asking for immediate action including suspension of the Principal. Ram Lal Anand College was a University maintained college and therefore the V.C.'s responsibility was immediate and greater. The V.C. immediately called the Chairman of the Governing Body for a meeting. Before the Chairman arrived the V.C. discussed his proposal to suspend the Principal in a meeting of his team.

Whereas other colleagues thought suspension of the Principal was the only way to deal with the tense situation in the University, I gave a different perspective. I perceived the incident as one where Dr. Krishna Bal was involved in the reported case not as Principal but as a student of Law Center-II. So he should be subjected to the same procedure for awarding punishment as was to be applied in case of any other student. In case he was found guilty and punished ultimately, there would arise a ground of misconduct for taking action against him as Principal. In case he was found not guilty of the use of unfair means in the examination the stigma on his name resulting from his suspension could not be wiped out. Therefore, I suggested that let the law take its own course. The Vice-Chancellor and other colleagues including the chairman agreed with me. Subsequent developments vindicated my stand. After completion of the processing of unfair means case Dr. Krishna Bal was found not guilty for the reason of want of clinching evidence and therefore he was given benefit of doubt and was let off.

Agitation Vegitation

(x) During almost the whole of the session 1988-89 a group of teachers in College of Vocational Studies continued their agitation for the removal of Dr. R.D. Pawar from the position of Acting Principal. They had the support of a vast section of the DUTA leadership though the President Dr. S.S. Rathi was quite impartial on the issue. He wanted matters to be settled peacefully by negotiations and discussions. However, the leftist and the rightist factions among the teachers forced him to call a meeting of the general body of the organisation. The main resolution passed was for the boycott of evaluation of answer scripts of the annual examination, 1989. In another resolution my efforts in rendering the agitation of the teachers ineffective in conducting the examination successfully came under attack. The second resolution prompted the Vice-Chancellor to remark, though in a lighter vein that I was appropriating what was his due (*aap hamara hak mar rahe hain*). It was his way of boosting my morale and thus continuing to be resolute in dealing with crisis sought to be created.

The DUTA activists had probably thought that since the evaluation work was to be carried out in a fixed number of centers, they would be in a better position to monitor the boycott and persuade teachers not to under-take evaluation work. Under the guidance of the V.C. we developed a strategy to counter the boycott. Since I was monitoring the evaluation centers for the previous two years it became easy for me to identify committed and trusted members of the teaching and non-teaching staff who were help to the Principals in running the centers. When examiners felt constrained to report at the evaluation centers, arrangements were made to prepare packets of answer books during the day to be delivered during the night to willing teachers at their residences. The evaluated scripts along with remuneration bills were collected from the examiners in a similar fashion. The progress of evaluation in this way was found to be speedy. We were able to get the co-operation of a large number of teachers who would volunteer for the evaluation work and persuade many others to do the same.

When all this was going on some teachers kept sitting on a protest sit in *(dharna)* in the open compound near the offices of the Dean of Colleges and the Director South Campus. The weather was unbearably hot. One day it became suddenly cloudy and it appeared that rain would pour during the night. I offered my retiring room for shelter if the teachers wished to move there in case it rained. They thankfully accepted the offer but did not have to make use of it as no rain came that night. The administration generally maintained cordiality with the teachers all through the agitation. In fact a group of teachers in economics was so highly motivated to do the evaluation at the Hindu College center that its members challenged and frustrated the efforts of the activists who were picketing in front of the center to dissuade or even prevent the examiners from doing evaluation work. This stance on the part of a good number of senior teachers eased the situation for us. The evaluation work was expedited and the results that year were declared earliest ever in five years.

Leakage Plug

(xi) The examinations of 1994 were going on when one morning a student of B.A.(Hons) economics came to my residence. He disclosed that the paper setter had divulged to the students of his college all the questions of the paper, examination for which was scheduled for the next day. He had somehow come to know the questions through a friend in that college. He further said that he was a bright student and had prepared thoroughly for the examination. The leakage of questions would put him at par with ordinary students who knew the questions beforehand. I thanked him for passing on to me such vital information and assured him that firstly no leakage could have taken place and in case such a thing was discovered after verification the paper would be replaced. Further, I advised him to proceed on the presumption that there was no leakage. The student left a copy of the set of questions with me. I immediately moved in the matter and brought the matter to the notice of the P.V.C. who was officiating in the absence of the V.C. The Controller of examinations, after comparing the set of questions with the question paper confirmed that there was a leakage. The Head of the department was consulted and immediate steps were taken to get an alternative question paper set and printed overnight and supplied to the Colleges early next morning. After the examination the student who had given the information about the leakage met me and thanked the University for taking timely action on his report.

The Trickle

(xii) With a view to combat the menace of some examiners reportedly leaking questions of the papers of examination to their favourite students, the University at one stage, introduced the system of getting double set of papers set by the examiners at the honours and post graduate levels. The Controller was free to choose either of the sets for use in the concerned examination. However, instances came to notice where determined elements could by pass the system. There was the case of a professor who prepared two sets of a question paper in which fifty percent of the questions figured in both the sets. The examiner had leaked to his favourite student only the questions common to both the sets. There being hundred percent choice of answering the questions the leakage amounted to hundred percent. This case was detected when another student who had managed to procure the questions some how complained a day before the examination of leakage citing the questions. Immediate action was taken by substituting the leaked questions with alternatives and a fresh question paper prepared and printed for use in the concerned examination. The then PVC had sought my assistance in the whole operation, which I willingly rendered. It is ironic that the examiner in question had the temerity to make a grievance of the moderators having altered the questions originally given by him It is a pity that the same gentleman was later appointed Vice-Chancellor of a deemed

University, from where he was unceremoniously removed though on a trivial charge of getting meat cooked in the kitchen at the Vice-Chancellor's official residence for his Canine companion.

In League

(xiii) Leakage of question papers as stated earlier was a rare happening in the University. But there was a shocking case of leakage by a teacher working as superintendent of examination for students of correspondence courses. The matter came to the notice of the University when one day a student activist flaunted a copy of the question paper for an examination to be held the next morning. He claimed that he had purchased the question paper from some one but he refused to divulge the source. The University after verification of the leakage gave the case to the crime branch of Delhi Police. Intensive interrogations brought out the disturbing fact of the superintendent of examination selling the question paper to his nephew, who made some fast bucks by further sale of its copies. The teacher involved was arrested and put behind the bars till he was granted bail. A case was launched against him. The College governing body placed him under suspension. The University debarred him from assignment of any examination work. The case provided grist to the factional mudslinging among the teachers for quite a long period. As public memory is short the case has almost disappeared from the memory of teachers. In due course of time the college governing body revoked the suspension order. The fate of the criminal case launched against the teacher is uncertain. It is pertinent to point out that the teacher concerned had secured the position of superintendent of examination at a particular center after a great deal of lobbying and by aggressive flaunting the fact of his being a handicapped person.

Right Overnight

(xiv) Prof. V.R. Mehta had joined as Vice-Chancellor a few days before the annual examinations of 1995 commenced. He was keen to ensure that the examinations passed off smoothly and had asked me to pay my personal attention to this area of administration though that did not fall under my normal responsibilities. One evening when I was in an Academic Council meeting I received an emergent message from the Joint Controller, officiating as Controller of Examinations that he needed my help in an urgent matter. I went out and found the Joint Controller standing tense in the lobby. I took him to my room where he told me that two open envelopes containing question papers of two separate subjects, examinations for which were scheduled for the next morning had been received by his staff from one of the examination centers mixed in the packets of used question papers. He had verified after counting that no question paper was missing.

Presumably the college staff had opened the packets by mistake and had quietly returned the same with used packets to escape responsibility for the mishap. However, I did not consider it prudent to take a risk of leaving things there. So we decided to make alternative arrangement. The first thing we did was to ensure complete secrecy in the matter. All the staff members in the know of the mishap were requested to stay in the office overnight (with no access to telephone). It was already past twelve in the night. I arranged some food for them from my house. Secondly we called the representative of a local printing press and persuaded him to under take the printing of alternative question papers, which were luckily available in the secrecy branch. At this stage I rang up the V.C. and apprised him of the incident and the steps taken by us. The V.C. was satisfied and said that the best possible action had been taken. As arranged, we received a call from the printing press at 5.00 a.m. informing that the papers were ready and would be supplied to the examination branch before 6.00 a.m. We started informing the colleges at this stage that the sets of question paper supplied earlier in the concerned subjects were not meant for that day's examination and that the correct sets would be supplied to them well before the examination time. The network for the supply had been worked out during the night and was put into operation immediately on receipt of the question papers from the press. Nearly all colleges got the fresh papers well in time. Never the less the timely action on the part of the University did leave a Principal peeved over the short delay that had occurred in replacing the question papers at his college center. Perhaps, he was expecting a major mishap.

Promotion Pangs

(xv) There were times when the degree examination used to be held at the end of three years. Students got promotion to second and third years of the course on the basis of examination conducted by individual colleges. At the end of third year there was a University examination covering the entire syllabus of three years. The performance in the college examination was not given any weight in the final result. With the passage of time the system started collapsing. Every college had its own criteria of promotion to the next higher class till a student reached the third year. Use of unfair means and intimidation of examiners became common in many of the colleges. An argument advanced in favour of mass promotions in college examination was that why detain students from reaching the stage of University examination on the basis of college tests which do not count ultimately.

The University experimented with an alternative scheme providing for a university level examination at the end of second year covering the papers of first year only. The second and third year papers were to be covered by the examination at the end of three years. The first batch of students to take their university examination at the end of second year under the new scheme was admitted in colleges during the year 1966. Such students took their first year examination conducted by the respective colleges in1967. Colleges followed different norms for promotion to second year. When the norms of promotion to second year were being discussed in a meeting of teachers in my (Shivaji) college, I pleaded for a lenient norm as I thought that it was illogical to detain students on the basis of first year papers as the same were going to be the basis of the University examination the next year. In other words we were depriving the students of an opportunity to prove themselves in the University examination. Only one teacher, Mr. S.K. Chawla agreed with me. Others present in the meeting decided upon certain norms of promotion, leaving both of us disappointed.

A year later in 1968 the results of the University examination held on the basis of the first year papers were declared. It was expected that the students would not be able to do full justice to the papers of first year studied the previous year. The results showed a high rate of failure. The failed students over all the colleges went on a warpath. Failing to control the agitation the University beat a hasty retreat and declared all examinees of the second year examination promoted to third year. But the University had learnt its lesson.

The very next year the scheme was replaced by another, providing for University examination at the end of each year. The same stood the test of time and survived for more than forty years in spite of the strains having developed on its working. Under the scheme there was a University examination at the end of each year with a provision for load shedding and load carrying. An attempt in 1998 to bring further reform in the system turned out to be abortive, as teachers in general did not favour an alternative to the prevailing scheme. It was a matter of some satisfaction to me that the seed of the idea sowed by the University during my tenure as Dean of Colleges had sprouted into action in some modified form subsequently. we had a more progressive scheme in place through delivery by a semester system, along with the dual option of four and three years degree programmes combined with the choice of a diploma after two years. But alas, the one year toddler became a casualty with the change of regime at the Center in 2014. However, it was the feeling of alienation among a vast section of teachers and also student groups of all hues over the issue that turned out to be the main factor before the powers that be in determining its fate. Also the dichotomy occurring as a result of jettisoning of the correspondence students from the reform was not an insignificant miss which queerly escaped attention of the critics of the new package.

System Schemes: L.L.B.

(xvi) The late eighties had witnessed a great amount of strain on the examination system for the B.E. and LL.B. courses. The semester system was being followed in both the courses. The promotion rules were quite rigid, but there was a provision for supplementary examination. The results getting generally delayed teaching for the higher semester could not be started in the right earnest. Students eligible to appear in the supplementary examination of a semester would not attend the classes of the next semester. With the results deteriorating progressively the students resorted to agitation for more and more relaxation in the promotion rules. Teaching suffered immensely. On the recommendations of Justice G.B. Deshpande committee, the promotion rules for the LL.B. course were relaxed and the system of supplementary examination abolished. In order to improve the quality of intake in the course an entrance test for admission was introduced. Both the reforms have proved quite useful in improving the quality of law education in Delhi University. A similar change was made in the B.E scheme of examination. A provision was made under which a student had the option to discontinue a paper and select a new one in lieu of that. Further, mid term tests were introduced for internal assessment. The supplementary examination was abolished. The faculty of technology was entrusted with the responsibility of carrying out all the operations of the examination. Since the time these reforms were made the engineering students have hardly been seen agitating at the door of the University on the issues of examinations. The system of centralised spot evaluation adopted in some measure has further improved things overall.

Subsidiary Subsides

(xvii) The pattern of Delhi University's three years Honours degree course with the components of main and subsidiary subjects had proved to be a great success over the years. But the non-reckoning of the performance in subsidiary subjects in the result of the main subject gave rise to the tendency among students not to take the subsidiary subjects seriously. Attendance in the classes of these subjects gradually declined to an alarmingly low percentage. Generally students would leave the subsidiary subjects during the annual examinations to be attended to only at the time of the supplementary examinations. The University appointed a committee in the mid eighties to examine the phenomenon and make recommendations to improve the situation. The committee recommended that (i) the pass percentage in subsidiary subjects be raised from 33% to 40% to bring it at par with the main subject, (ii) the marks obtained in the subsidiary subjects be added to the marks obtained in the main subjects while determining the result and ranking of students and (iii) the chance to appear in supplementary examination be given only after the part three examination. The academic Council accepted the recommendations. At this point of time my term as member of the Council had ended.

In my opinion the decision was not well thought out. The demerits of the new system far outweighed the merits. The weightage given, for example, to performance in subjects like Mathematics and Sanskrit to students of honours in English could present a distorted picture of their standing in the main subject. The vice-versa was also true. The students themselves were alarmed at the decision. The DUSU President, Mr.Balram Yadav launched an agitation demanding a review of the decision. He sat on an indefinite *dharna* outside the office of the V.C. AS DUSU adviser I tried to persuade Mr. Yadav to end the agitation. But he asked me whether the decision of the University was going to do any good to the students and further requested me to put across to the V.C. my considered view in the matter.

I met the Dean of Colleges Sardar Mohinder Singh and shared with him my views and wanted him to convey the same to the V.C., Professor Gurbaksh Singh. He quietly went into the room of the V.C. and got me summoned there. When I told the V.C. of the flaw in the decision, he retorted that I thought too much of myself. In a lighter vein though, he went to the extent of saying that I thought I were *khuda*. My retort in an equally relaxed manner was that the V.C. probably did not think I too was human. Thereafter the V.C. became serious and asked the P.V.C., Professor P.C. Mukherji about his opinion in the matter. The P.V.C. endorsed my views. On being questioned by the V.C. why he did not express his views in the Academic Council meeting the P.V.C. giving a meaningful smile said, "You never asked me for that." The V.C. felt concerned that the issue had not been taken seriously by senior academicians and wanted that I should explain to him the implications of the decision earlier taken in the Academic Council and the alternative to be followed if necessary. I came back saying that I would meet him whenever he required.

Next day while I was busy in a UGC workshop at the Arts Faculty building, the Secretary of DUSU, Mr. R.P. Singh came with a letter from the V.C. requesting me to meet him at his residence in connection with the issue of subsidiary subjects after the workshop was over. I met the V.C. as desired and explained to him the issues involved. It did not take him long to be convinced of the need to review the decision. He authorized me to convey to the students his decision to place the matter before the Academic Council for review. A letter to this effect was given to the President of DUSU and with that ended the agitation of the students. The V.C. was gracious enough to voluntarily arrive at the scene of *dharna* and offer juice to Mr Yadav to mark an amicable solution of the problem. Shri Vijay Goel and a couple of other former student leaders were hovering around with no particular role there. Subsequently the matter was taken to the logical conclusion. The Academic Council reviewed the earlier decision and decided that the performance in subsidiary subjects be not counted to determine the result of the main subject. However, the percentage of marks to pass the subsidiary subjects was retained at forty.

Stalling a Miscarriage

(xviii) I was appointed Acting Head of the department of Sanskrit on 6th June 1976. Soon after taking charge of the office I had to deal with a couple of very sensitive issues. One of the matters was an anonymous complaint received by my predecessor in connection with the Ph.D. thesis submitted by Shri Swaminathan, the then Deputy Educational Advisor (Sanskrit) in the Ministry of Education. The allegation in the complaint was that the thesis was a verbatim copy of a project report earlier submitted to the office of Shri Swaminathan by a teacher of Tirupati Sanskrit Vidyapeeth. I scrutinized the thesis very closely and found no commonality with the project report either in form or contents. Similar was the finding of an independent referee appointed by the University earlier.

Having regard to the sensitive nature of the matter I dealt with this file in the examination branch itself and handed it over to the Controller of Examination, Shri Madan Mohan personally. My predecessor was keen to know the progress of the file. Instead of asking me about the same he demanded the file from the dealing assistant in the department who pleaded ignorance about the matter. The assistant however, thanked me for having saved him from the dilemma of divided loyalties by directly dealing with the file and leaving it in the examination branch. It may be mentioned that my predecessor was also the supervisor of Shri Swaminathan and was supposed to have direct knowledge of the contents of the thesis. It was curious therefore, that he entertained an anonymous complaint and chose to forward the same to the Controller for instituting an Inquiry contrary to the procedure followed in such cases as per Government of India's circular on the subject. Ultimately the fair name of Shri Swaminathan was vindicated. I had the satisfaction of being instrumental in averting a miscarriage of justice.

Scheming Re-evaluation

(xix) The late seventies and the early eighties witnessed a phenomenal growth in the number of students in the University. The examination branch came under severe pressure by the mere burden of numbers let alone the complexities arising as a result of growing multiplicity of courses. Tendency of the unsuccessful candidates in the examination to blame it on the system gave rise to a demand for re-evaluation of answer books. A few mistakes discovered in the results were magnified and cited in support of the demand. A committee appointed by the University in 1982 to examine the demand did not favour the introduction of re-evaluation but at the same time recommended several measures to streamline the evaluation process. The recommendations of the Committee came up for consideration of the Academic Council. As a demonstration by a group of students led by the DUSU President, Sudhansu Mittal was going on outside, the doors of the Council Hall had been bolted from inside as a precautionary measure. The matter was discussed in all its aspects and the recommendations of the committee were accepted unanimously. At this stage I noticed an elected teacher representative, Sudesh Sharma of P.G.D.A.V. College going out of the Hall, leaving the door open. The Dean of Students' Welfare, A.S. Kukla followed him.

Within a few minutes a group of students demonstrating outside barged into the Council Hall unhindered demanding the introduction of re-evaluation system. The group also declared a *gherao* of the Council members till the demand was accepted. The V.C. Professor Gurbaksh Singh had huddled consultations with senior members of the Council. On assessing that the consensus was in favour of re-evaluation he announced the acceptance of the demand in principle, the modalities to be decided by the A.C. in due course of time. Later a committee was constituted in which I was also included as one of the members. The committee worked out the modalities, which were accepted by the A.C. and the system of re-evaluation was introduced w. e. f. the session 1982-83 in courses other than professional courses and wherever there were joint examiners. Though the system entailed heavy burden on the examination branch it has served a useful purpose in rectifying possible errors. Stray cases of its misuse have come to the notice of the University for which remedial steps have been taken. The credibility of the examination system has, however, been enhanced by this system.

Fairly Unfair Means

(xx) There was a case of use of unfair means by a number of students in Shyamlal College during the tenure of Professor Baxi. It was detected at the valuation stage by the examiner. She had observed that ten examinees (later known to have their seats in close proximity in the same room) had answered some questions in the same manner also committing the same errors. The examiner reported the case to the University. While the case was under process and notices were served to the concerned students for explaining their position a group of persons led by some DUTA activists barged into the examination branch premises protesting against the action initiated by the University and caused damage to property. In the mean time the examiner made a complaint to the University against a couple of teachers of her own college who allegedly threatened her of dire consequences for making out a case of use of unfair means against the students. A faction of teachers supporting her took cudgels on her behalf and demanded from the University the setting up of an inquiry in the matter.

A preliminary inquiry in the incident at the examination branch was conducted by Professor Badal Mukherji who after a brief quest advised for a more thorough and high level inquiry in the totality of the matter. Eventually Justice (retd.) A.R. Desai was appointed inquiry officer in the case. Justice Desai in his report blamed the factional fights among the various teacher groups responsible for much of the ills. He however, did not fix any onus on any individual teacher. Therefore no action was taken on the report when the same was placed before the Executive Council. However, the case of use of unfair means was taken to its logical conclusion and the concerned students were punished as per norms. A queer aspect of the case was that one of the students involved in the case was the son of a senior teacher activist of the same college.

Abbreviating a Ruling

I joined as Reader in the department of Sanskrit in July 1972. Around the same time the election of teacher representatives to the Academic Council was scheduled. Several friends in Shivaji College and the Sanskrit department had desired that I become a candidate for the election. As Mr. J.P. Jain, a colleague in Shivaji College had already declared his candidature for the election and had met me for securing my support I did not think it appropriate to offer myself as a candidate. Mr. Jain however, did not win the election. The election for the next term due in 1974 was postponed to February 1975 in order to comply with the technical requirement of including the election rules as appendix to the Statute 7. The issue had been raised in a writ filed in the Delhi High Court by Shri S.S. Goyal a teacher of Ramjas College. Out of the twenty (later increased to 26) seats four were reserved for teachers appointed in the University departments. Hoping for a comfortable win I offered myself as one of the candidates. At the scrutiny of nomination papers a constructive role was awaiting me. My nomination paper was duly accepted.

The nomination paper of another candidate Dr. A.P. Shrivastava proposed by Dr. J.N Saxena, Reader in Law department was initially rejected on the ground that the proposer had written on the nomination paper his name in full as Jagan Nath Saxena whereas the voters' list contained the name as J.N. Saxena. The scrutiny officer, Professor F.C. Aulakh had ruled that the name did not tally with the one entered in the voters' list as required by the election rules. Strong pleas by Dr. A. P. Srivastava, himself a Reader in law in favour of the nomination were turned down. In the mean time I had closely examined the election rules. Raising a point of order I invited the attention of the scrutiny officer to an equally significant provision in the rules that the name of the candidate should be written in full. I also demonstrated how J.N. Saxena was the only abbreviated form of Jagan Nath Saxena and there was no ambiguity with regard to the identity of the proposer. The scrutiny officer graciously accepted my plea and revised his ruling declaring Dr. Srivastava as validly nominated candidate. Several teachers present on the occasion wondered how I had advocated the cause of a rival candidate. Such thoughts were far from my mind. I felt happy that my intervention helped in resolving the matter justly.

Direct Access

My political views were well known in the University circles. I believed in the Congress ideology but was not a formal member of the Party. A local Congress leader wanted me to be formally associated with the Party and offered a sum of one thousand rupees as the token help from the Party to meet my election expenses. I politely declined the offer, as I believed a formal attachment with a political party in dealing with the matters of the University was not appropriate. The election was a smooth affair. I was elected with a comfortable margin. A couple of days after the results of the election were declared a Principal, who later became the Dean of Colleges, came to see me in the Sanskrit department. He wanted that as member of the Academic Council I should play a role helpful to the administration. He also offered to introduce me to the V.C. and the P.V.C. at a personal level. I did not appreciate the approach of the gentleman and told him about my views on the role of a member of the Academic Council. As regards my meeting the V.C. and the P.V.C, I told him politely not to worry about that as I could have direct access to both of them when required.

Peaking to Speak

Incidentally the first meeting (June 1975) after the election of the new representatives of teachers was also the first meeting presided over by the new Vice-Chancellor, Professor R.C.

Mehrotra. The first item on the agenda was consideration of the letter of the UGC regarding the revision of pay scales for teachers. The UGC had stipulated certain conditions for the grant of revised scales of pay. The teachers in general were highly exercised over the issue. This was also an occasion for the newly elected members to demonstrate their oratorial skills. Speaker after speaker took the floor uninvited by the chair. I tried to catch the attention of the V.C. to allow me to speak by raising my hand intermittently. After a long wait when I found that the V.C. was helpless in controlling the order of speakers I stood up sprightly and raising my voice a bit I asked the V.C., "Mr. Chairman sir, shall I have to wait till eternity to get my turn to speak?" A complete silence descended in the meeting hall. The V.C. regretted his failure to give me an opportunity to speak in spite of my continued efforts to catch his attention and ruled that I would be the next speaker and that no one else should stand up to speak unless invited by the Chair. This brought some order in the proceedings. I quietly sat down and waited for the V.C's next call. I stood up to speak on being called by the Chair. First I apologised to the V.C. for having raised my voice saying that I had not intended to be impolite to him, that was only a device to catch his attention. Then I enunciated the approach for responding to the UGC communication.

I suggested that we accept the new pay scales and negotiate with the UGC on the conditions attached there with through a process of discussions. Teacher representatives having affiliation with different political parties were echoing discordant opinions on the issues before the Council. Ultimately a resolution by majority vote was passed accepting the revised pay scales and appointing a committee to draft a response to the UGC on the conditions attached. On a later occasion the V.C. confided in me how he was impressed by my very first performance in the Academic Council. I made it a habit to speak in the Academic Council only if I had to say something different from what had already been said or if I thought I could give new dimension to an issue. I also made it a point to always speak with the permission of the chair. On one occasion while I was making a submission the chairman interrupted me saying that enough had been said on that day's subject. I immediately sat down even without completing my last sentence. My stance made an instant effect on the mind of the Chairman. He was apologetic and asked me to complete my speech. I stood up and made my full submission. There was much substance in what I stated. He chairman thanked me for my contribution to the debate. I received approbation of many members present in the meeting. These stances paid me rich dividends.

Principles and Principals:

Bharati College

After the retirement of Dr. Panigrahi in 1991 the post of Principal of Bharati (Mahila) College was to be filled up. The selection committee had met and made its recommendations on the last day of the tenure of the Governing Body. The Chairman of the Governing Body forwarded the recommendations to the Vice Chancellor late at night the same day. The University could process the matter earliest the next morning. But the appointment could not be made even if the Vice-chancellor were to dispense with normal provision of invoking the apex committee as there was no Governing Body to make the appointment. The Governing body was reconstituted after a gap of couple of months and a new Chairman (Shri Bhiku Ram Jain) had been elected. The case was processed further and the recommendations were placed before the (apex) selection committee. The committee did not recommend any one and decided that the post be re-advertised. The chairman of the G.B. did not agree with this recommendation and was insisting on the name of a candidate who was not even eligible as per provisions of the Ordinances. In any case, the other members had arrived at the recommendation on merit. After initial reservations the chairman re-advertised the post.

The selection committee met and recommended only one name- that of the same candidate who was not technically eligible and on whose name the chairman had insisted on the earlier occasion. After taking legal opinion and with due application of mind the Vice-Chancellor disapproved the recommendation in a detailed order giving reasons. The Chairman was not happy with the decision of the University. He articulated his protest formally and informally and even threatened to go ahead with the appointment irrespective of the University's position. Efforts were made to convince him about the correctness of the stand of the University. Ultimately better sense prevailed and the chairman did not go ahead to act unilaterally and arbitrarily. The candidate who had been found ineligible by the University however, filed a writ petition in the Delhi High Court. Finally the High court upheld the Position taken by the University.

With passage of time the Governing Body chairman was changed. The post was re-advertised once again. The selection committee met and made a unanimous recommendation, which was forwarded by the chairman to the Vice-Chancellor. The candidates selected were listed without any order of merit or preference. As such the University had no alternative but to place the names before the (apex) selection committee for final selection and ranking of candidates as per requirement of the relevant ordinance. The selection committee with the chairman of the Governing body as one of the members unanimously made a panel of names in order of preference. The University forwarded this panel to the chairman with the request to make appointment on the basis of preference given there. Strangely enough the chairman developed second thoughts without any valid reason and wrote to the University expressing his fresh preference. Evidently this stand was untenable and the University wrote back indicating the same. After vacillating for a couple of days the Chairman relented and appointed the Principal (Dr. Asha Gupta) in accordance with the panel sent by the University. It is a different matter that Dr. Asha Gupta resigned after a couple of years caving in to pressure brought on her by a group of teachers of the College. Ultimately another senior and able teacher of the College was appointed Principal. It may be mentioned that this teacher had figured in the panel of names submitted by the Chairman in the first instance. She had in the intervening time obtained the Ph.D. degree.

Gargi College

The selection committee for appointment of Principal had met and unanimously recommended a panel of names. As per provision of the Ordinance the panel should have been placed before the Governing Body. But for reasons best known to him Prof. S.K. Vij, one of the University representatives in the selection committee brought the unanimous recommendation to the Vice-Chancellor for approval. The V.C. had hardly opened the envelope when he received a letter from the Chairman. The Chairman in his letter had stated that he disagreed with the other members of the selection committee and that the person put at number three in the panel should be appointed. The V.C. discussed the matter in his team. After careful consideration it was decided that the matter be first placed before the Governing Body. The Officiating Principal (incidentally the person being favoured by the chairman) was asked to call a meeting of the Governing Body urgently. The meeting was called and the G.B. members first passed a vote of no confidence against the Chairman and then elected Ms Joy Michael as the new Chairperson. The outgoing Chairman (Shri Ahuja) fumed and fretted and left the meeting in huff. Thereafter the G.B. unanimously approved the unanimous recommendations of the selection committee and authorized the chairperson to appoint the Principal after obtaining the approval of the Vice-Chancellor. The Director South Campus, Professor G.K.Das and I sat at a colleague's house nearby to keep abreast of the developments in the college. The colleague (Shri Sikandar Lal of Shivaji College) and his family were kind enough to give us food and company till late in the night. The Vice-Chancellor gave his approval to the decision of the Governing Body the same day. The next day Dr. Hema Raghavan was appointed Principal who later became Dean of Students' Welfare in the University. She has finally retired and a worthy successor has been appointed.

Sri Aurobindo College

After the denial of second stint of re-employment to Dr. Ranbir Singh in 1987, the post of Principal of Sri Aurobindo College fell vacant. Officiating arrangements continued for a long time. The post was advertised in1989 and the process of selection was set into motion. Before the selection could be made the term of the Governing Body expired and the Delhi Government nominated a new set of persons. Hectic lobbying started for getting the position of chairman of the G.B. Some candidates for the post of Principal took active part in it. One of them in fact went about canvassing for one of the members with the declared assurance that he would be appointed Principal of the College. But the member was not sure of his success unless he got the support of the University representatives and the teacher representatives in the G.B. He started spreading word to the effect that the University administration was opposed to him. At the same time he approached the Delhi Congress strong man Shri H.K.L.Bhagat to intervene on his behalf and persuade the University to help him get elected as chairman. On Shri Bhagat's invitation the V.C. deputed me to meet him and discuss the matter. In our meeting I conveyed to Shri Bhagat the thinking of the V.C. in the matter. It was pointed out to him that the Chairman should give up his bias in the selection of the Principal and a person generally acceptable to all members of the selection committee should be recommended for the post. If that were the approach of the gentleman the University representatives will have no objection to his election as chairman. Shri Bhagat found this position of the University unexceptionable. In fact he went a step further and arranged a meeting at his residence where the prospective chairman, the V.C., a senior Delhi political leader and I myself were present. At the meeting all matters were cleared and Shri Bhagat emphasized that a person of proven merit should be selected and for this the University could best guide the College. Even some names cropped up, which Shri Bhagat whole-heartedly commended.

In a matter of days the Governing Body met and unanimouly elected Chaudhary Mukhtiar Singh as chairman. The chairman on his part proceeded with speed and fixed a meeting of the selection committee. In exercise of his emergency power he himself nominated two members of the selection committee instead of getting them nominated in a meeting of the Governing .Body. The University received certain representations objecting to the procedure followed in nominating the two members. The University sent the case for legal opinion. The senior Counsel opined that since the matter was that of the appointment of Principal the Governing body in a meeting should nominate the two members. The V.C. discussed the issue in his team. It was felt that there was a need and scope to review the matter.

I was deputed to meet the Senior Counsel and explain to him the provisions of the ordinances and how the eleventh hour cancellation of the meeting of the selection committee would result in avoidable inconvenience to the candidates and others. The selection committee was scheduled to meet at 4.00 p.m. I met the senior Counsel in his chamber in the Supreme Court at 1.00 p.m. and explained to him all that was discussed in the V.C.'s team meeting. The senior counsel reiterated his earlier opinion and advised that the meeting of the selection committee be postponed and reconvened after the procedure as suggested by him had been completed. Disappointed over the failure of my mission I headed for South Campus where I was to meet Prof. Abad Ahmad, the Director of South Campus. I had hardly gone a kilometer when a thought crossed my mind for the solution of the problem. I went back and told the senior counsel that a meeting of the Governing Body was scheduled to be held immediately after the meeting of the selection committee was over. I suggested that the action taken by the chairman in nominating the two members on the selection committee could be placed before the G.B as the first item. In case of its approval the recommendations of the selection committee should be considered. The senior counsel was in full agreement with me. So he reviewed his earlier opinion and recorded accordingly.

I informed all concerned about this denouement and attended to my assignment of monitoring the completion of the process of the appointment of the Principal. A minor problem had cropped up. Dr. D.S. Mann selected for appointment was a teacher of physics. At the time of selection the introduction of science subjects including physics in the College was under process and had yet to be finalized. Therefore it was decided that Dr. Mann should join as Principal only after the subject was introduced in the College with the approval of the UGC. The UGC sanctioned the introduction of the subject. Dr. Mann took over as Principal and was responsible for developing the college academically by introducing several other relevant courses and promoting sports. It is a pity that he was refused re-employment beyond the age of sixty three years. His political affiliation did not gel well with the party controlling the governing body. Even my personal pleading to a very otherwise upright and just chairman could not help things.

Maitreyi College

During 1989 Begum Abida Ahmad was the chairperson of the Governing Body(G.B.) of Maitreyi College. She felt highly harassed by the behaviour of the treasurer both during the proceedings of the meetings and in dealing with matters of the College in general. The vacant post of Principal had been advertised and a meeting of the selection committee was to be held. As per convention Shri Goel would have been included as a member of the selection committee as a nominee of the G.B. But Begum Ahmad would not venture to deal with Shri Goel in the selection committee. In the circumstances it was decided to replace the treasurer. Shri Arjun Dev of NCERT was appointed in place of Shri Goel by a resolution of the Governing Body passed by circulation of papers among the members of the Governing Body. Obviously Shri Goel had opposed the resolution. A former Professor (Amba Prasad) of the University had also not agreed with the rest of the members. Scared as Begum Ahmad was of the possible disruption that Shri Goel could create in the G.B. meeting she fixed her residence as the venue of the meetings of the selection committee as well as the G.B. scheduled to be held one after another the same day. The V.C. deputed the Proctor (Prof. I.P.S.Monga) and me to be available at the residence of Begum Ahmad for consultation on any matter related to the meetings if required. Mercifully both the meetings went off smoothly except some fretting and fuming on the part of Shri Goel. Mrs. Sudesh Bhalla of Lady Shri Ram College was selected for the post of Principal. A question was raised in some quarters about a reference to Mrs. Bhalla in the inquiry report in the case of alleged misdemeanour on the part of the then College Principal Miss Luthra whose niece had appeared as a candidate for an examination at L.S.R. The University accorded approval to the selection only after satisfying itself on obtaining legal opinion, that the inquiry report had not indicted Mrs.Bhalla for any impropriety. Mrs. Bhalla administered the college with distinction till she retired.

St. Stephen's College

The Chairman of the Governing Body of St. Stephen's college along with the outgoing principal met me to ascertain whether the college was free to appoint as Principal a candidate who did not have a post graduate degree in any of the subjects taught in the college. I invited their attention to the provision which made it mandatory for the principal to do some teaching either in the College or the University department. The Chairman heeding my advice proceeded strictly in accordance with the University norms. Eventually the management of the College appointed Dr. Anil Wilson, a Reader in English in the Himachal Pradesh University, Shimla to the post of Principal.

Later after a few years Dr. Anil Wilson, Principal of St. Stephen's College was appointed Pro-Vice-Chancellor of Himachal Pradesh University Shimla. The College Governing Body selected Dr. Bhattacharya, a teacher of Jesus and Mary College for appointment as Acting Principal after open advertisement for the same and sent the name for approval of the University. The office of the Dean of Colleges pointed out that the relevant ordinance provided that the Vice-Principal, if any, and if there was no Vice-Principal, the senior-most teacher in the college would be appointed Acting Principal. After approval of the Vice-Chancellor the attention of the College was drawn towards the provision of the ordinance XVIII on the subject with a request to accordingly proceed in the matter. After some hesitation the Governing Body appointed the Vice-Principal, DR. Horace Jacob as Acting Principal of the College. It may be mentioned here that Dr. Bhattacharya a reputed teacher is the daughter of former cabinet secretary and former Governor of Punjab, Shri N.K. Mukherji and the grand daughter of Mr. S. Mukherji, a former reputed Principal of St.Stephen's College.

A similar situation again obtained later in January when Principal Anil Wilson proceeded on leave for the same destination-Simla-to take over as the Vice-chancellor of the Himachal Pradesh University. The College management appointed Dr. Thampu, a senior teacher of the College concurrently member of the Minority Institutions Commission as OSD. This arrangement also turned out to be controversial and the OSD resigned. The post of the Principal had already been advertised. The senior most teacher Mr. Frank was appointed Acting Principal, till the appointment of a regular Principal .Eventually DR. Thampu was appointed Principal, though not without fluttering of a few feathers in the College community.

Hindu College

Hectic lobbying took place when the Principal of Hindu College was to be appointed after the retirement of Dr. P.C. Verma. The selection committee with Dr. Bharat Ram as Chairman recommended Dr. Ashok Mittal, a teacher of the College for appointment. As soon as the name became known protests started pouring before the Chairman against Dr. Mittal. There was vehement opposition from several members of the Governing Body. The track record of Dr. Mittal was discussed in not very healthy atmosphere. The Chairman wondered if the University could do something in the matter to bail him out. He had a personal meeting with me to discuss the matter. I told him that the University would come into picture only when the Governing Body sends a list of persons for final selection. On being asked if the Governing Body could reject the panel recommended by the selection committee I reiterated the provision of the Ordinance XVIII stating that the University would respond on receipt of a list from the Governing Body. Later the Governing Body rejected the panel and advertised the post again. The selection committee recommended a panel of three names but the Governing Body chose to send only one name. This was in violation of the procedure laid down for the purpose. Accordingly the University pointed out the lapse, which the College promptly rectified. It was for the second time that the College Governing Body made a faux passé in the process of appointing Principal. On receipt of the full panel the V.C. gave approval for the appointment of Principal in accordance with the order of preference mentioned by the selection committee. Dr. Kavita Sharma became the first woman to be appointed Principal of Hindu College. It may be mentioned that the name of Dr. R.D.Panwar also figured on the panel recommended by the selection committee.

Shivaji College

Dr. Tulsi Ram resigned from the post of Principal of Shivaji College in July 1975 and the post was advertised. Those days I was working as Reader in the Sanskrit department of the University. Inspired by the spirit of serving my former College I applied for the post. At the interview, among other things the chairman (Shri Jag Pravesh Chandra) asked me if I was in favour of religious instruction in colleges. I replied that compulsory instruction in religion was not desirable in a multi-religious society like ours and optional instruction in religion was not feasible for want of infra structure and competent teachers. The chairman was seemingly unimpressed with my reply and entangled me into a longish discussion on the subject. I sticked to my views on the subject and gave cogent reasons in support thereof. The focus was shifted to other questions, which I tackled with equal confidence. The selection committee prepared a panel of nine persons listed alphabetically from among whom the final selection was to be made by an apex committee headed by the Vice-chancellor. It took nearly an year's time for the apex committee to meet.

At the interview the Vice-Chancellor (Prof. R.C.Mehrotra) read out my bio data underlining the fact that I had scored first class in all examinations including also an All India NCC course. One of the members, Prof. M.V.Mathur asked me why I was shifting to administration when in light of my bright record a promising career in academics could be easily foreseen. My reply was that in educational administration there were ample opportunities of maintaining academic interest. I further pointed out with due apology that among the members of the selection committee were persons, who were the best examples of such a combination.[I am sure my reply must have pleased all the members of the Committee.] At the end of the interview the V.C. asked me if I would advance any special claim for the post. I replied that I had no special claim except the qualifications, which I had mentioned in my application. The selection committee put only my name in the list to be sent to the college for appointment of Principal.

The chairman of the Governing Body (Shri I.K. Trehan) kept the issuing of appointment letter to me pending for about two months in the impression that he would get another name to be included in the list. But the University pointed out that nothing can be added to the minutes of the selection (apex) committee to which he himself was a party. That ended the suspense. The chairman ultimately issued the appointment letter to me. I joined as Principal of Shivaji College on 27th August 1976.

On my appointment as Dean of Colleges in 1988 I was on leave and lien till 1996. The post of Principal was advertised in 1997 and the selection committee recommended three names. The chairman of the Governing Body, Dr. J.K.Jain sent only one name for the approval of the University. It took me several sessions of discussions with Dr. Jain to convince him to send all the three names for consideration of the Vice-Chancellor. By the time the remaining names were received the qualifications for the post of Principal had undergone an alteration. After taking legal opinion the University asked the college to re-advertise the post as per new qualifications. The matter dragged on for several years for one reason or the other. Ultimately the post was filled up in mid 2002 with the appointment of Dr. (Mrs) Rama Patnaik of Indraprastha College. Unfortunately she failed to enlist the support and co-operation of a large majority of teachers. Things went wrong after a couple of months of initial romance of having a lady Principal in a co-educational college. The confusion got worse confounded with the politicking by some members of the governing body. Placing an ex- Principal of a women's college as chairperson of the governing body proved counter productive. The demolition squad pushed hard and succeeded in securing the suspension of the Principal. With the prospects of alternative employment in sight Dr. Patnaik went for voluntary retirement jn stead of fighting in the court waiting for years for uncertain outcome. I had some role to play in the denouement.

Sports Science

Driven by the vision of Professor Moonis Raza, the then V.C of Delhi University the Delhi Government opened the Institute of Physical Education and Sports Sciences in 1987. Initially the Institute was housed in a corner of a government school at Ludlow castle in Civil Lines area. The Director of Physical Education of the University was entrusted with the additional job of putting the Institute in place. Since the number of students admitted in the first year was small paucity of space did not pose any immediate problem. Soon after my joining the University as Dean of Colleges the OSD of the Institute accompanied by another teacher met me putting forth a number of demands. The major one was that the Institute be shifted to the premises of the Directorate of Physical Education in the University. The V.C. had already briefed me about the issue and had desired that the Delhi Government should take the responsibility to maintain and run the Institute and that the University was to provide academic help and guidance. Therefore I found no difficulty in explaining to the OSD what was obvious to me. Apparently unsatisfied he went back but not without clumsily insinuating that he would not be able to contain the unrest among the students spreading fast due to the unsatisfactory arrangements for needed space. I took note of what he had tried to convey in a veiled manner and kept my eyes and ears near the earth.

It did not take long before a fierce but short of violent agitation was launched by the students (working as proxies) of the Institute demanding shifting the Institute to the University area and starting of postgraduate courses in sports science. The University administration showed firmness but simultaneously proceeded to persuade the Delhi government to make a spacious school building available for the Institute (where it continues to run till now). One year Diploma course in physical education (D. P. Ed.) was instituted. The agitation was left with no legs to stand on. It died a natural death.

Power to Punish

Dr. S.C. Jain, a teacher of Physics in Hindu College used to be irregular in taking his classes on one pretext or the other. His behaviour with his colleagues in the department was far from cordial. He was also very abrasive in his dealings with the staff in general and hardly cared for the exhortations of the Principal to mend his ways. In fact he often challenged the authority of the Principal. Matters came to such a pass that the association of the

College went to the extent of passing a resolution demanding action against him. The Principal, Dr.P.C.Verma met and informally told me one day that the Governing Body was contemplating dismissal of Dr. Jain on the grounds of misconduct. I was concerned over the turn of events and advised Dr.Verma to use caution as the punishment of dismissal may not go well with the University community in the prevailing conditions and that the issue might trigger a big agitation by DUTA. Dr. Verma's assessment was that in the first place no agitation in support of Dr. Jain was likely as he had lost sympathy of the teachers in general and those of his own college in particular. He further said that if at all such a situation developed he would be ready to plead with the Governing body to reduce the punishment to withholding of some increments. I found this approach reasonable for bringing a derelict teacher to book. I shared this piece of personal conversation with Prof. Baxi, the then Vice-Chancellor. He was not sure if dismissal was the right punishment. He thought a corrective action would be a better option. But he left the matter there hoping for the right thing to happen.

The Governing body of Hindu College proceeded to dismiss Dr. Jain. The V.C. was initially reluctant to give his approval to the action of the Governing Body. He got a questionnaire prepared for the opinion of the Senior Counsel, the central point being that could the V.C. reduce the punishment or could he refuse to approve the dismissal. The Senior Counsel's opinion on both the queries was in the affirmative. My reading of the University law was different. In my opinion the provision for approval of the V.C. of the action of dismissal was incorporated in Ordinance XII to put a check on procedural flaw or a mala fide action. I explained to the V.C. the various provisions regarding the service conditions of college teachers and how the V.C. was not contemplated as a disciplinary authority higher to the G.B. The V.C. appreciated the point I was making and ultimately gave his approval to the action of the G.B in dismissing Dr. Jain.. However, he personally felt that the punishment was harsh and hoped that the issue would not invite an agitation in the University. I recalled for his benefit the approach of the Principal in this case as shared with me earlier.

Ready to Review

During a meeting of the EC held around this time one of the teacher representatives in the Council, Dr. N. K. Kakkar came in the well of the house obstructing the proceedings and resumed his seat only after obtaining an assurance from the V.C. that he would take up the matter of dismissal of Dr. Jain with the College authorities. But he gave no assurance as to the outcome. The DUTA also had taken up the case of Dr. Jain; agitating for his reinstatement. The Teachers' Association of Hindu College also developed second thoughts and describing the punishment as harsh demanded the reinstatement of Dr. Jain. In these circumstances the V.C asked me to discuss the matter with the College authorities to explore the possibility of a review of the punishment. I called the Principal and explained the situation developing at the University and reminded him of his promise earlier made to get the punishment reviewed. The Principal was gracious enough and responded positively. He only desired that since it was a matter of the powers of the Governing Body, two things should be done. Firstly, Dr. Jain should request the College for a review of the punishment with an undertaking for submitting to the discipline of the College. Secondly, at least the P.V.C. if not the V.C. should meet the chairman Dr. Bharat Ram to put across the University's point of view. The V.C. agreed to the above modality. The P.V.C. Prof. A. L. Nagar and I met Dr. Bharat Ram and explained to him the dynamics of the case. Dr. Bharat Ram straight away said that it was solely a matter for the University and the Principal to decide upon. He, on his part, as Chairman of the G.B. was willing to accept any proposal brought by the Principal, which was to the satisfaction of the University. Consequently Dr. Jain applied for review of his case. The Governing Body decided to modify the punishment from dismissal to withholding of three annual increments with cumulative effect. The teachers, both in the DUTA and the Staff Association of Hindu College heaved a sigh of relief over saving the job of a teacher. The College management had the satisfaction over the implementation of the principle of punishing the derelict. The University administration was happy that its intervention could bring about resolution of a sensitive and ticklish issue.

Abortive Attempt

Dr. Mrs. Raj Wadhwa was one of the distinguished Principals in Delhi University Colleges. She had built up Vivekanand (Mahila) College from a scratch and brought it to the position of one of the leading colleges of Delhi. She deserved and got the first re-employment for three years after superannuating. Before the University could process the case for approval, the term of the Governing Body expired and new personnel were appointed. Shri K.G.Bhagat, an eminent lawyer got elected as chairman with the active support of Mrs.Wadhwa. Shri Bhagat had solicited her help through the good offices of Mr.R.K.Dhawan. The approval of the University to the re-employment of Mrs. Wadhwa was conveyed to the chairman Shri Bhagat in due course of time. He took no action in the matter for quite long and also did not take the other members of the G.B. into confidence. Nor did he call a meeting of the G.B. requisitioned on the subject by some members. A couple of days before the due date of her re-employment Mrs.Wadhwa requested the chairman to issue her the necessary letter. He told her that he would issue the letter in due course of time. Suspecting the bona fides of Shri Bhagat, Mrs.Wadhwa prepared herself to file a writ in the Delhi High Court. Her hunch came out to be true as Shri Bhagat on the last day of her tenure issued a letter asking her to hand over charge to the senior most teacher and that the re-employment granted to her by the previous G.B. was not valid as per law. Mrs.Wadhwa immediately moved the High Court in a writ petition. She won the case after a couple of hearings. When confronted by hard facts and provisions of the Ordinances and rules of the University Shri Bhagat beat a hasty retreat and offered in open court to give Mrs.Wadhwa the required letter for her re-employment. It is pertinent to mention here that the High Court rejected the clarification of the provisions of the Ordinance XII relating to re-employment offered by the Ministry of Education in response to a query made by Shri Bhagat ruling that the ministry had no role in the matter and that it was curious and improper that such a letter was at all sent to the Chairman of the governing body.

His Whim

Mrs. Wadhwa was happy that her stand was vindicated. However, the saga of her re-employment was to continue for one more episode. She had justified her first re-employment by taking the College to greater heights. When the time for the second stint of her re-employment approached a different person (Shri Ram Phal Bansal) was the chairman of the G.B. He was politically aligned to the B.J.P. As per popular perception politically Mrs.Wadhwa was pro BJP though she was also known for functioning without political considerations. It was expected that there would be no hassles in Mrs. Wadhwa getting the second stint of re-employment for a further period of two years. But this expectation proved elusive as did Mr. Bansal's stand on the issue. In spite of the overwhelming opinion in the Governing Body being in favour of granting further re-employment to Mrs. Wadhwa Mr. Bansal went on postponing the issue for formally placing it before the G.B. When several members protested to Mr. Bansal he called Mrs. Wadhwa and requested her to accept only one year's re-employment instead of for two in the first instance. She agreed and the needful was done. When one year expired Shri Bansal was no more on the G.B. This time there was no problem and Mrs.Wadhwa got her final re-employment honourably. She relinquished office on attaining the age of 65 years.

Troubles in Daulat Ram

Mrs. Sita Lakshmi Nambiar Principal of Daulat Ram College was very popular and believed in and practiced democratic functioning. She was very considerate and helpful to the staff and students and did not countenance the interference of the members of the family of the management in the day to day functioning of the College When Mrs. Nambiar superannuated the College management did not favour giving her re-employment. The chairman, Shri Dharmavira when approached told the V.C., Prof. Gurbaksha Singh that an important member (Shanta Mohan, whom Mrs. Nambiar had taught at M.A.level) of the family of the College management wanted to have a new Principal and that he being a close family relation would not like to oppose that family member as she had lost her husband some time back. Some DUTA activists met Mrs. Nambiar and asked her if she would like the

DUTA to take up her case. She politely refused such an offer, as she did not want any controversy on her account.

Mrs.Deepali Chandra succeeded Mrs. Nambiar. She presented a contrast with her predecessor in functioning. Controversies started cropping up around her very early. A feeling of alienation started developing especially among members of the teaching staff. The calm and homogeneous climate of yester years gave way to bickering and agitations. The College management was being fed with one-sided version given by the Principal. Decisions taken at the Governing Body level with limited and sometimes biased inputs were flawed and in several cases opposed by various groups. The agitating staff meeting with repeated rebuffs from the Principal also got into the syndrome of rigidity and hostility. Their posture attracted some extremist elements in the University who were always on the lookout for a hunting ground. Situation in the College degenerated day by day. The University administration gave friendly advice to the Principal from time to time to be realistic in her approach in solving problems and devise strategies to win over the confidence of her staff. But the Principal generally took it with a pinch of salt.

Upendra Baxi, Professor of Law in the University was appointed V.C. on May 11, 1990. Some teachers of Daulat Ram College living in his neighbourhood on the campus had been talking (at times in a biased manner) to Prof. Baxi about the goings on in the College. On his appointment as Vice-Chancellor they became more active and aggressive. Their direct access to the V.C. turned their ever increasing arrogance into some sort of mania for the removal of the Principal and super cession of the Governing Body. This group of teachers being very vocal had succeeded in enlisting the following of the majority of teachers in the College and support of some Professors in the University departments. But things had changed. Prof. Baxi was in a different role now. From a disinterested listener he was now in Vice-Chancellor's chair expected to follow and protect the Act, Statutes and Ordinances of the University. The Agitating teachers were impatient and wanted things to happen their way. They did not let any opportunity slip their way and would take cudgels on any issue and on anybody's behalf.

In a meeting of the Governing Body of the College one of the members, Mr. Mittal was reported to have made a remark which was construed to be derogatory to the dignity of Women. The teachers immediately rushed to the V.C. who was a reputed feminist also. They demanded Mr. Mittal's removal from the membership of the G.B. The feminist in Professor Baxi got the better of the V.C. and the Jurist in him, and in spite of the note of caution striked by me he decided to remove Mr. Mittal from membership of the G.B. He himself signed the removal order. This I thought was quite an unusual act on the part of the V.C. Mr. Mittal filed a writ petition in the Delhi High Court against his summary removal. Predictably Mr. Mittal won the case. The court held the action against natural justice, as no show cause notice had been served before taking action..

Kidding on 'Kidnapping'

Another incident presented an opportunity to the teachers to agitate and pressurize the V.C. A student from eastern region, who was resident of the College hostel had not returned after spending the week end with her parents in New Delhi. The college informed her parents about it. Presumably she was taken as missing. When her parents approached the College for help a story was spread by the teachers that the girls in the hostel were not safe, as one of them had been kidnapped. It was for the College and the Police to look into the matter and take such action as was appropriate. But these teachers queered the pitch on the 'kidnapping' story and succeeded in persuading the V.C. to institute an inquiry in the matter to be conducted by the University Proctor who was ever more than willing to jump into any fray. Later on her return to home it turned out that the girl had taken leave from the hostel for the week end and was living with her father, an I.A.S. officer at his official residence at New Delhi on the date of her disappearance and that instead of being kidnapped she had voluntarily gone away from her home with her boy friend and had returned on her own in due course of time.

You Hold, I Go

Yet another point of pressure brought upon the Vice-Chancellor by the group of agitating teachers was the issue of re-employment of Mrs. Vijayan one of the active members of this group. Mrs. Vijayan due to her personal and family circumstances was not interested in getting re-employment and as such had not applied for the same. But on the contrary in a letter addressed to the G.B. she had blamed the management for their alleged mala fides and stated that it would be below her dignity to accept re-employment in the College. The teachers were alleging that Mrs. Vijayan was being denied re-employment. On the one hand the concerned teacher was doing everything to spoil her own chances of getting re-employment and on the other the group supporting her was pressurizing the University to intercede on her behalf. When the V.C. asked for my opinion on the issue I gave my assessment as stated above and offered to make efforts to persuade the management to act unilaterally to grant re-employment to Mrs. Vijayan, who was known to be a good teacher. On clearance from the V.C., I proceeded to take up the case with the chairman of the G.B. On my explaining the various angles of the issue, particularly of Mrs. Vijayan being a good teacher and there being hardly a chance of her accepting re-employment the chairman readily agreed to get the clearance of the case by the G.B. The G.B. decided to offer to Mrs. Vijayan re-employment for one year in the first instance, to be reviewed well before the expiry of that period. As was my hunch Mrs. Vijayan did not accept the offer and the matter ended there. The College administration thus escaped another salvo from the agitating teachers.

Conspire to Perish

Finding the management reluctant to proceed against the Principal the teachers turned their ire against the Governing Body itself. They raised the question of mismanagement and improper investment of College funds. A case was being built up to pressurize the University to take action in accordance with the Provisions of Statute 30 (D) (i) to add 50 % additional members to the Governing Body. The Governing Body replied to questions and queries whenever made by the University on the alleged irregularities. There did not appear to be substance in these allegations. But certain vocal members of the EC working in tandem with the agitating teachers of the college succeeded in getting a notice issued to the College for action under provisions of statute30 (D) (i).The reply of the College was not found satisfactory and the EC decided to add five members to the G.B. The Chairman filed a writ petition in the High Court challenging the action of the University. A good number of teachers of the College attended the Court on days of hearing. On one of the hearings they got a strict reprimand from Justice P.N. Kripal when they tried to intervene during the arguments. Justice Kripal questioned their presence in the Court and asked whether they were on leave from the College and whether they were not neglecting their basic duty of teaching. The writ was allowed mainly on the ground of law of natural justice not having been followed without going into the merit of the case on other counts.

The V.C. was of the opinion that the High Court had not fully appreciated the procedure followed by the University and that the case of the University had good chances of succeeding in the Supreme Court. Accordingly it was decided to file an SLP in the Supreme Court. The Supreme Court upheld the verdict of the High Court. It was a set back to the agitating teachers of the College and the University had burnt its fingers twice. But instead of cooling down, tempers got heightened up in face of successive setbacks. Demand for drastic action became almost a crescendo. In these circumstances the EC appointed a committee under the chairmanship of Prof. Namvar Singh, the Visitor's nominee on the E.C. to draft a charge sheet against the Governing Body. The other members of the committee were the two teacher representatives in the EC. The same committee was authorized to study the replies of the College and offer its comments thereon.

Path of Peace Paved

I had my doubts and reservations on the course adopted by the University all along and had been expressing the same to the V.C. in strict confidence. But at the same time I kept these reservations entirely personal and did my best to implement the decisions of the V.C. and the University unreservedly and sincerely. The V.C. fully appreciated the position taken by me. In this background I considered it my duty to advise the V.C. not to repeat a process which had already resulted in loss of face to the University. I could demonstrate to him how loosely drafted the charge sheet was and how it lacked substance to stand judicial scrutiny. The V.C had full trust in me (and I think, in my legal acumen as far as university rules were concerned) and therefore, asked me to suggest an alternate course of action. I suggested that in place of adding members to the G.B. as a punitive measure we should explore the possibility of the College *suo motu* requesting the University for nominating an agreed number of additional representatives on the G.B. I offered my services to negotiate with the College management. I also pointed out to the V.C. that such a course was well within the provisions of Statute 30 (C), which prescribed a ceiling of twenty for membership of the G.B. The prevailing number was only fifteen.

The V.C. being a law expert expressed his surprise and happiness at the discovery of the space for the new strategy workable within the statutes of the University and gave me full authorization to proceed in the matter. Without any loss of time I organized a meeting with the Chairman (Shri Mahendra Narain Gupta) of the Governing Body. Professor P. B. Mangla, close to the chairman also joined us. I explained to the chairman the advantages of such a solution. It was based on mutual trust and faith and confrontation was foreign to the proposed arrangement. The chairman was gracious enough to accept the suggestion and sent a proposal accordingly. The EC considered the proposal and decided to send five additional representatives authorizing the V.C. to decide upon the names. The V.C. on his part was very fair to all concerned and nominated five reputed Professors known for their integrity and administrative ability. The arrangement proved of such a great help that the College continued to follow it for a long time even though not called for in the improved situation.

The major hump had been crossed and the College appeared treading on a smooth course. But one irritant still remained. It was the almost impossible chance of improvement in inter-personal relations of the Principal with the staff. Dr. Ashok Jain, a distinguished academician became chairman of the College governing Body. He along with the seven representatives of the University served as a convenient bridge between the management and the teachers. With patient parleys where I also joined when required a formula was worked out according to which the

Principal Mrs. Deepali Chandra would seek pre-mature voluntary retirement. The College in turn would give her all admissible benefits and in addition some amount of compensation in the form of advance salary for the unexpired period of her tenure. In due course of time the formula was implemented and the College witnessed much needed peace. Subsequently Dr. Malati Subrahmanyam, a moderate and a distinguished teacher of the College was appointed Principal.

Acharya of Bhaskaracharya

Delhi Government opened the Bhaskaracharya College of Applied Sciences in 1995.Dr. Chibber, a senior Professor of Chemistry was appointed OSD pending the appointment of Principal. The newly constituted Governing Body elected Dr. B.R.Grover, a retired Professor of history in Jamia Milia as its chairman. He presided over the selection committee for making recommendations for appointment of the Principal. After the interviews were over, he read out three names to be selected for the purpose without asking the other members even once to give their opinion in the matter. When they challenged him he swore by non-existent powers of the chairman and adjourned the meeting saying that he had made the selection and whatever the other members had to say had been considered by him. That amounted to ultra-constitutional act on the part of the chairman. The other members of the selection committee (one of them being Professor Deepak Pental, who later became V.C.) lodged their protest with the University. Therefore when the chairman put his recommendation before the Governing body the same were turned down on the ground of *ultra virus*. University took note of the style of functioning of the chairman and did not approve his name proposed by the Delhi Government for the next tenure. Some other gentleman was elected chairman. The process of the appointment of the Principal went off smoothly. The University extended full co-operation to the College management. Dr. G.R.Chopra was appointed Principal. He proved a very successful administrator. Within a couple of years of his taking over as principal the college got its own new building and several innovative courses were introduced.

Rumblings at Ramjas

Ramjas College (1917) is one of the oldest three colleges (the other two being St. Stephen's (1881) and Hindu (1899) of the University of Delhi, which happen to be senior in age even to the University. The College has had such distinguished persons as its Principals as Rai Kedar Nath, Gurmukh Nihal Singh and Shri B.B.Gupta. Shri P.D.Gupta, long time Bursar of the College succeeded Shri B.B.Gupta. He was an expert in finance and examination matters but was not well equipped wit skills in human resource management. Some how, he could not enlist the confidence and support of his colleagues, vital for managing the College during a period when the radical ideology was on ascendance in the academic world in India. He gradually found himself surrounded by controversies. A vocal section of the staff went on a warpath against him. Even student leaders got involved in the confrontation and the forum of students' union was used to fight the battle against the Principal. The University administration could not remain unaffected by the heat of the events at Ramjas College. The Inquiry committee headed by Justice S.S.Dulat indicted the extremist elements among the staff and students. No follow up action on the report could be taken as the events moved faster than the process of decision making.

The University thought of taking Shri Gupta away from the scene of controversies by appointing him Controller of Examinations in the University. But the pressure brought about by some vested interests in the University administrative staff scuttled the move. However, very soon Shri Gupta was appointed Controller of Examinations of the Kurukshetra University where he proved his mettle in streamlining the examination system. Dr. Govind Rai Chaudhary, who had briefly served as Principal of Swami Shraddhanand College and had to leave amid controversies, succeeded Shri Gupta as Principal of Ramjas College. Dr. Chaudhary found the seat quite hot. He had already failed to manage things at Shraddhanand College and it did not take very long for him to realize that managing Ramjas College was a hurculean task beyond his capacity. He resigned leaving the College in a crisis. Dr.B.M. Bhatia, the then Principal of Hindu College was appointed OSD to look after the College in addition to his responsibility as Principal of his college. Feeling frustrated Dr. Bhatia gave up the charge within a short of time. Shri Ruddar Dutt, who later became Principal of School of Corresponding Courses and Continuing Education, then took charge as OSD. He also left after some time with the realization that things could not be improved there in the given circumstances.

With the declaration of emergency in the country in June, 1975 agitations gave way to disciplined behaviour on the part of all concerned and the life in the College appeared to be normal. Dr. Kartar Singh, a senior teacher of Botany in Kirorimal College was appointed Principal of the College. Taking advantage of the environment brought about by emergency, he worked hard for the development of the College. There was appreciable improvement in the College, especially in creation of infrastructure and development of the campus. Ramjas looked like having cast away the ominous shadows. The withdrawal of the emergency in 1977 and the emerging political culture not leaving the College untouched very soon exposed the deceptive calm. The elements earlier fomenting and leading the agitation and which were dormant during the emergency resurfaced with renewed vigour. Dr.Kartar Singh failed to realize the difference in the environment and continued to function in the style perfected during the days of emergency which met with hostile opposition from the staff.

All sorts of controversies arose and confrontation rather than discourse became the preferred course in tackling issues and solving problems. This started telling upon personal relations of the Principal with several activists in the College. An unfortunate incident of a murderous attack on one of the teachers, Mr. Dilip Simion by some students allegedly on the inspiration of the Principal and the then Director of Physical Education, Dr. J.P. Jain triggered off a crisis. The teachers demanded immediate suspension of the Principal and Dr. Jain. The agitation spread to the University administration. All efforts to contain the agitation, which grew stronger day after day proved futile. Most unwillingly, the Governing Body placed the Principal and Dr. Jain under suspension and decided to institute an Inquiry into the unfortunate incidence. But peace could be restored in the College on the governing body agreeing to institute an inquiry against the Principal by a retired high court judge.

OSD Ramjas

Officiating arrangements were made by appointing the senior most teacher as Acting Principal. This experiment failed, as one after another Acting Principal would resign within a short period of taking charge. It was at this stage that the Vice-Chancellor (Prof. Gurbakhsh Singh) persuaded me to work as OSD of Ramjas College. I took charge of OSD in addition to my responsibilities as Principal of Shivaji College in July 1983. I took up this responsibility with the understanding that it would be for a couple of months during which period the College would have solved the problems and appointed a new Principal. Apart from the normal work of the post of Principal I was required to organize and process the Inquiry in the case of Dr. Kartar Singh to be conducted by Justice (retd.) S.N. Shankar. I under took my work with earnest devotion and objectivity. My day started with my reaching Ramjas College at 8.00 a.m.(even earlier if a meeting with Justice Shankar was fixed for the morning). After meeting the staff and visiting the science departments I left instructions with the administrative staff regarding matters to be attended to during the day. Around 12.00 noon I left for Shivaji College where I spent three to four hours. The ungrudging help and co-operation of my colleagues in Shivaji Colege, especially the Vice-Principal, Mr. Prithvi Chand proved a great source of strength for me in performing the onerous task that I had under taken. I returned to Ramjas College by four o'clock and dealt with the papers brought for my consideration and paid attention to all pending issues. I devoted the evening to the work of the Inquiry committee and returned home normally around 9.00 p.m.

I picked up the threads of the cobwebs of issues at Ramjas College one by one and tried to sort out things. I got full co-operation of the teachers in general excepting a few endemically negatively oriented elements. It was equally true of the non-teaching staff. I had made it known to all concerned that I was not in Ramjas for a job, which I already had in Shivaji. My motivation was to do some good to a sister institution to the extent

I could. However, I realized in a couple of months that the road for the smooth passage of Ramjas College needed patient toiling for a period longer than I could afford to devote with two assignments at the same time without affecting my efficiency and straining my stamina. I therefore, requested the College Governing Body to relieve me from the responsibility of OSD with effect from the beginning of January 1984. The Governing Body acceded to my request, though reluctantly, and I returned carrying rich experience of working in difficult situations. A few examples of my interactions in Ramjas College are worth mentioning:

Ruling on Rules

(a) A few days after my joining as OSD a meeting of the Staff Council was called. Confirmation of the minutes of the last meeting was the first item on the agenda. The very first resolution in the minutes was regarding condemnation of the Acting Principal's way of functioning. The meeting had been held in the absence of the Acting Principal and was presided over by a teacher elected by the members present. I pointed out that firstly the meeting was not valid as the same had been held without the consent of the Principal who was ex-officio chairman of the Council (there was no provision in the rules for an elected chairman). Secondly the Staff Council was not empowered to discuss and adjudicate on the conduct of the Principal. Therefore, I as chairman of the Council was duty bound to uphold the rules and not to become a party to an *ultra virus* proceeding. I requested Shri S. S. Goyal, one of the teachers known to be an expert in University laws and rules, to give his reaction on my observation. Shri Goyal agreed with my interpretation of the Staff Council rules. After some discussion the suggestion of a senior teacher for leaving the item as dead without any comments or ruling was unanimously accepted.

Win Win for All

(b) The term of appointment of the Bursar of the College was about to end when the office-bearers of the Staff Association met me and referred to a resolution of the Association laying down the procedure for appointment of the Bursar. Accordingly they expected me to invite the name from the Association for the purpose and forward the same to the Governing Body for appointment. My stand was that Ordinance XVIII provided for the appointment of the Bursar on the recommendation of the Principal and the Staff Association did not come in the picture. I did not wish to be rigid and therefore suggested that the teacher currently performing the duties of Bursar should continue for the period I was to work as OSD of the College as I was quite satisfied with his work. The office bearers had no objection to this. I continued to get the help and assistance of the incumbent. The Staff Association was happy that I did not precipitate matters by selecting a person for appointment disregarding the procedure set out by the staff Council for the purpose I had the satisfaction of not being party to adopting a procedure not contemplated in the relevant ordinance. Dr. Gupta enjoyed an extended tenure as Bursar.

Reciprocity Pays

(c) Among the problems that I had to tackle immediately as OSD was opening of the canteen. The spacious building meant for the purpose was locked by the previous caterer who had entered into litigation with the College management Efforts made earlier to get the canteen opened had not shown any result. The new session had already started and the students and members of the staff were demanding the opening of the canteen. I called the contractor and told him to vacate the premises as his contract had already expired. His response was very positive. He told me that he was prepared to vacate the premises immediately provided his outstanding bills running into thousands of rupees were paid by the College. I took steps to get the bills paid expeditiously with the approval of the governing body. Consequently the contractor vacated the canteen premises.

Not Their Business

© One day a group of students and karamcharis led by a couple of teachers assembled outsie my room wanting to see me immediately to discuss something important, aon being allowed to enter they made quite a crowd. I requested them to take the available chairs in the room. Those getting no chairs were rfequested to wait till enough number of chairs were arranged.The intervening g moments set the tone of the discussions. They informed that they had formed a co-operative society to run the College canteen and wanted my permission for the same. I told them that the matter of giving permission for running a canteen in the College was under the purview of the Governing Body and that the society formed by them could not *suo motu* decide upon the matter. They could compete with others as and when the tenders were invited for the purpose. In any case, there was no immediate arrangement required to be made as an ad-hoc arrangement had already been made, I told them. The members of the group had no ground for further argumentation. The matter ended there and they went back.But before they left I asked in a lighter veinnot expecting a reply why they were making tt heir business.

Promotion in Motion

(d) When I joined Ramjas College in July1983 I discovered that the cases of promotion of teachers under the Merit promotion scheme were pending. I processed the cases and fixed the dates for holding meetings of the respective screening/evaluation committees in various subjects. I also wrote letters to the concerned teachers to be present in the College and make them selves available to the selection committee if required. A delegation of teachers met me to protest against my decision to call the teachers to appear before the committees. I explained to them the norms and the procedure as set out in the University norms. I further impressed upon the teachers to extend their co-operation in building up a dignified promotion process and not to give an impression of having fear from peers. The teachers went back satisfied that what was being done was in their own best interest. The meetings passed off smoothly and cases of promotion of most of the eligible teachers were processed by the time I relinquished charge as OSD.

Not Negative Alone

(e) As soon as the news of my appointment as OSD became known in ramjas College I received the most unexpected visitor at my residence. It was Shri S.S. Goyal who had been at the fore-front of all agitations in the College. He had been on a course of perpetual confrontation vis a vis the authorities whether in the

College or in the University. We had known each other during interactions at University fora like the DUTA and the Academic Council and were aware of each other's approach to things. I was impressed by his thorough knowledge of the University law and rules but disappointed over the way he would himself follow the same. I expected some fire works from him in the College upon my appointment. But he revealed to me an entirely different Shri Goyal. In the first place he welcomed my appointment as OSD of the College. Then he went on to explain how he had been wronged and denied his rightful dues by successive Principals. He also apportioned blame to the teachers who, he thought had used him for serving their own selfish interest. He offered to extend his full co-operation to me. It was a pleasantly refreshing meeting giving me new insights in the understanding of human relationships. I had the satisfaction of mitigating the grievances of Shri Goyal without delay.

It was a co-incidence that one day I happened to be around when he developed some cardiac problem while he was taking his class. I immediately took him to the University Health Center in my own car and got him first aid and then arranged to send him to a specialist. One day he confided in me how inspired by some teachers he had landed himself in the position of the hostel warden, an assignment perceived to be a bulwark against the Principal which he no more wanted to hold on to. I could appreciate his dilemma and relieved him of the responsibility.

All Together

(f) Elections of the college Unions and the DUSU were scheduled as usual in the first week of September 1983. I had to organise the elections both in Shivaji College and Ramjas College. The system had been streamlined and tested at Shivaji College. So I entrusted the work of election to a team of senior teachers led by the Vice-Principal there. I had received several representations at Ramjas College regarding the weaknesses in the system. In consultation with the teachers associated with the election work I introduced the system as practiced in Shivaji College. The main element of the system was transparency and precision. Ballots of different colours were used for the various posts. All the ballots in a polling booth were cast in a single box. After the polling all the ballot boxes were brought on the stage of the college auditorium and emptied in one pile in full view of all present there. The ballot papers were then sorted out post vise and put in separate bundles to be later taken to the respective venue for counting. Only authorised persons were allowed entry at such venues. Result for each post was announced at the venue concerned. Earlier counting for each post took place separately at each polling booth. This entailed computing the totals arrived at several booths. The candidates and their agents had to run around the booths to find out the progress of votes polled by them. Moreover teachers-in-charge of counting at different venues for the same post had variation in norms of declaring votes invalid. The students welcomed the new system. It worked smoothly and all concerned were satisfied.

Suspension Agitation

Prof. S.N. Singh was in-charge of the admissions to Law Courses during the Year 1999. The admissions were to be made through an entrance test. In some quarters he was perceived to be functioning arbitrarily in the matter of taking decisions on admissions. There appeared press reports of all kinds of irregularities allegedly being committed by him in admissions. In one of the responses to the press Dr. Singh jointly with Professor B.P. Singh made a statement that the Vice-Chancellor (Prof. V.R. Mehta) had asked them for the admission of a student which they refused as it was not permitted under rules. The report infuriated the Vice-Chancellor as it was not based on facts and was aimed to defile his fair name. Both the Professors were asked to explain their conduct in leveling a false charge against the Vice-Chancellor. While the reply of Prof. B.P. Singh was evasive and dilatory, Prof. S.N. Sigh chose to take the stand that he had done no wrong and that whatever was known to him had been stated to the press. It was clear that Prof. S.N. Singh was in mode of confrontation with the Vice-Chancellor. Wiser counsel from well meaning quarters did not have any effect on him and he continued to be belligerent. Some of my other colleagues and I were advising the Vice-chancellor to exercise patience in the hope that Prof. Singh would come round to express regrets for his conduct.

After the flag hoisting and tree plantation ceremony in the University on 15th August, 1999 the Vice-Chancellor told some of us that he was not going to wait for more than a day for suspending Prof. Singh. I in turn requested Dr. Mool Chand Sharma, Proctor and Professor of law to use his good offices with Prof. Singh and persuade him for expressing regrets. Before Prof. Sharma could take an initiative in the matter the next morning, Prof Singh left a copy of a writ petition that he intended to file in the Delhi High Court the same day praying for stalling of action contemplated against him. The Vice-Chancellor, convinced that Prof. Singh was snatching the initiative in the case, suspended him with immediate effect and also ordered an inquiry against him. The V.C. spoke to me on phone in the evening and informed me of the action taken by him saying that the circumstances were compelling and he could not wait and talk to me before suspending Prof. Singh. My response was that whatever action he had taken had my full support and we all would together tackle the issue with solidarity.

Feathers Flutter

The news of the suspension of Prof. Singh spread in the University circles like a wild fire. Suspension of a teacher and all the more of a professor was an unthinkable thing to the current generation of teachers. Further, Prof. Singh was also the election officer for the ensuing elections of the DUTA. A group of activist teachers of all political hues barged into the residence of the V.C. and started shouting and using rough language in the presence of his family members. The V.C. remained quite composed and took them along and sat outside in the lawns of his residence to discuss the issue. In the mean time I was telephonically informed of the incident while I was in a meeting at Hindu College. I rushed to the residence of the V.C. and on arrival found the V.C. and P.V.C sitting in the lawns surrounded by a group of teachers. I joined them and sat there quietly listening to the provocative remarks being made by teacher after teacher. As DUTA elections were near, I took these speeches as compulsions of competitive politics. But when personally prodded to respond to some of their questions, I left no doubt about the justness of the action of the V.C. in suspending Prof. Singh. I also underlined the determination of the administration to deal firmly with any eventuality. There being no common ground to meet on, the teachers dispersed giving an ultimatum to remove the V.C. if he did not revoke the suspension of Prof. Singh by five o'clock of the evening next day. My aside was that in that case the teachers would have to stop their watches working.

Posturing apart the teachers frantically started exploring the avenues of negotiations for an amicable settlement of the issue. The V.C. on his part was open minded and kept the doors of negotiations open. I enjoyed his full confidence and trust and reciprocated the same by doing my utmost to uphold his honour and dignity of his Office. Several elements made insinuations against me but failed to draw a wedge between us as all that I was doing in dealing with the situation was in full knowledge and with the guidance of the V.C. In fact I made no single move unless the same had been discussed with the V.C. The unity of purpose, solidarity and firmness of the V.C.'s team was a phenomena witnessed rarely in earlier regimes.

In the meanwhile as the date (31st August1999) of elections of DUTA approached nearer the activists shifted their energies to electioneering. This provided to the administration an opportunity to consolidate its strategy to deal with the already petering out agitation. Mr. Shriram Oberoi of NDTF, a front organization of the BJP was elected President. He started his tenure with renewed zeal to enliven the sagging spirit of the agitation. By this time there were more on lookers than supporters of the agitation. The rigid posture of Prof. Singh in not resiling from his position of declared hostility to the Vice-Chancellor cost him dear. The observations of the Court, made on different days of hearing of a writ of public interest litigation filed by some students, also demoralized the protagonists of the path of agitation.

Way Out

Finding himself in an unenviable position the DUTA President started exploring escape windows. He approached the Vice-Chancellor for an amicable settlement of the problem. The Vice-Chancellor told him (and all others who approached him in this connection) to discuss the issue with me as I stood fully authorized to reach at a settlement on his behalf. After a series of negotiations in which some saner elements helped him a draft agreement was finalized late at night in my room. It was to be shown to the V.C. the next morning for approval and implementation. The DUTA President was keen to settle things the same night and therefore rang up the V.C. seeking an immediate appointment to settle the issue. The V.C. however, had received some guests that night and expressed his inability to attend to the issue at that hour of the night but at the same time fixed 7.00 a.m. next morning at his residence for discussing the matter. The DUTA President reached the V.C. residence in time. I also joined the meeting along with the Pro-Vice-chancellor (Prof. Abad Ahmed) and the Director, South Campus (Prof. Abhai Mansingh). After a brief discussion the DUTA President Shriram Oberoi addressed a letter to the Vice-Chancellor stating that the DUTA appreciated the circumstances under which the University had taken action against Prof. Singh. Adding that the DUTA stood for upholding the dignity of the Office of Vice-Chancellor he declared the agitation closed and assured full co-operation for making up of the teaching time lost as a result of the agitation. The Vice-Chancellor was satisfied at that and therefore, he ordered the revocation of the suspension of Prof. Singh forthwith.

Recognition Cognizance

Ever since Shri S.R.Oberoi had been elected President of DUTA he had been involving himself in controversy of one type or the other. Perhaps he wanted to demonstrate to his electorate how active and strong a President he was. Though as a person he was mild mannered and friendly he adopted tough postures, which could not be sustained. Once he was leading a *dharna* outside the venue of the Academic council meeting. A group of students were also around agitating on some issue. Police had been deployed at the gate of the hall. When the A.C. meeting was in progress some persons led by Shri Oberoi barged into the hall and indulged in violent behaviour. Shri Oberoi was alleged to have physically threatened the V.C. and assaulted the Registrar. At that point of time I was outside the hall pacifying the agitating students. On hearing the noise inside the hall I went in and found that the V.C. had already been escorted safely to his residence. I reached the V.C.'s residence and learnt about the whole incidence. It was being said by some people there that Dr. S.S. Rathi and Shri I.M. Kapahi were also responsible for inciting the students to barge into the hall and indulge in violence. I had observed no such action on the part of the two colleagues. However, the V.C. was himself very emphatic about their alleged activity. He had strong feelings in the matter and wanted to derecognise the three teachers. Some elements close to the V.C. fueled the fire of anger overtaking his mind.

Notices of withdrawal of recognition were served on the three teachers. I must confess that I acquiesced in the matter and did nothing beyond gently advising the V.C. to show magnanimity and forget about the incident, as there was nothing personal involved. The teachers responded by moving the Delhi High Court in a writ petition for the revocation of the notice for withdrawal of recognition. Positions taken on both sides had hardened but after some time there was a thaw in interpersonal relations through the efforts of some well-meaning persons. The V.C., a graceful person agreed to mutually resolve the tangle. The three teachers in separate letters to the V.C. expressed their faith in peaceful resolution of issues and regretted if an adverse impression had been created by their behaviour. The V.C. revoked the notices of withdrawal of recognition. The High Court was accordingly informed. The episode involving very senior and respected members of the teachers' fraternity ended happily. I draw satisfaction from the fact that with help from Dr. P.C. Patanjali I was instrumental in arriving at an amicable settlement.

Vigil at V.C. Villa

The year 1989 saw a host of agitations for the removal of Dr. R.D.Pawar as Acting Principal of College of Vocational Studies. One evening having frustrated in their attempt to force the governing body of the College to take a certain decision the DUTA activists rushed to the residence of the V.C., Professor Moonis Raza. The V.C. had gone to attend a marriage. The teachers were informed accordingly. But they staged a *dharana* at the gate thinking that the V.C. was inside his house. I reached the V.C.residence soon after the teachers' arrival. My repeated pleas to them to lift the *dharana* bore little result. The teachers were determined not to leave before meeting the V.C. It was getting late in the evening. On being contacted the V.C. that in the first place he was likely to reach late at night and even if the teachers wait till late hours he would not be able to meet them. Even this message had no effect on the teachers and they refused to leave and rather hardened their posture by obstructing the entry passage especially by deploying lady teachers in the front rank.

The V.C. had been kept informed of the developments. At about midnight he arrived at the residence of the P.V.C. Professor Gangrade. Mediatory attempts by Professor Sumit Sarkar and Professor Manoranjan Mohanty also did not bring any result to solve the tangle. The V.C. decided that he would enter his residence unhindered and the Police should ensure that. The Police officer on duty, CH. Suraj Bhan (former champion of wrestling) was more than ready to remove the teachers from the gate forcibly. But I advised him to wait till lady police persons arrived, requisition for which had already been sent to the Police camp at Jharoda Kalan. We waited till 2.00 o'clock in the night when the lady police arrived. They neatly picked up the couple of lady teachers squatting in front of the gate. I recall Miss Sonia Ghosh putting some resistance initially. All other teachers present there, left in a few minutes' time. The V.C. entered his residence unobstructed and I believe, had a peaceful night's sleep. It took me barely half an hour in reaching home, having dinner and thanking God before falling in deep sleep.

Blockade Braved

Ever since Dr. Sunita Puri had been appointed Principal of the Lakshmibai College in 1998 a section of teachers were confronting her and wanted her to resign and leave the College. Pressure was being mounted on the University administration to dislodge Dr.Puri. Once when the V.C. was not in town the teacher activists of the college led by Mrs. Kiran Walia announced blockade of the office complex under which no member of the V.C. team would be allowed to enter his office. I made it a point to reach my office even before the teachers arrived and squatted in front of all the entrances to the complex. When I left for my residence at lunchtime no one stopped me but at the same time I was warned that I would not be allowed to enter again. I went home, took my lunch and sat thinking about ways to re-enter my office. I had a fair idea of all the entry and exit points in the office complex. There was one exit door, which the teachers had failed to identify for picketing. It was the rarely used door for taking out discarded papers of the examination branch. I requested the Controller's office to keep the bolt of the door open from inside. I abandoned my official car and rode in the covered jeep of the examination branch. I also changed my clothes to *dhoti* and *kurta* to effect, in some measure, a disguise. I arrived at the entry point and before the group of teachers squatting only a few yards away could realize what had happened I was inside the building. I went near the main entrance and greeted Mrs. Kiran Walia and others blocking the gate. They were surprised not so much over the fact of my managing to find entry as over my sartorial guise. Mrs. Walia simply said, "You look impressive in your new attire." I had no answer and thus beat a hasty retreat to my office.

Parleys Apart

As the completion of the term of appointment of Professor V.R. Mehta as Vice-chancellor drew nearer, the agitation against the Principal of Lakshmibai College grew more vehement. It got a further fillip from the election of Professor V.P. Dutt as chairman of the governing body of the college. DUTA leadership also got involved in the agitation. Events culminated in the suspension of the Principal by the governing body. The chairman wrote to the V.C. seeking his approval of the decision. While the case was under consideration of the V.C. the Principal moved the Delhi High Court in a writ petition for stay of any action against her. The High Court passed an interim order asking the V.C. to take a decision in light of the material on record and any other record that he may like to see and also after giving a personal hearing to the Principal if he so desired. The V.C. was holding a team meeting at his residence. Some DUTA representatives gained entry inside his residence on the pretext of discussing a formula of settlement of the issue. After discussing the issue for a few minutes they demanded that a particular type of formulation be made in replying to the college chairman. In an aside talk in the adjoining room I suggested that the V.C. and other members of the team should engage the teachers in negotiations and I should be able to prepare and send a reply to the chairman on lines decided upon by the V.C. But problem arose when the lady teachers of Lakshmibai College blocking the gate did not allow me to go out. I told them in a lighter vein that I would turn into a fly and manage my exit.

'Though the remark was made off the cuff it set me thinking of exploring alternative point of exit. I went in the backyard of the V.C.'s residence and found a spot on the boundary wall from where I could easily cross over to the compound of the School of Corresponding Courses. Fortuitously there was a ladder lying on the School side. Some employees who were around helped me jump over the wall. By coincidence a driver of a teacher of the School was available on the spot along with his car. He was good enough to give me a ride to my office. I got the reply prepared in a few minutes, arranged its dispatch and returned to the V.C.'s residence by the same route as described above. It was such a quite affair that no one among the teachers present at the V.C. residence came to know about it. On my arrival the V.C. gradually changed the stance and finally declared that the University had already replied to the chairman almost on the lines that the teachers were suggesting. Suspecting that a reply might not have been sent they agreed to leave if we showed the office copy. The V.C. took advantage of the situation and immediately flaunted and read out from the copy of the letter. The teachers were not satisfied with the contents of the letter but they had no alternative. The scene had been shifted to the College and the teachers could little afford to miss the opportunity to meet the chairman and impress him. So all of them left to continue their own private parleys. The case dragged on and it was only during the tenure of the next V.C., Professor Deepak Nayyar that the High Court gave a deadline for the V.C. to take a final decision. The V.C. after taking legal opinion and considering the matter in all its aspects gave approval for the suspension of the Principal, Dr. Sunita Puri. Later the governing body terminated her services. It is another story that a subsequent order of the Court in favour of Mrs. Puri did not prove of any help to her as a determined governing body ensured that she remained in wilderness.

Attempt to Intimidate

A few days after Prof. Mehta joined as V.C.(1995) I was in a meeting, which was going on in a room adjacent to his office. I noticed through the window a group of teachers led by Dr. R.D. Pawar going towards the office of the V.C. In a few minutes'time noise of shouting reached the committee room. As the noise got louder I went into the room of the V.C. to be available for any help that may be required. I found that the members of the group were asking the V.C. to issue immediate orders for the re-employment of a teacher (Mr. Khan) of the College of Vocational Studies. The V.C. told them that the matter was in the purview of the Governing Body of the College and that they should discuss the matter with the Chairman. I requested the teachers to be calm and patient and understand the position as explained by the V.C. In turn they challenged my very presence there and accused me of interference in their matter. I affirmed my presence there as a member of the team of the V.C. and told them that they had no right to question my presence there.

The verbal exchanges with the leaders of the group including Dr. R.D. Pawar and Dr. J.P. Sharma turned hot. Dr. Pawar went to the level of making uncomplimentary remarks about my role as an Officer of the University. I rebuffed him and suggested that instead of making a scene in the room of the V.C. he should go out and wait for me in my room where we could discuss any problem that he might have with me. The V.C. was shocked at the remarks made by Dr. Pawar against me. He desired that action should be initiated against Dr. Pawar for his unruly behaviour. But I preferred to ignore it and wished to make Dr. Pawar realize his mistake by giving him sane counsel in calmer moments. Thanking the V.C. for his offer of action against Dr. Pawar I went back to attend the meeting in the adjacent room.

In the meantime I sent instructions to my staff to make the group led by Dr. Pawar seated in my room and offer cold drinks. After the meeting was over I reached my office and asked Dr. Pawar about the problem he had with me. He moved down from the chair and squatted on the floor in front of me and asked me to shoot him. I advised him to refrain from such drama and come to the point if there was anything to be discussed for sorting out. On learning about the 'drama' the P.V.C., Prof. A.L. Nagar and the Registrar, Prof. S.K. Wasan came to my room to intercede. But I politely told them that they did not need to worry, as I was sure of resolving the matter peacefully. Appreciating the situation both left but not before Dr. Pawar had culled this itself as an example of my stubbornness. He also pretended that I had threatened him and that I was free to execute my threat as he was at my disposal. I impressed upon him about the futility of his attempt to provoke me and politely but firmly advised him to develop positive attitude and to seek harmony instead of confrontation. The episode ended with a happy note to be followed by a personal visit of Dr. Pawar to my office a few days later expressing regret over his behaviour. I reciprocated by assuring him of my continued goodwill for him.

Resignation Resort

(i) Shri Vijay Goel was an elected member of the Executive Council during early nineties. It was his second and last tenure. Around this period an incident of ragging occurred in Ramjas College, which got blown out of proportion due to inapt handling at various levels. The media played a major role in distorting the episode. Mr. Vijay Goel first staged a *dharana* at the University gate demanding a certain course to be followed in the case. Failing to get his demand met he addressed to the V.C. a letter of resignation from membership of the EC. He attended the ensuing meeting of the EC and asked the V.C. to announce the acceptance of the resignation. I raised a point of order saying that Mr. Goel's letter was not a valid resignation letter, as the same had not been addressed to the Registrar as per provision of Statute 38. The V.C. ruled accordingly and in a lighter vein remarked that if Mr. Goel was sincere in resigning from the membership of the EC, he should submit the letter of resignation to the Registrar in which case it would become effective immediately. Mr. Goel was visibly embarrassed.

(ii) Another member of the EC, Miss Veena Majumadar was highly dissatisfied by the amount of punishment awarded to the culprits in a case of ragging at Ramjas College. She wrote to the Vice-Chancellor, Professor Baxi expressing her unhappiness and demanded that a special meeting of the EC should be held to discuss the issue. The V.C. discussed the matter in his team. My view was that discipline being in the sole jurisdiction of the powers of the Vice-Chancellor a reference of the same would not be in accordance with the provision of law. Further that would amount to the EC deciding over the action of the V.C., which he had taken by virtue of the authority given to him by the Statutes of the University. The V.C. and other members of the team agreed with the above view and it was decided not to place the matter before the EC. Apparently Miss Majumdar felt agitated over this decision and sent a letter of resignation from the membership of EC to the V.C. The V.C. sought my advice in the matter. I pointed out that since Miss Majumdar was a nominee of the Visitor no action was called for at the University level as far as her resignation was concerned. She was free to take up the matter of her resignation with the Visitor. The V.C. agreed with the above analysis on the basis of the provisions of the University Statutes. The matter stood there. The University did not hear any thing on the issue from the Visitor. Miss Majumdar did not attend the ensuing meetings till the end of her term of nomination a couple of months later.

Fun at 'Funeral'

Professor Moonis Raza had superannuated in February 1990. Pending appointment of new Vice-Chancellor Professor K.D. Gangrade, the P.V.C. was acting as Vice-Chancellor. As was their wont, the laboratory employees of the University and colleges went on strike when the time for practical examinations approached. They were insistent on certain demands, which could not be acceded to. The University decided to postpone the practical examinations till after the end of the vacations. To keep their agitation alive the employees resorted to an indefinite *dharna* at the University gate. The P.V.C. entrusted the job of handling the situation the way I thought fit. Several interactions with the employees failed to bring them to resuming work. They had thought that the interim administration would cave in under the pressure of their tactics. They made me the target of their ire. One day they prepared an effigy of mine and took out a 'funeral' procession through the roads of the campus.

On learning about their plan I decided to follow the procession in my car driving a few yards' behind. The procession ended at the compound inside the main entrance of the University where the employees performed my 'last rites' by burning the effigy. After watching the fun unobserved from a respectable distance I went home to have my lunch. The word went round how sportingly I had taken the incident and how demoralized the employees felt. Eventually they approached me through Principal Krishnamurthy of Sri Venkatesvara College for a meeting on 11th of May 1990. I discussed the matter with the P.V.C. and fixed the meeting to be held at 11.00 A.M on the above date. Before the meeting could take place the event of the appointment of Professor Upendra Baxi, the new V.C. on the same morning changed the context. So the meeting stood cancelled. In stead the new V.C. went round the campus and also met the agitating laboratory staff and asked them to lift their *dharna* and let him examine the issue in a congenial atmosphere. Consequently the agitation was called off. The V.C. came to know of the frivolity of the demands of the laboratory staff.

Computer Compulsion

The Vice-Chancellor Professor Mehta wanted to modernize the administration in a big way. As one of the measures he approved a scheme of providing computers to the senior administrative offices. A committee constituted for the purpose had negotiated with a government of India concern and brought down the quoted price substantially. The Registrar and the finance officer were associated with the negotiations. It was 31st of March when the other members had cleared the papers for placing order by the Registrar for supply of computers. But the Registrar had some personal reservations and was dilly dallying in the matter. I was performing the functions of Pro-Vice-Chancellor on that particular day. I called the Registrar and requested him to place an order for the purchase of computers as that day happened to be the last day of the financial year. Finding the Registrar non-co-operative I sought guidance from the Vice-chancellor. The Vice-Chancellor reminded me that I was functioning as Pro-Vice Chancellor on that day and that I should use my authority to decide the issue. I in turn sent a written note to the Registrar asking him to do the needful. Hoping for a positive response I waited in my room for some time. When no response came from the Registrar for quite some time I called the Registrar's office. To my utter surprise and disappointment I was told that the Registrar had left his office for some unknown destination. Frantic enquiries were made at several plausible destinations without any result. Ultimately I requested the Finance Officer to send an order under his hand for the supply of computers, which he did.

The next day I learnt from the Vice-Chancellor that the Registrar had called on him late in the evening and had sent in his resignation requesting to be relieved of his charge after three months. The V.C had accepted the resignation and given three month's time to the Registrar to relinquish his charge. It was an enigma to me that the Registrar, who had been quite co-operative throughout took such a uncooperative and rigid stand on that particular issue. Perhaps he had already made up his mind not to seek further continuance of his current appointment which was to end in three months' time.

III

Vortex of Work

Shivaji College

In the summer of 1961 I had gone to Manali with my friend Gyan Datt Jha. At that time I was part time lecturer in Khalsa College, New Delhi. World Agriculture Fair Memorial (W.A.F.M) Shivaji College was opened that very year. While at Manali I received a letter from my former teacher Dr. Dev Raj Chanana informing me of the same and also advising me to return to Delhi immediately and apply for the post of lecturer in the College. Coincidently my return journey was already scheduled to commence a day after. I reached Delhi after halting for a day at Ambala at my friend O.P.Rana's place. I met Dr. Chanana who posted me with all the necessary information. The next day I submitted my application at the residence of Dr. Punjabrao Deshmukh, the Chairman of the governing Body of the College. His secretary, Mr. Korde was gracious enough to accept my application though I was late by a day. At the interview my rural background and a helpful attitude of the Head of the department, Dr. N.N.Choudhuri apart from my bright academic career, matched with three year's teaching experience played crucial role to boost my performance. I was selected for the post.

I joined the post on 3rd of August 1961 after resigning from the temporary post in Hindu College, Delhi. Shivaji College turned out to be my destiny. I progressed serving there by leaps and bounds in the literal sense. I got my selection grade in time. I was awarded the Ph.D. degree of the University of Delhi on my thesis 'A Study of Skanda Cult' which I completed while in service of Shivaji College. From there I moved to the University department as Reader in 1972 only to return as its Principal four years later. I was fortunate to preside over the destiny of the College for twelve years during which period the College witnessed phenomenal growth, both in academic depth and physical expansion. I finally left the College in 1988 to become the Dean of Colleges in the University of Delhi but only to turn into a pensioner on its roll in 1996. In between I remained on leave and lien from the College. I feel having received from the College the best any one could aspire for. I can't say how much I gave back to the College, but I can certainly say that Shivaji College has taken my heart away.

Manali Man

The decision to visit Manali was taken at the eleventh hour. We had got reservation of seats made in the train up to Pathankot from where we could proceed to any of the hill resorts reachable from there. A chance meeting with some colleagues of my friend Jage Ram Rana who had come to the railway station to see us off clinched the issue. Jage Ram introduced us to his colleagues. They were to be on duty at Manali during the visit of Pandit Jawahar Lal Nehru commencing a day later. They encouraged us to be there at least to have a closer peep of the Prime Minister and his grand children, Rajiv and Sanjay. We reached Manali to find it turned into a government colony. There was hardly any accommodation available. There was no private accommodation either or even an economy hotel where we could look for our stay. Both of us lingered on in the Tourist Office till late in the evening. In this while we had struck a friendly cord with the Tourist Officer, Mr. Mathur. Another gentleman, Sardar Satbir Singh Kohli, who studied History at Delhi University joined the two of us. He was an acquaintance of Mr. Mathur. Things moved our way and we were allotted a two-room aluminum hut for a week to begin with.

As we moved out of Mr. Mathur's office we found an envelope containing a wad of photographs lying on a sofa. On closer scrutiny the photographs turned out to be those of doubtful characters who were under the surveillance of the police while the Prime Minister was in Manali. Obviously some Intelligence Officer had left behind the envelope in the Tourist Office. Realising the importance of the photographs we straight away headed for the office of the

Deputy Commissioner, Mr. Prakash Kathpalia, whose camp office was nearby. He felt relieved and happy at the retrieval of the sensitive material. I also told him my having been a college mate of his younger brother, Ravi Kathpalia. In the process our identity and bona fides got established and verified. Later it appeared to us that Mr Kathpalia had left instructions with his staff to take care of our well being. The security staff took us as part of their team. It became easy for the Tourist Officer to renew the reservation of accommodation for us till we required. In fact, Mr. Mathur himself shifted to our hut for the period we remained there. Our hut also became a rendezvous in the evening for several officers in the entourage of the Prime Minister for relishing endless cups of hot tea and for having a vintage view of the river front in addition to other fun. We had carried with us a few utensils and a kerosene stove and other arrangements for making a quick meal. One day we played host to Mr. Buesgin, the Director of Max Muller Bhavan, New Delhi. He was staying in a private guest house not very far from our hut. He reciprocated the invitation and treated us to a sumptuous breakfast. He had liked Manali as he found its flora and fauna almost similar to that in which he had lived in Germany.

Rohtang Pass

A day's trip to Rohtang pass was an exciting and exhilarating experience. We traveled by bus up to Rahla from where we made a steep and long climb to reach Marhi, a vast and beautiful spur dotted with small white tented huts of the Tibetan traders selling their wares and hot tea and snacks. The residuals of snow lingering on the newly sprouted green grass presented a feast to the eyes. We could broadly figure out in the snow clad white expanse the contours of the pass which was still a couple of miles away. But since the gradient in most parts was not very steep we managed to reach the top of the pass speedily negotiating our way amidst the showers of snow crystals thrown by the snow cutting machines deployed at different points to clear the way . It was for the first time in my life that I walked on snow. I also saw the deeper spot on the surface of the pass where the melting snow had formed a water receptacle to serve as the source of the river Beas. A make shift shrine named Beas Kund had been put up there. The very thin number of tourists present there only betrayed the lack of the sense of adventure among our country men.

Luggage Lag

The return journey from Manali was not only hectic but also full of anxious moments mixed with a comedy of errors. My friend Gyan Datt Jha and I boarded a bus from Manali which was to take us to Pathankot from where we were to catch a train for Delhi. We had put our luggage including two hold alls on the roof of the bus. We were watchful in ensuring at each stop that our luggage was secure. A stop ahead of Palanpur a smart girl in her late twenties got down to change her bus for reaching Dharamshala and off loaded her luggage including a hold all and a suitcase. The lady being the only passenger to get down at the stop, my friend and I both became complacent and did not bother to check the safety of our luggage. A light drizzle also added to our complacency. However, to our surprise we found one of the hold alls missing when we made a check at the next stop at Palanpur. Instead an unclaimed hold all was lying near other items of our luggage. It became clear to us that the lady had off loaded our hold all by mistake, leaving her own behind. The bus was to halt there for half an hour.

We reported the matter to the driver and requested the driver to wait at Palanpur till the bus bound for Dharamshala arrived there. The driver did not agree to wait beyond a few minutes. As he started and drove the bus a few yards I sighted the Dharamshala bound bus approaching the bus station. Both of us asd also several other passengers pleaded with the driver to co-operate. He halted the bus enabling us to exchange the miscarried articles. Both of us as also the young lady were happy at the timely retrieval of our respective belongings. Our bus resumed its forward journey. One gentleman closely watching our predicament earlier administered a long lecture to us on the need to be particularly vigilant while traveling. We thought he was a wise man with experience and were in agreement with him in all that he had said.

By the by the bus reached the outskirts of Pathankot. The gentleman referred above got down from the bus taking away a small box from the roof of the bus. We had neither the inclination nor any doubt so as to keep a watch on him while he took away his luggage. After all he was so well versed in matters of travel and the attendant hassles I had come to believe after listening to his exhortations a little while ago. On reaching the last bus stop we discovered that our box was missing and another box with lighter weight was lying unclaimed on the roof of the bus. We were now certain that the gentleman who had got down from the bus at the previous stop had taken away our box. We took the unclaimed box the nearest police station. The police officials broke open the box. Luckily the home address of the gentleman was found among the papers in the box. We hired a rickshaw and headed for his house in the city. On reaching his house we learnt to our dismay that he had gone to his office some distance away and was carrying our box with himself. We were in a fix as the time of the departure of the train for Delhi was drawing near. We returned to the police station leaving a message for the gentleman to reach there at the earliest. Time was ticking. We were waiting at the police station with baited breath for his arrival. At long last he appeared on the scene. He returned our box and was profusely apologetic. We only wondered what ever happened to his sermons travel tact !

We hurried to catch the train just when it had received the green signal. We could not even get our return tickets endorsed at the station. Technically speaking, we were traveling without ticket. We made a day's halt at Ambala to meet my friend O.P. Rana. In this while we managed to make a short trip to Chandigarh. I was impressed with the lay out and architecture of the city, modernity incarnate indeed! I won't forget to mention the warm hospitality extended to us by Satbir Singh Kohli at his restaurant, 'Aroma' in Sector 17.

Second Coming

I happened to visit Manali the second time in 1964.The occasion was special this time. I had married in May the same year and had desired to spend a few days with my wife in Manali the best part of the mountainous tract I had known. Our journey which was originally scheduled to commence on seventh of May had to be postponed for about a month for the reason of compulsion of attending to an important assignment in the College. The night train of seventh June reached Pathankot on the morning of eighth. From there we took a direct bus to Manali and reached there by the evening. Nothing much had happened to Manali since my last visit. The green rice fields and forests of the dark green cedar trees dominated the landscape as ever before. There were not many tourists either. Perhaps only those cared to reach there who were not looking for big bazaars and modern means of entertainment and posh hotels. It was a paradise for the lovers of nature and those who wanted a calm and peaceful environment. But there was a difference. Manali had lost against Time in the death of Pandit Jawaharlal Nehru on 27 th May. The bonding of Pandit Nehru with the place had been legendary. As a Kashmiri he was in a better position to compare the heaven on earth with the mystique of Manali. He would rush to this place whenever he wished to escape the hum drum of life in the the Capital. The river Beas wending its way through the valley produced a gurgling and sonorous sound, especially during nights serving as a balm to the strung nerves. The small streams all over the slopes hastening to merge with the river down below at the bottom of the valley helped in producing energy just enough for the working of the mini flour mills presented a spectacle of its own kind. A bath in the hot water coming out of the sulphur springs at Vashishtha was quite refreshing.

The second tryst with the Rohtang pass was equally exciting and enjoyable for me. My agile wife hardly needed any help for the arduous climb. So we went up to the saddle of the pass speedily. The time thus saved was utilized in moving around on the snowy expanse. We were able to start our return journey well before any possible blizzard might hit the place. I shared the sense of pride of my wife over the fact that she was perhaps the only Indian lady to have made it to the top of the Pass that day. The climb down over the steep course was turning quite strenuous on our legs. I managed a pony from a caravan passing our way for my wife to ride for small distances intermittently. We had hardly realized that a longer stay on snowy field with thin canvas shoes on could lead to frost bite. On our return we had to nurse our feet by soaking them in hot salty water for hours for getting the desired relief.

Watery Grave

Shivaji College in its early years functioned in a temporary building in village Matiala, which was linked to Najafgarh road by a narrow lane of about a kilometer's length. The place was much better than the dilapidated bungalow at Najafgarh where the College was housed for the first three months of its existence. However, there was no electricity or water connection available there. A small well in the premises of the College served the needs of water, which was infested with bacteria, most of the time. The Principal carried his own water can in his car. The other inmates risked their health by using the water available from the well. Blissfully ignorant about the possible consequences all in the College failed to appreciate the gravity of the situation. It was only in1964 that things changed for the better with the initiative of Dr. Sarup Singh, who took over as OSD of the College after the Principal Dr. R.K. Bhan had moved to Hastinapur (later renamed as Motilal Nehru) College opened that year in Moti Bagh, New Delhi. He took immediate measures to get the sanction of the University Grants Commission for procuring potable water from the city by hiring a horse driven cart for the purpose.

One day the cart along with the horse pulling it overturned and fell into a deep watery pit while negotiating a flooded part of the approach road near the College. In the mishap a student who was riding the cart for fun got drowned. The loss of a young life came as a great shock to the College community. The tragedy came handy to the students and the staff to bolster their demand for shifting the College to a safer place in the city. Dr. Sarup Singh consulted Principal Shanti Narayan of Hansraj College. It was agreed to hold classes of Shivaji College in the Hansraj College building in the afternoon session. As an overwhelming number of students and all teachers came from the city the decision was greeted as a welcome measure. Everybody thought that the temporary sojourn in the city might turn into a permanent abode there. But two of us, Mr. S.K. Chawla, lecturer in English and I did not have any such illusion in our minds. We two were former students of Delhi University and personally knew many teachers of Hansraj College. We thought holding classes in building of another college in the given circumstances was an infra dig.

As soon as we came to know about the decision both of us met Dr. Sarup Singh at his residence in Kirori Mal College and explained to him our reservations regarding the decision. We volunteered to get the approach road repaired with the help of the government and by involving the NCC volunteers within three days, the period for which the College had already been closed. Dr. Sarup Singh appreciated our point of view and also our gesture of service by self. He promised to wait till the situation normalized. As good luck would have it the weather improved the very next day. The water receded instantly as if under the influence of some charm of prayer. The Municipal authorities took prompt action in getting the approach road repaired within a day. The College reopened to continue to function in its own premises at village Matiala.

Tryst with the Titan

Shivaji College had weathered the storm of instability in 1964 with the helping hand of Dr. Sarup Singh. Dr. Tulsi Ram had been appointed the new Principal. Things were looking sanguine and smooth. To assure the College community of his support the Vice-Chancellor, Shri C.D. Deshmukh had agreed to visit the College and give an address. I was deputed to escort the Vice-chancellor to the College from his residence at India International Center, of which he was the president. I reached the Center at the appointed time and was received by Dr. Deshmukh personally. He took me to his study and asked me to wait there till he got ready. Before I could proceed to occupy the front seat with the driver Dr. Deshmukh asked me to sit beside him on the back seat. Very soon he made me comfortable by engaging me into conversation. After getting my personal introduction he went on to put me a number of questions on education and discipline, curriculum and culture etc. After initial hesitation, which Dr. Deshmukh dispelled by his affectionate demeanor, I managed to give free expression to my views on the issues raised by him. I was in favour of twelve years of schooling in place of the then prevailing eleven years. I advocated more class contact hours for languages than those for social sciences. I also expressed the view that science subjects needed a continued updating of curriculum to keep abreast of the latest knowledge. Problems of indiscipline among students should be handled with a positive approach, I opined.

Our journey to the College covered in more than an hour turned out to be a rewarding experience for me. It was a rare occasion to be in continued conversation for such a long duration with a person of Dr. C.D. Deshmukh's caliber. I felt quite happy that I had acquitted reasonably well in what I considered a grilling interview for an unknown job. But my sense of self-esteem rose considerably when Dr. Deshmukh made the content of our conversation the subject of his speech at the function in the College. He referred to and commended my views on various issues. He even offered to consider proposals based on those if the College wrote to him. After the function was over several of my colleagues thronged me and congratulated me for having created such a positive impact on the Vice-Chancellor. The Principal felt proud of me and gave expression to his happiness in his own inimitable way. The event did not swell my head, though. Greater modesty dawned on me, which gave me an inner happiness. But more was yet to come.

The next day I received a telephonic call from Dr. Sarup Singh, then Princopal of Kirorimal College. He congratulated me on how I had impressed Dr. Deshmukh, who had mentioned about my views on education in a meeting of the Principals that morning. Dr. Deshmukh had prefaced his observations by referring to his interaction with a young lecturer of Sanskrit in Shivaji College the previous day whose name he was trying to recall. Before Dr. R.K. Bhan, the former Principal of Shivaji College could grasp the query and give out the name Dr. Sarup Singh filled with joy gave my name. Dr. Sarup Singh wondered what recipe I had administered to Dr. Deshmukh to make such a lingering impact on his mind. I replied that it was in the nature of the great that they would discover extraordinariness even in the ordinary. I happened to be one such medium, I told Dr. Sarup Singh.

The staff association of the College had organized dinner in the evening that very day. Dr. Sarup Singh had also been invited. At the dinner party he narrated the gist of my encounter with Dr. Deshmukh as shared by him with the Principals in a meeting earlier in the day. Every one present again congratulated me. I could not agree more with Bhartari Hari that the great always tend to magnify several fold the good points of others, ignoring their shortcomings. I came to know more about the greatness of Dr. C.D. Deshmukh later in life on reading his writings and the legendry notes he had left in the official files of the University and from accounts of the officials who had worked closely under him.

Cynicism Scores

Deciding against a temporary camp life did not mean that the college community was happy to continue to live with depravity. The fact that the College utterly lacked in infrastructure continued to agitate the minds of all sections of the College. Allotment of a permanent site for the College at Raja Garden had brought some cheer to all of us. But the financial position of the Bharat Krishak Samaj, the parent trust of the College was not sound. Therefore the prospects of the College having its own permanent building in the near future looked bleak. All the teachers including the Principal, Dr. Tulsi Ram were not sanguine about making any headway towards raising the academic standards of the College in the given circumstances. Thwarted hope and throttled aspirations started giving quarter to cynicism in the minds of some of us. One day in a conversation during a walk with Shri Dayakishan Mudgil in the College compound I remarked that we would have to forcibly lift the College and shift it somewhere in the city to enable it to breathe academic oxygen for its survival.

Shri Mudgil endorsed my cynic remarks and further added that the act should be performed well when the Principal was away on leave. It was my turn now to support his idea elaborating how the cool headed Principal could not be a part of such an adventure. The cynical part of our conversation ended and both of us reverted to serious talks about the means for progress of the College. But our foray ended without any concrete suggestions emerging. Shri Mudgil carried the earlier part of our conversation to the Principal's ears in a lighter vein. The Principal's reaction was prompt and polite. He stated in my presence that he would very much like to be part of any action, howsoever hazardous to improve the lot of the College. It was clear from the events that followed in the coming months that my cynical remark had stirred the conscience of the Principal. He started exploring avenues to achieve the common goal.

Merger Verger

The Delhi Administration had opened a couple of colleges in 1967. In the search for suitable persons to head the colleges the name of Dr. Tulsi Ram, Principal of Shivaji College cropped up. Some of us teachers in the College got an inkling of the approach of the Delhi Administration in the matter. Some of us who were close to Dr. Tulsi Ram talked to him about the issue and suggested that the best course would be to request the Delhi Government to take over Shivaji College. Dr. Tulsi Ram was in agreement with this suggestion. Taking the Chairman of the Governing Body, Shri Ram Niwas Mirdha into confidence the matter was followed up. Shri Mirdha not only agreed to the suggestion but also used his good offices to persuade the Delhi Administration headed by Shri Vijay Kumar Malhotra to take over the College. Dr. Sarup Singh played a very helpful role in the matter, especially in dousing the fire of discontent among a section of the teachers ignited by certain vested interests. The Delhi Administration decided to take over the College as a going concern and caused its merger with another college started by the Administration that very year in a school building in Karampura. The merged entity was named as Shivaji College after dropping the words 'World Agriculture Fair Memorial' which prefaced it earlier. The seniority of the staff was settled in accordance with the length of service in permanent capacity in each institution without disturbing the inter-se seniority within the same unit. Karampura was again a temporary halt. The perambulatory course of the College ended only in August1976 when it moved into its own elegant and spacious building at Raja Garden. The event coincided with my taking over as Principal of the College.

Search for Research

Ever since I passed my M.A. examination I was in search of a suitable topic for doing research for the degree of Ph.D. I met several scholars inside and outside the University of Delhi to discuss the subject. But the more pressing need was to get a permanent job of lecturer. After having worked in temporary capacity in different places for a couple of years I was appointed lecturer against a permanent post in Shivaji College in 1961 I had been reading extensively the literature available on the subjects of my interest. I finally decided to work on 'Study of Skanda Cult', a topic on which not much work had been done. Dr.Mrs. Sita Nambiar agreed to be my superviser. I went about doing my work earnestly. I corresponded with scholars like R.N.Dandekar (Poona), Vasudev Sharan Aggarwal (Benaras), V.Raghavan (Madras) and Swami Raghavacharya (Bareily). All of them responded promptly and gave me useful information concerning my subject of research. Apart from my official superviser my old teacher Dr. Dev Raj Chanana was a great help.

As I was doing a full time job and had added responsibilities after my marriage in 1964 my research work progressed by the by and bit by bit. But at the same time my target never got blurred. I had done sufficient work but was still not satisfied with the standard. One day Dr. Chanana took me to the University library and showed me a couple of theses on which Ph.D. degree had been granted. He advised me to compare their standard with the standard of work already done by me. He further told me that the more I worked the higher would be my aim.

I followed what he wanted to convey to me. I took two months' study leave from the College. long summer vacation followed the period of leave. I sat writing my thesis regularly. The final draft was ready by June 1970. I went to Swami Shivanand Ashram in Rishikesh to discuss it with Dr. Nambiar, who was there for a holiday. She introduced me to Swami Krishnanand and told him about my research work. He invited me to deliver the weekly lecture one evening. I accepted the invitation hesitatingly as there was no escape. The lecture was meant to last for about forty minutes. I spoke for over one and a half hour. It was the essence of my research work, which I reproduced in my own words. All present were impressed. Dr. Nambiar patted my back for rising to the occasion and doing her proud. Swami Krishnanand complimented her on turning her disciple a shade better than herself. She took it as a compliment to her as she believed in the adage putrat parajaya, shishyat parajaya -one would always wish to be excelled by one's son or a disciple. I was instilled with greater confidence with regard to the quality of my research work.

I submitted my thesis by the end of August 1970. The reports of all the three examiners were received before the annual convocation scheduled for February 1971. But for one reason or the other viva-voce examination could not be arranged for a considerably long period- almost a year after the reports had been received. All kinds of rumours were floated by some mischievous elements. I was not disheartened. At last the viva voce examination was fixed for 31 December 1971. A large number of teachers and research students witnessed my viva-voce examination, which lasted for more than an hour. The examiner, Professor Venkateshvaran of Annamalai University was thrilled by the clarity and thoroughness of my understanding of the subject of my thesis. He profusely praised me for producing a thesis of excellent quality. The rumours got nailed truly well. The thesis was published later and stands the scrutiny of the scholarly world.

Cool Head

In the absence of Dr. Tulsi Ram who was on long leave during 1972 Shri Prithvi Chand was acting as Principal of Shivaji College. The Acting Principal terminated the services of Shri Suryakant Gautam, a temporary laboratory attendant in the department of physics on the recommendation of the teachers. Shri Prithvi Chand had also consulted the then Secretary of the staff council of the College. I was Bursar of the College but I was not consulted in the matter. However, I fully supported the decision. The College non-teaching staff went on an indefinite strike. The teachers took command of the work of the College office in turns during their vacant periods and did not allow work to suffer. I was in the forefront of a group organizing all the work including cleaning of bathrooms. On the other hand a couple of teachers gave indirect support to the employees. It was abundantly compensated by the silent and tacit support that a large number of employees gave to the College Administration. But we never tried to break their unity. Initially the central employees union (DUCKU) had kept itself aloof but joined the agitation after their efforts for an amicable settlement did not bear the desired fruit.

The University-wide strike by the employees alarmed the University Administration. On the advice of the Vice-Chancellor, Dr. Sarup Singh the matter was placed before the governing body of the College at an emergent meeting. I had prepared myself well to convince the other members of the justness of the action of the Acting Principal as it was feared that one of the University representatives, Prof. M.D.K.Choudhary might oppose the same. But I found the intervention of Prof. Choudhary quite positive and constructive. The governing body unanimously endorsed the action taken by the Acting Principal. But at the same time it wanted some initiative on the part of the teachers to settle the issue of strike at an early date. Dr. B.P. Dubey and I, the two teachers' representatives in the Governing Body were entrusted with the responsibility to hold consultations with the teaching staff and others and report back. The position of the Acting Principal having been vindicated we could start afresh to deal with the case. After consultations with the teachers we had discussions with the Acting Principal to evolve our strategy.

Armed with all the details of the case and the references of relevant rules we held negotiations with DUCKU representatives Sarva Shri Shraddhanand Sharma, K.N. Thusu and T.C. Verma. The third member of our team P.C. Ganguli, the Secretary of the Staff Council of the College did not join the negotiations due to certain personal compulsions. The DUCKU representatives were seasoned trade unionists well equipped with negotiating skills. We, the two teacher representatives, on our part were fully prepared for the maximum we could do for a settlement. So without going into polemics we straight away spelt out a formula, which after minor modification was accepted unanimously. The formula stated –'Shri Suryakant may be given another chance temporarily to work in the College for a period of six months to end on 1 January 1973, after which period his case may be reviewed in light of his performance.' The Governing Body graciously approved the formula at its subsequent meeting. The strike was called off with immediate effect. Suryakant got a fresh letter of appointment on temporary basis for six months. He mended his ways to earn continuity in service in the College later.

Udasin Akhara

Nearly an acre of the land earmarked for the playground of Shivaji College had been under encroachment for a number of years. The encroachers had given the area the semblance of a religious place by setting up an akhara of the udasin sect of Baba Shrichand, the estranged son of Guru Nanak. I had taken up the matter on behalf of the College with the local police in 1974. I was working as Reader in the University at that time. As suggested by the police authorities I persuaded the then Acting Principal Shri Prithvi Chand to file a formal complaint. Prosecution was launched in due course of time. But it appeared from the progress of the case that the college authorities did not pursue the case earnestly. The College had moved to its new building a couple of days before I joined as Principal in August 1976. I found the encroachment had hampered the construction of the boundary wall of the playground. I took up the matter as one of my immediate priorities. I met the concerned magistrate to expedite the judgment. I had hoped that the judgment would be in favour of the College and the encroachers would be soon evicted. Several letters addressed to the concerned quarters could not elicit any response.

The matter was raised in a meeting of the Governing Body held in late 1977. Shri Kanwar Lal Gupta was the chairman. Since the matter was informally taken up for discussion I told the chairman that as Principal there was little left for me to do, but perhaps in my personal capacity I could achieve the desired result. I sought the protection of the Governing Body in case any crisis happened in handling the issue. The chairman was gracious enough to say that the Governing Body would support me in any action that I might take in the best interest of the College. This assurance though verbal filled me with a new sense of determination to solve the problem of the encroachment.

Courting Court

It was in early February 1978 that I met the SDM of the area, Shri Charan Singh Kherwal. in his chamber in Tis Hazari courts. I explained to him my problem and sought his help in the matter. The SDM told me that the case earlier filed by the police had already been decided in favour of the encroachers for want of appropriate witness. He further informed me that on the contrary when interrogated as a witness, the Acting Principal had failed to recognize the encroachers and had also testified before the court that they were not causing any nuisance to the College. However, the SDM was still ready to help the College. He had summoned Sant Jagir Singh of Udasin Akhaara to join us a few minutes later. I was surprised to see Shri O.P. Wadhawa, an old student of the College accompanying the Sant as his advocate. Shri Kherwal told the Sant in no uncertain terms that not withstanding the court's earlier verdict, he would have to vacate the piece of land, which belonged to the College. The Sant was co-operative and promised to vacate the encroachment if an alternative piece of land was made available to him. After the Sant and his lawyer had left the SDM suggested that since a formal channel would take years for settling the matter I should take possession of the College land through my own means. Any problem arising out of my action would be taken care of by the administration. He also promised to render police assistance if required. I returned deeply enthused to achieve my objective of removing the encroachment at the earliest.

Direct Action

I formed a small group of teachers and the office bearers of the Students' Union to finalise the strategy of the proposed action. A cultivator tractor was hired to plough the play- grounds for a couple of days. The encroached area was scrupulously avoided while ploughing and leveling the playground in order to ensure that nobody got an inkling of our plan of action. We had the inspiration and support of a senior functionary of the University belonging to the Sikh community. He was with us on the D-day. Our group went ahead with the demolition of the temporary structures on the area and cleared it of all signs of occupation by the encroachers. Our Sikh students handled the sensitive part of the structure where Guru Granth Sahib had been ensconced with due religious decorum. The whole area was cleared in about an hour's duration. In the mean time representatives of the sant had contacted the police to intervene in the matter. Accordingly a senior police officer arrived in the College. I explained to him the whole background and the understanding given to me by the SDM. He desired that I should ask everybody to stop any further activity at the ground. There was nothing much left to be done for us. Therefore I asked all teachers and students to leave the place and return to the College building. I thought we had achieved our objective so very easily without any hurdle. But more tense moments were to follow.

Rash Reaction

Thinking it advisable to be away from the scene I ensured that all members of the College had left for their homes. Thereafter I also left the College to reach home. An hour later I received a telephone call from Mr. Saini, the proprietor of the petrol filling station near our College ground, informing me that a gentleman had staged a sit in at the ground cleared by us earlier during the day. I ignored it thinking that it was a gimmick, which would come to an end after some time. Next day was Sunday. I got information in the morning that a room like structure (without roof) had been built up at the site during the previous night. I immediately rushed to the College and after assessing the situation spoke to the police authorities requesting them to keep a check on any negative developments from the point of view of the College. The Police authorities assured me of their best possible co-operation and help. Satisfied by the assurance I came back home. At this stage I called up Shri Kedar Nath Sahni, the Chief Executive Councilor on telephone giving full details of the incident and also apologizing for the delay in informing him. Shri Sahni's response was sympathetic and he assured me of all possible help.

Akhand Path

Next day on reaching the College I found an Akhand Path going on at the site of the demolished structure. Various newspapers had splashed the news of the demolition giving their own colour to the whole episode. I devoted the better part of the day in sending press releases to newspapers clarifying the position of the College. The Akhand Path was to continue till the evening of the next day. So expecting no special development during the day we all in the College went back home. Next day some teachers and a few students lingered on in the College even after the classes were over. Some of us were basking in the sun in the College lawns. Around 5.00 p.m. we noticed a group of Sikh youths advancing from the

Ring Road side towards our College. The police was around in sufficient number. Perhaps thinking that the youth might be joining the Akhand Path the police did not stop them. But after they went past the venue of the Akhand Path the police became suspicious and challenged them. Shouting slogans they ran towards the College. We realized of their real intention of attacking us only after they jumped over the boundary wall of the College. All of us present in the College ran for cover as the miscreants were armed. Dr. S.L. Gupta a senior teacher in the College virtually dragged me out of my office exhorting me to run away or else I was sure to come to physical harm at the hands of the miscreants. His premonition came true as they made the Principal's office their prime target. They had smashed the windscreen and the door panes of my car and some furniture in my room before the police chased them out of the College building. Some of my colleagues and I crossed over to the residential area on the western side by jumping the boundary wall. Some hid themselves in the bathrooms. Alertness on the part of the police saved the day for us.

No Foes

As the authorities at higher levels were monitoring the situation it did not take long for the area SSP Mr. Nikhil Kumar to arrive at the College to be followed by the Deputy Commissioner, Shri Basant Kumar Goswami and DIG Shri Mandher. My very first interaction with Mr. Nikhil Kumar was quite dramatic but cordial and served as the foundation for relationship of mutual regard and admiration for times to come. Since the College had been attacked it could lead to very serious developments if caution was not used in handling the situation. The DC picked up my telephone and started briefing the Chief Secretary about the incidence. As soon as he uttered the words, "Sir, some students of Khalsa College had attacked ...." I put my hand on the mouthpiece of the telephone and said, "Mr. Goswami! they were not Khalsa College students." Upon this he asked me, "How do you know that?" In reply I put the counter question, "How do you know that they were Khalsa College boys?" I further said, "At best they could be described as antisocial elements. We should not involve the name of a sister college." Promising to talk later Mr. Goswami snapped the conversation with the chief Secretary. He was all agog. He had not imagined that the issue could be made so simple by the aggrieved party. He appeared to be visibly relieved. But he was anxious to know from me what was going on in my mind. I simply told him that I was interested only in the College land, and nothing else. He asked me to give him one week's time to solve the problem. I told him that he was free to take as much time as required but the people in the College would be happy if he could solve the problem in a week's time. Then Mr. Nikhil Kumar asked what more he could do for us. One of my colleagues present demanded that the police should escort us all safely to our respective homes. I however, did not agree with the suggestion and offered my own services to whosoever wanted a safe passage to his home. Undaunted by the events of the day we all went home looking forward to better developments in the coming days.

Friendly Flavour

Apprehending that students' reaction to Tuesday's incident in the College could be violent I deputed a group of teachers to properly brief them and educate them about the positive role played by the police. On such occasions the ire of the students is generally directed against the police. But in the case of our students it turned out to be different. The next morning the students assembled in the College compound but remained restrained and raised pro police slogans something new to the police people, accustomed to receiving brickbats for doing thankless jobs. I considered it to be the best moment to disperse the students and send them home. We declared the next day as a holiday in order that tempers get further cooled down. I utilized the day in getting my car windowpanes fixed. When I returned home from the market my wife told me about the frantic messages received from the office of Mr. Nikhil Kumar, the last being that I should reach my College for a meeting at 4.00 p.m. I took Dr. R.D. Mishra and Shri S.P. Shukla (who happened to be at Mishra's house) along and made for the College wondering about the purpose of the meeting. We made several conjectures but ultimately thought it to be a meeting for a solution. We were unanimous in believing firmly that any solution should include the restoration of the disputed piece of land to the College.

As my car reached the turning point from ring road towards Shivaji College, the in-charge of the local police post, Sub-Inspector Rajpal Singh joined us and gave the good news that the wind was in our favour. On reaching the College I was received at the gate by Shri Nikhil Kumar and Sardar Jaswant Singh Phul, member Delhi Metropolitan Council, a good friend of mine from my Khalsa College days (He later became Principal of GGS College of Commerce, Delhi). Before Shri Nikhil Kumar could have a word with me I walked up to the elderly Sardarji with a flowing white beard standing nearby and by reflex action touched his feet. He embraced me saying, 'o kaka tusi is college de Principal ho, tusi thoda guru granth sahib di be-adbi kar sakde ho!' (o my child! you are the Principal of this College! It can't be that you show disrespect to the guru granth Sahib). At this stage he was introduced to me as Sardar Sethi, the President of the Delhi Gurudwara Management Committee (DGMC). Sardar Jaswant Singh remarked that he had anticipated how I would respond in given situation. Shri Nikhil Kumar stood amused. He told me later how his suggestion of my expressing regrets to the Sikh representatives was not acceptable to Shri Kanwar Lal Gupta, the chairman of the Governing Body of our College when approached for the purpose. A meeting was held in my room under the chairmanship of the Deputy Commissioner. An agreement was signed between the College, Sant Jagir Singh and the Delhi Administration and witnessed by the President of the DGMC. The main features of the agreement were as follows:

1. Sant Jagir Singh will forthwith vacate the encroached piece of land.
2. The Delhi administration will allot a suitable piece of land to Sant Jagir Singh.
3. The Principal expressed regrets over the incident at the college grounds.
4. The Delhi Administration will withdraw criminal cases if any against all concerned parties.

All Ends Well

After the meeting was over we all moved to a make shift pandal in the play ground where an akhand path was going on. The representatives of the DGMC and the Deputy Commissioner made conciliatory speeches to pacify the Sikh sangat present there. I was also invited to speak on the occasion. I spoke in Punjabi (which I had picked up during my service in Khalsa College) and underlined the fact how high esteem we all in Shivaji College and I personally had for holy Sikh traditions. My colleagues and some police officers known to me personally present there marveled at my Punjabi. I myself felt elated for having risen to the occasion. The assembly dispersed after distribution of karha prasad. Later I joined a press conference at the office of the Deputy Commissioner. While the press conference was in progress Shri Nikhil Kumar read out a message 'received' according to which the representatives of Sant Jagir Singh had already shifted to the new site earmarked for allotment to him. I was advised to take possession of the piece of land vacated by him immediately. I went home and contacted my resource persons to make arrangements for erection of the boundary wall early next morning. Every arrangement was in place by day break. In a few hours' time the construction work was complete except the fixing of barbed wires which were fixed a couple of days later. As I stood on the playground free from encroachment with some of my colleagues I felt it was a moment of great satisfaction.

Days of Development

The years that followed were the years of growth and development for the College. I received wholehearted co-operation from my colleagues, both teaching and non-teaching. With their help I was able to instill a spirit of pride and dignity in doing the maximum for the progress of the College. At the undergraduate level new courses like Geography, Sociology, Computer Science, B.A.(Hons) Physics and B.Sc.(Hons) Biochemistry were started. At the postgraduate level Sanskrit, Political Science and Economics were approved. However, the College could not start Economics for want of students. The new courses attracted better students. This helped in improving the academic environment. The extensive playground was developed. Grassy courts were laid for different sports. The cricket pitch attracted players from far off places apart from our own students. The two lawn tennis courts were daily thronged by teachers and students interested in the game. The

College won championship in the University in several sports and games on several occasions. Our players figured in the University teams at inter-university events.

Silver Jubilee

The year 1986-87 happened to be the Silver Jubilee year of the College. Different departments organized throughout the year activities and events commensurate with the occasion. The huge and detailed model of the 'Cell' put up on a wall as part of the Science exhibition on the occasion was a big draw. A special Souvenir published reflected the progress of the College over the past years with a liberal presentation of photographs and graphics concerning admissions, results and finances of the college. The finale was marked by an impressive function on 11 February 1987 where Shri Balram Jakhar, Shri Ram Niwas Mirdha, Shrimati Krishna Sahi, the Vice-Chancellor Prof. Moonis Raza and many other prominent guests graced the occasion with their presence. Every member of the College community was enthused by the shape the College had taken. The usually tumultuous audience on such occasions turned out to be exceptionally disciplined and responsive during proceedings on the dais. The silver lining had after all appeared on the horizon. The Chief Guest, Shri Balram Jakhar's speech was so emotive and inspiring that it surprised the speaker himself. When the Chairman of the College Governing Body speaking on the occasion suggested to the ministers present that my services should be utilized at the national level, the Vice-chancellor promptly remarked that there are many who could serve the government but there are important roles awaiting me at the University. Was he anticipating my impending appointment as Dean of Colleges, many wondered.

Colleague's Call

Shri Dhananjaya Sharma, a lecturer in Economics in Shivaji College had gone on a tour of Rajasthan during the summer vacation some time in the early eighties. He had grown a long beard and traveled alone in the manner of an explorer. He often talked to people especially the poor to assess their economic condition. Engaging himself in this hobby he strayed into Indian Territory very close to the border with Pakistan. The Indian Intelligence agencies took him for a Pakistani spy and held him for questioning. Shri Sharma revealed his identity but could not prove it as he had carried no supporting document. At last he gave to the Intelligence officer my telephone number for the purpose of verification of his identity. The officer talked to me on phone. I satisfied him with regard to the bona fides of Sri Sharma, whom I described as a law abiding citizen with concern for the poor and the deprived. Shri Sharma also talked to me briefly on the phone and thanked me for my support. Otherwise generally critical of my working he had all the personal regard for me. The above incident further deepened the regard. I never had any misgivings about his critical responses on several issues. After all our critics help us tread the right course.

Central Evaluation

The annual examinations of 1987 had been delayed Sas the University teachers had gone on a long drawn out strike on the issue of pay revision. Once the strike was over the teachers offered all co-operation to compensate for the loss of time that had occurred because of the strike. They suggested centralized evaluation of scripts. The V.C. called me one day to discuss the matter with him. The Controller of Examinations, (Dr. Ravi Bhatia) was also present. Presumably Dr. Bhatia had earlier told the V.C. of his helplessness in organizing the system. With a view to support Bhatia I started pointing out the difficulties in switching over to the new system. The V.C. told me that the merits and demerits of the new system were not under discussion because he had already made up his mind to adopt the new system. He added that his purpose in calling me was to request me to organize and monitor the centralized evaluation. He expressed the hope that I would not disappoint him. As there was no scope for further arguments I agreed to shoulder the responsibility.

I went about the job systematically. Evaluation centers were opened in 18 colleges. Subjects/papers were allocated to the centers in such a manner that there was no glut of answer books at any one center. Coding of roll numbers was also entrusted to the centers. Evaluation work continued with speed. Substitute examiners could be appointed with speed in consultation with the concerned head of department. The evaluated answer scripts along with the award lists were sent to the examination branch in regular installments. The tabulation work was started simultaneously. It became easier for the University to declare the results in time. The bills of the examiners were received at the evaluation centers and forwarded to the Examination Branch. Later during the tenure of Prof. Mehta remuneration bills of the examiners were paid at the evaluation centers. Such an arrangement proved a motivating factor for teachers to come forward for evaluation work. A further improvement was made in allowing the teachers to have the option to either evaluate the scripts at the centers or take them home without losing the pro rata per day conveyance charges. The latest system resulted in reduction in paper work of the examination branch and the finance branch. It also motivated a good number of teachers including women to associate themselves with the evaluation work.

Central Admissions

With the progressive increase in the number of students passing 12 th class examination from Delhi schools together with the growing influx from outside Delhi, especially from Bihar, admission to under-graduate courses in the colleges of the University turned highly competitive year after year. Nearly fifty percent of the students had no choice except join the School of Correspondence Courses & Continuing Education. Professor Moonis Raza mooted the idea of organizing the admissions on centralized basis in the very first year (1985) of his joining as Vice-Chancellor. Presumably his team members had amply briefed him on the subject. He put the proposal in a meeting of the Admission Advisory Committee, which was immediately endorsed by several members present there. I was also present in the meeting as OSD Examinations. I expressed my desire to speak on the issue. But the V.C. in a lighter vein dismissed my request saying that I should forget for the moment that I was a Principal and should tell the members as OSD Exams by what date I would be able to declare the results of the entrance tests for admissions to medical and engineering courses held that year. As far as the question of centralized admissions was concerned I did not need to apply my mind to the same. The University was going to switch over to it for the current session.

I sat quiet in the hope that the modalities for the new system to be introduced would be announced in the meeting. There were vague references to computerization of the system but nothing concrete emerged. I felt alarmed at enormity of the exercise and the perils of the University undertaking such an onerous responsibility where angels would fear to tread. The V.C. declared the meeting closed hoping that all concerned would make the new system a success. I could not contain myself and striking a humorous note I told the Vice-Chancellor that the decision was turning the stomach of the Principal in me and sought his permission to express my views on the issue of centralized admission inn my capacity as a Principal. The permission was granted. I briefly dilated on the demerits of the proposed system and pointed out how that could boomerang on the University administration. The V.C. appreciated the point I had made and declared the meeting adjourned to be held the next day. He also invited members to come with replies to the questions I had raised concerning the centralized admissions.

The next day I reached the venue of the meeting at the appointed time. Finding none there I went to meet the Dean of Colleges Sardar Mohinder Singh, who had been asked by the V.C. to organize the meeting. He informed me that the V.C. had decided to give up the idea of centralized admissions and therefore, the meeting also stood cancelled. Later on it came to my knowledge that the V.C. had expressed his unhappiness over the manner of bringing the proposal for centralized admissions without any preparation and without examining the implications. I felt relieved that the University was saved from being landed in a situation of chaos. However, to mitigate the hardship of admission seekers a centralized application form was devised which was made acceptable at all colleges. Later when I became Dean of Colleges the form was improved by adding the information about availability of courses college-wise. That format is still prevalent and serving a useful purpose.

The issue of centralized admission was raised during the tenure of successive Vice-Chancellors. Prof. Baxi had strongly opposed the move. He took the view that wherever it was necessary and feasible centralized admissions were already being made. Prof. V.R.

Mehta was ready to accept this demand soon after he joined as Vice-Chancellor. On being consulted I explained to him the disadvantages and difficulties in administering the system both for want of infrastructure and manpower. More-over sufficient time for preparations was not available. Prof. Mehta abandoned the idea with a heavy heart saying that he would personally see to it that centralized admissions were organized in all undergraduate courses with effect from the next session. As he went into the knitty gritty of the admission process during the days to come he fully grasped the implications of centralized admissions and was the first to oppose it whenever the question was raised in any quarter during the rest of his tenure. That continues to be the policy of the subsequent administrations, though not without tasting the pudding themselves.

Election Faction

As soon as I received the names of the nominees of Delhi Administration on the Governing Body of Shivaji College for the year 1987 duly approved by the University, hectic lobbying started in several quarters for the post of Chairmen, who was to be elected in a meeting. Before I could call a meeting for the purpose I received a telephone call from a gentleman among the nominees who knew me personally asking me about my opinion as to who should be elected as Chairman. I innocently named an elderly experienced person. The gentleman at the other end closed the conversation, saying that he agreed with me. A couple of days later Shri Jagpravesh Chandra, the Chief Executive Councilor of Delhi telephoned asking me to do him a favour, which he was ready to spell out only if I gave a promise in advance. I regretted my inability to give promise without knowing what Shri Chandra had wanted. But at the same time I told him that I held him in high esteem and if his request was reasonable and just he should have no hesitation in spelling out the same and I would have no hesitation in acceding to it. Shri Chandra then opened up and gave the name of a person whom he wanted to be elected as Chairman. The name turned out to be the same as I had in mind and which I had shared with another member as mentioned above. I promptly shared my view with Shri Chandra who expressed his happiness over our commonality of approach in the matter.

After the date of the meeting for the election had been fixed one of the University representatives on the Governing Body informed me that a certain gentleman was canvassing for his election as Chairman. Similar information came from some other quarters. This gentleman happened to be the same who had telephoned me first of all and had Okayed the name I had suggested. The meeting was held on the day fixed for the purpose. Fourteen out of a total of fifteen members attended it. Sardar Santokh Singh was elected protem Chairman to conduct the election. Some one proposed the name of Shri B.S. Bhalla and it was duly seconded. Another person proposed the name of Mr. H.S. Josh which too was duly seconded. Some well meaning members suggested that the election should be unanimous. In their opinion Shri Bhalla could be elected Chairman and Mr. Josh could be appointed Treasurer. I supported the suggestion pointing out that never in the past there had been a contest. But the proposition was not acceptable to Mr. Josh who said that there has to be a first time for every thing, so why not have election for the first time. Finally the election was held. Shri Bhalla won polling eight votes while Mr. Josh polled six votes. The earlier offer of appointing him Treasurer was withdrawn and Dr. Verma was appointed to the post. Mr. Josh did not attend any of the meetings of the Governing Body for the rest of his tenure. This incident, however, did not come in the way of my helping Mr. Josh later when he contested successfully the election to the membership of the executive Council of Delhi University.

Dean of Colleges

The post of Dean of Colleges had acquired a special position from the beginning of its creation in 1971 during the tenure of Prof. Sarup Singh as Vice-Chancellor. The first incumbent was Principal Shanti Narain, a very reputed educationist. His successor, Sardar Mohinder Singh was appointed during the tenure of Vice-Chancellor, Prof. R.C.Mehrotra. The next Vice-Chancellor, Prof. Gurbaksh Singh appointed Dr. P.L.Malhotra, Principal, College of Vocational Studies as Dean of Colleges in 1980. Dr. Malhotra left in July 1983 to take up the appointment as Director, NCERT. Sardar Mohinder Singh was again appointed Dean of Colleges for the residual term of about two years. Prof. Moonis Raza reappointed him in 1985. He vacated the post in 1988 on attaining the age of 65 years. I was appointed Dean of Colleges in a meeting of the Executive Council held on 26th October1988 and I joined duty the next day. My term of appointment was ordinarily co-terminus with that of the Vice-Chancellor i.e. till February1990.

Speculations regarding the person to be appointed Dean of Colleges each time since 1983 had invariably included my name among the probables. Reliable sources told me later that Prof. Gurbaksh Singh had thought of appointing me to the post. He was however, advised by a senior educationist friend of his to appoint the experienced Sardar Mohinder Singh saying that I was quite young (I was 47 years old) and would have ample opportunities of reaching to that position. Prof. Gurbaksh Singh had later confirmed to me that he had discussed such a thing with a friend whom he did not name but I knew who he was. Now when I dispassionately think over the matter I find the advice of that friend of the Vice-Chancellor objective and mature and in a way prophetic in my case. I would like to mention here the background preceding my first appointment as Dean of Colleges.

Great Guru

When Prof. Moonis Raza joined as Vice-Chancellor I was working as OSD examinations. I had frequent interaction with him on matters of examination. He happened to like my way of dealing with issues. I got deeper insights of university administration from him. Even after my relinquishing charge as OSD Examination I was frequently summoned by him to discuss various issues. He had put me to the work of preparing data concerning different alternatives to be offered to the teachers' organizations agitating in connection with the revision of pay scales in 1987. He was quite appreciative of my projections of suggestions with statistical tables and graphs. He also started including me in the group, which he took along with him at discussions with the DUTA representatives and elsewhere. He also asked me to plan and organize the centralized evaluation of answer books for the examinations of 1987. When the time for appointing a new Dean of Colleges drew near speculations on names started. Different people would meet him to fathom his thoughts in the matter. But he kept everybody guessing. Driven to respond to the anxious queries from those near him, he would reel out four or five names out of which any one could be appointed. My name was included among those. Other names were those of equally competent persons.

As the date of Executive Council meeting in which the appointment was to be made drew closer the guessing game became hot. Several persons would meet me to give their good wishes and advice (as they might have been doing with others) as to how I should make efforts for getting the post. In fact I received queries from several quarters on the day of the E.C. meeting whether the V.C. had called me to make the offer already. At least this was the general impression of people regarding such appointments made in the past. Some well meaning friends, on learning that I have had no interaction with the V.C. on the issue till the starting of the EC meeting, observed that I could not have been in the reckoning for the appointment. I too believed it to be the case. I was in my office in Shivaji College till about 6.00 p.m. when I received a telephonic message from the Information Officer of the University, Shri Deepak Malhotra saying that things were moving favourably for me in the meeting of the EC (I later came to know that the EC had already decided to appoint me and the Vice-Chancellor had asked him to inform the press accordingly). Wondering what the cryptic remark of Shri malhotra could mean, I left the College for my home.

On reaching home I found my wife and children cheerfully excited and keen to know if I had been appointed Dean of Colleges. On my expressing ignorance about the matter they told me that several press persons had called them on phone and given the news of my appointment. Within minutes I received a few more calls from press persons congratulating me. I could neither deny nor confirm the news and accepted their congratulations conditionally. But they asserted that their source of information was reliable and I could take the news as confirmed. At this point the Registrar, Shri Madan Mohan, arrived at my residence to give the news and congratulate me. For a moment I went into a trance thanking God for bestowing on me such an unexpected favour. At the same time I cursed myself for entertaining all the misconceived notions regarding how appointments to such high posts were made. However, my respect for Prof. Moonis Raza, whom I admired as an administrator, was further enhanced for appointing me without ever disclosing his mind to me on the subject. In my thanksgiving meeting with him he told me that he did not make the matter known to me before the appointment was actually made because, as he put it, he would have been deprived of the services of a person like me had I been disinclined to his offer, but once the matter became a fait accompli I would not disappoint him. I marveled at the greatness of the person. I have learnt a lot in University administration from him during the time I worked in his team. His term of appointment ended in February1990.He was a great Guru He knew better and taught well.

Second Stint

Upendra Baxi, a renowned Professor of law was appointed Vice-Chancellor of the University on 11th May1990. The United front government headed by Shri V.P. Singh as Prime Minister was in power at the center. The government was supported by the BJP. When Prof. Baxi called the first meeting of the Executive Council it was expected that he would announce his new team. But he did not even make a mention of the subject in the meeting. In the next meeting some members asked the V.C. to name the members of his new team. He merely said that he was thinking about the matter and would take a decision in due course of time. When no proposal regarding the matter came from the V.C. even in the meeting held next time the same members demanded that the continuing members of the team be dropped and a new set be appointed without any further delay. Prof. Baxi reacted to this demand quite sharply asserting that while he considered the matter to be important, he was not going to be forced by any one to appoint whom or when and said that as and when he made up his mind he would bring the recommendation before the EC. The next meeting of the EC passed off without any one raising the question of appointment of new team members. But when the meeting next to that was held a demand came from the same familiar quarters that the V.C. should appoint his team members and that if he wanted to retain the current members he should formalize the same. The issue had gone almost full circle. Was it in any way connected with the BJP's withdrawal of support to the V.P. Singh government ? But Prof. Baxi would not oblige any one by charting his time-table of appointments according to the diktat of others. He only promised to expedite the matter. In the next meeting held on 17th November1990 he announced that Professor A. L. Nagar would replace Prof. K.D. Gangrade as P.V.C. and I would be the Dean of Colleges. The appointment of the Director South Campus was, however, deferred. After the meeting ended two EC members went up to the V.C. and said that they were disappointed with his decision. The V.C. did not respond except giving them a telling smile.

Baxi Won't Bend

The developments preceding the above appointment need to be recalled. Soon after Prof. Baxi took over as V.C. one or the other delegation used to meet him almost with a regularity to impress upon him what kind of persons should be appointed as members of his team. Some of these delegations would insinuate against me suggesting that I should be replaced. They even cited some cases where decisions taken by me were reported to be questionable. In such cases the V.C. soon after the concerned delegation leaving him would call for the files along with a covering note from me in each case. I would promptly respond as desired. Invariably the files came back to me with interesting remarks like 'very good', 'well done', 'keep it up' etc. recorded thereon by the V.C. I was amused, certainly not by the noting on the files but by the situation in which my detractors were putting themselves by making unfounded allegations. The Vice-chancellor also relied upon me for preparing drafts of communications to be addressed by him to persons holding important positions in reply to their letters seeking one or the other kind of favour on behalf of some one. In most such cases it was to be a polite regret. I enjoyed my work and strived hard to develop better administrative skills.

High Soul

There was a case, which I had fully examined in light of the exiting rules and given my advice to the V.C. in a long note. Presumably the V.C. was under some pressure to accept an interpretation as given by a group of teachers which was at variance with my advice. The V.C. chose to get the observations of his PS (a Deputy Registrar) who concurred with the version of the teachers. The V.C. returned the file to me with the noting 'place before the EC for approval.' I was quite perturbed thinking that the V.C had over ruled me on the basis of the Deputy Registrar's note. Before leaving office for my home in the evening I rang up the V.C. seeking immediate appointment saying that I would not be able to get sleep at night disturbed as I was over the method adopted by him in dealing with the case. He responded by saying that he had only casually looked at the file while traveling in his car and that he was open on the question and would certainly like to discuss the same with me as the first thing the next morning.

It was already quite late in the evening, but I prepared a self contained comprehensive note for perusal of the V.C. I also discussed the same with the Director South Campus, Prof. Abad Ahmed and then both of us met the V.C. in his office the next morning. The V.C. carefully went through the note and declared that my interpretation of the issue was correct and therefore, there was no need to place the same before the EC. He accordingly put a note on the file. I went back thanking him for having spent his time in going through the details of the case in light of the rules cited by me. The meeting of the EC was held the next day (17 November 1990). Prof. Baxi d announced my appointment as Dean of Colleges in the same meeting. I wonder if my appointment by Professor baxi had any connection with the stand I had taken the previous day. Only the high souls do such things. Professor Baxi was responsible for creating the myth about my memory of the University Calendar page wise and clause wise. He trusted me and I did my best to keep his trust. He gave me respect and regard more than what I could have deserved.

Third Inning

Professor Baxi resigned in August 1994, nine months before the expiry of his term for taking up an assignment in England. The process of appointment of the new V.C. was set in motion earnestly but it was in March 1995 that the new V.C. Prof. V.R. Mehta was appointed. He was an old student of Delhi University and had also taught at Ramjas College for some years. As such he was not new to the University. He had a number of friends working in Delhi University who must have briefed him about the latest in the University. As on earlier occasions several delegations and individuals met him to advise with regard to the formation of his team. Prof. Mehta was very candid, at least with some of the people who talked to him on the subject. He told a member of the Executive Council, who had met him to discuss the subject that I would be continued as the Dean of Colleges for reasons that were explained to him. That member admittedly having no interest in me was impressed by the frankness of the V.C. and his reasoning. This also set the member thinking afresh about my performance as Dean of Colleges in my previous term. His attitude towards me turned positive. This helped us both in resolving many a ticklish issue with mutual trust and understanding. The Vice-Chancellor declared his new team in a meeting of the EC held on 29th May1995. I was reappointed Dean of Colleges for the third time.

Lame Duck

Prof. Mehta's term ended in March 2000. The new V.C., Professor Deepak Nayyar joined on 16th May 2000. I was left with a period of less than a year to reach the age of 65 years beyond which a person could not continue to hold the office. It was therefore, clear to me that the new team of the V.C. would have a new Dean of Colleges. It was only a matter of time for the V.C. to make up his mind about the new members. Professor Nayyar first wanted to understand the working of the University. So he took a couple of months to take up the matter of appointment of his new team members. He would hold meetings of the team daily and take copious notes regarding several matters. He took decisions on several ticklish problems after extensive discussions in the team meetings. After developing a fair comprehension of the University scene through these interactions the V.C. went ahead to hold a meeting of the EC on 8th August 2000. A couple of hours before the meeting he called the members of the team and confided in them about his decision to appoint a new team. He worked out the modality in such a manner that he would first thank the outgoing members and then the names of the new members of the team would be declared. A short tea break would follow where the new team members would be invited. On the EC reassembling the new members would take the place of the old ones. The process was gone through amid a feeling of fulfillment in the old team and enthusiasm among the new. For me that was not only the end of an era but also the culmination of a rewarding career in the University. I cherish the sweet memories of my interaction with a wide section of the University community, first as a student and then as a teacher and administrator for more than forty-five years.

Mandal Days

The government of India accepted the recommendations of the Mandal Commission for reservation of 27% of jobs for members of the Other Backward Classes in 1990. Country wide agitations started in protest against the decision. Public property at many places became a target of violence and arson. Strikes and bandhs resulted in disruption of normal work in offices and commercial establishments. Educational institutions turned into rallying points of the agitationists. Delhi University was no exception, but the administration under the enlightened leadership of the Vice-Chancellor, Professor Upendra Baxi managed to restrict the agitation to minimum disturbance in the University with no disruption of teaching. A suggestion from the highest quarters for closure of the University and evacuation of the hostels for some time was discreetly turned down with an assurance of keeping the campus peaceful. The agitating students appreciated the decision of the University and in turn co-operated with the administration throughout the period of the agitation. Barricades put up at different points on the roads passing through the campus did cause some inconvenience to the public. But ways and means were found to solve the immediate problems. On couple of occasions when the police arrested the agitating students the University officials arranged to get them released with a promise of maintaining order. I played an active role in monitoring the situation as it developed from day to day. Often I rushed to the campus late at night responding to the summons from the V.C sometimes sneaking into his house by jumping over the boundary wall to escape notice of the crowd of agitating students squatting at the gate. The cordiality between students and officials of the

University transcended to the ranks of the police too. The University came out unscathed from the agitation.

However, a tragic incident on the road out side Deshbandhu College remained a regret of the University. The incident was more a result of the politicking relating to the ensuing elections to the students' union of the College. A student of the College, Mr. Rajiv Goswami was almost pushed into an attempt for immolation in a bid for upmanship in the agitation. He over did the act and in the process got severely burnt. Intensive care in the hospital saved his life. The apparent wounds healed in course of time, but Rajiv never regained his essential health. However, he turned out to be the hero of the day. The next year (1991) he fought and predictably won the election of the president of Delhi University Students' Union. A vestige of the agitation in the Campus is a small platform raised in the middle of the Chhatra Marg at its crossing with Arun Bose Road near Delhi School of Economics. The platform in a slightly trimmed size still stands there raising questions regarding its odd shape in the minds of those who are unaware of its history.

Parliamentary Committee

It was around 1992 that the University was summoned to appear before the Parliamentary committee on SC/ST. The matter was the non-reservation of seats for SC/ST in the admissions to post graduate courses in medicine. Delhi University had adopted a system of giving five percent weightage to candidates of the SC/ST category in determining merit for admission to such courses. Some candidates seeking admission to the Lady Harding Medical College had petitioned to the committee for giving them percentile reservation in the number of seats available. The V.C. deputed me to represent the University. The Secretary Education, Shri Giri and Chairman UGC, Professor Ram Reddy were also present. I explained to the committee the benefits that had accrued to the candidates of SC/ST category under the system adopted by the University. I submitted that percentile reservation of seats was not favoured in order to maintain standards in a critical area like medical education. I also pointed out to the committee the provisions regarding the powers of the Academic Council and the Executive Council given in the Delhi University Act. The Chairman of the Committee asked the Secretary Education and the UGC Chairman whether they favoured an amendment in Delhi University Act in order to incorporate a provision for issuing directions to the University on reservation. Both of them expressed the view that such a move would not be conducive to the autonomy of the University and that a persuasive policy could achieve the desired results. The meeting ended with the committee expressing the hope that the University would on its own pursue a more affirmative policy in the case of the candidates of the SC/ST category in the admissions to the medical stream in post graduate courses also. It may be mentioned here that the Supreme Court, some years ago ruled against reservation of seats in post- graduate medical courses.

Joint Committee

The Ministry of Human Resource Development had proposed an amendment in the Delhi University Act to enable the Guru Gobind Singh Indraprastha University to give affiliation to Institutions in Delhi. The bill was before the Joint Parliamentary Committee for its recommendations. The Committee had invited the Vice-Chancellors of both the Universities some time in June 2000 to give evidence. The notice of the meeting was short. Our Vice-Chancellor was abroad and was scheduled to return after the date of the meeting. On telephonic contact the V.C. deputed the P.V.C. and me to appear before the Committee and make provisional submissions as may be decided by us. We were also asked by the V.C. to request for holding another meeting to take a final decision. We both attended the first meeting of the Committee. The P.V.C., Prof. Abad Ahmed after making the preliminary observations asked me to explain the objections of the University on the draft amendment. I explained the flaws in the bill, which had gone much beyond the intent of the proposed legislation. It amounted to opening doors to any university in the country to affiliate colleges in Delhi. While explaining the position of the Delhi University I had to contradict the arguments given earlier by the Additional Secretary of the Ministry on some point of law. The chairman (Shri S.B.Chavan) and members of the Committee were convinced of our stand and as requested by us the Chairman adjourned the meeting to be held again after about a fortnight.

The Secretary for Education, Shri M.K .Kaw organized a meeting where Vice-Chancellors of both the Universities were invited. The P.V.C. and my self assisted our Vice-Chancellor. We had done our homework and had carried a draft of amendment sufficient to serve the purpose, which the proposed amendment sought to achieve. All concerned agreeing on a common draft the meeting came to an end within a few minutes. The agreed draft was later submitted to the Parliamentary Committee, which commended it to the Parliament leading to a suitable amendment in the Act as act 43 of 2002 coming into force on 25th September 2002.

Interaction with Students :Teacher's Wear

I started my teaching career at S.G.T.B. Khalsa College in January 1958. I was below 22 years of age at that time. My lean and thin appearance was responsible for my being taken as a student by students of disciplines other than Sanskrit on several occasions. I had to resort to the device of carrying a leather portfolio bag to flaunt my identity as a teacher. I left Khalsa College to join Hindu College in November 1960. My interaction here too was restricted to students of Sanskrit who were not many in number. In between I had taught students of Sanskrit at the Post-graduate (evening) Institute of the University for a couple of months. It was at Shivaji College, which I joined in August 1961 that my interaction with students of all disciplines started in my capacity of NCC Officer (NCC was compulsory for all students till1967). Though young in age, I was one of the senior teachers responsible for organizing various student activities in the College. As an old student of the University I saw in the young students my own image of yester years. My dealings with them were friendly, though firm and formal. I maintained this basic attitude throughout my career, which proved quite helpful in tackling problems. I wish to recount here some episodes.

Second Thought

(i) Hardly a year had passed after my joining Shivaji College as lecturer when one day I noticed a student on the back bench of a classroom creating noise by rubbing his shoes on the floor. The noise was loud enough to disturb the class where a newly appointed teacher was lecturing. I happened to pass by that classroom and heard the noise. I immediately called out the student, took him aside on the pathway and without thinking gave him a slap. The student was tall, well built and had an impressive personality. On second thoughts I realized that I had made a mistake in slapping the student. My reflexes worked sharply and raising my voice I asked the boy if he realized what grave wrong he had done. He was quite repentant and expressed regret for what he had done. But my agenda was different. I told him that his mistake was not so much grave in itself but its byproduct in provoking me to make a mistake was graver. He continued to be humble and said that I was a teacher and had all the right to correct him by any means, even by giving a slap. I praised him for his decent behaviour and wished him a bright future. Later he was selected to be an Officer in the Army.

Ever for Students

(ii) A central NCC parade was held at Hansraj College ground on 15 August 1963 in which contingents from all the colleges took part. I led the contingent of Shivaji College. The Prime Minister, Pt. Jawaharlal Nehru took the salute and addressed the parade and filled all present with a patriotic fervour. After the parade was over an altercation took place between the cadets of ITI, Arab ki Sarai and Shivaji College on the road outside the parade ground. When I reached the spot I found one of my cadets fallen on the ground being beaten with sticks by the ITI cadets. I immediately covered the cadet with my body thrown over him. I was in uniform. The cadets of ITI having noticed me (an officer) stopped hitting and immediately disappeared from the scene. However, I received my share of the blows, which fortunately turned out to be not so severe. This action of mine further won the hearts of my cadets who over the years turned the incident into a legend. I on my part experienced a feeling of fulfillment. We all took the incident in its stride.

Students Saved

(iii) A similar incident happened years later when I was Principal of Shivaji College. The office bearers of the student's union wanted to buy some furniture for their office. They desired that I accompany them to the market to help in buying the same at reasonable rates. We were to board a bus from Rajourie Garden to reach Mayapuri. There was rush in the bus. The secretary of the Union forced his way from the driver's door. A quarrel ensued. The students demanded that the bus be taken to the Police station. My intervention proved futile, as the tempers had gone rather high. The bus crew took the bus to the Mayapuri bus depot in place of taking it to the Police Station. They segregated the students from the other passengers and invited them to come inside the depot to lodge their complaint. As soon as the students entered the compound of the depot several members of the staff of DTC pounced on the students and started hitting them with blows. I yelled and shouted at the staff but they continued beating the students. Then I physically came between the students and the staff. In the process I too received a few blows. But some saner elements in the staff could visualize the seriousness of what was going on. They intervened and the staff stopped their violent activity and disappeared from the scene. In the meantime some student had called the police which arrived immediately. The depot in-charge and other officials also arrived. They all expressed their regrets over the incident. The police DCP offered to register a case against the staff members involved if the students so desired. But the students wanted to leave the matter there. We left for the College hoping that the DTC authorities would take appropriate action in the matter.

Army Attachment

As NCC officer I was deputed to attend a month's Army Attachment Camp in Summer of 1967.With me was a group of cadets from Rajasthan. We were received at Pathankot railhead by a young Sikh officer, who escorted us all the way up to the position of the 6 Garhwal Rifles deployed close to the Line of Control in the Poonchh Sector. He had taken all care of our needs during a full day's journey. He had arranged Breakfast and Lunch at the Army Units on the way. It was raining heavily when we reached our destination. A young Captain received us and escorted me to my place of stay during the period of the Camp. It was afine small double fly tent well protected by an encircling snake trench.

Without wasting any time the Captain asked me what shall I have first, Whisky or Rum? He looked a little puzzled when I told him to send just a cup of hot tea. Tea was served to be followed by a sumptuous dinner. Next morning the Commandant of the Unit received me in the mess over breakfast and introduced me to all other officers. The cadets were lodged with the troops. I made it a point to join the daily Physical training programme in the morning.

The daily schedule included visits to various posts of our army overlooking the line of control from vintage points. I saw how our officers and soldiers lived a tough life in make shift bunkers. We could see some activities going on the other side of the border. We could see first hand how difficult it was to maintain vigil at posts located at heights of more than nine thousand feet. Our group was taken to some of these posts. The climb on Kalatop turned out to be most arduous but a rewarding experience. Black stumps of trees burnt by enemy shelling during the 1965 conflict with Pakistan could be seen at different spots on the slops of the mountains. Similar must be the scene on the opposite side. The most exciting part of our Camp was the experience of firing arms like Sten gun, machine gun, 2 inch mortar in addition to rifles of different makes. The high point was firing of rocket launcher and throwing with accuracy hand grenade. The last one required alertness both before throw and after the arsenal had been released.

President and Punishment

(iv) I removed the President of the student's union (1978-79) of my college from the post after an inquiry committee had found him guilty of beating a fellow student. All his efforts to coerce the College administration in getting reinstated to his post failed. Even a hunger strike undertaken by him fizzled out. It had become evident that he did not enjoy the sympathy and following of large section of students of the College. The annual sports meet of the College was to be held in a couple of days. The ousted President felt that his isolation from students will be sealed if he continues to be shorn of the title of President. Failing to get support from the fellow students in the college he decided to enlist the support of some student union leaders of other colleges.

One day before the sports meet was scheduled to be held a group of about twenty student leaders from different colleges barged into my room and demanded the restoration of the office of President to the student concerned. First of all I asked them to take their seats, as there were enough chairs in my room. Then I served them some cold drinks, which they accepted with some reluctance. I told them that I would treat them as guests and expected them to conduct themselves as such. By this time their ruffled tempers had turned cool and they pleaded their case with cordiality. I expressed my helplessness in accepting their plea at that stage and suggested that their friend should follow the normal course of giving a representation for consideration at appropriate forum. They went back disappointed but at the same time claiming that the students in general were not willing to participate in the sports meet without the President. I invited them to come the next day and try to find out from the students themselves if they were in agreement with them.

I gave them one hour for the purpose. After that if the students responded to the call of the College authorities to report for the meet nobody should forcibly stop them from participating in the events. The student leaders from other colleges led by the DUSU President Shri Hari Shankar came to the college at 9.00 a.m. and after trying for an hour gave up. At the very first call for the first event of the meet the students started entering the grounds. The deposed President posted himself at the entrance of the ground and started physically stopping the students from entering. I reached the spot and reminded him of the agreement arrived at the previous evening. When he appeared to be adamant some students came forward and removed him from the scene. Within minutes the first event of the meet was on. I could see Shri Hari Shankar witnessing the goings on from a distance. A few minutes later the deposed President came in to seek permission to witness the events which was granted. He sat through the progress of some events and then left assuring his best co-operation for the success of the meet. I thanked him for the gesture. Later the staff council having been satisfied by his conduct recommended the restoration of his office. Accordingly the suspension was revoked and he was once again the President of the student's union of the College.

Open Door

(v) One day the newly elected (1989) President of DUSU Miss Suniti Wadhwa entered my office and asked in a rather raised voice as to why no officials including the members of the V.C.'s team were available in their seats. I had not met her earlier but guessed from her sartorial choice and tomboyish look that she was Suniti. I asked her to sit down and told her that I, the Dean of Colleges was very much present in my office and willing to help her. Then in a lighter vein I asked her how she had marked me absent when I was present. She sat down and apologized to me profusely for her misdemeanor. She was full of regard for me and continued to show it throughout her tenure as President.

On another day when the V.C. was away on leave Suniti managed to enter his office room along with a couple of her followers and bolted the door from inside. The Security officer had called the Police. Suniti refused to come out and threatened to break the furniture of the room in case attempt was made to remove her from there with police help. At this stage the Security officer apprised me of the situation. I immediately rushed to the V.C.'s room and pleaded with Suniti to open the door. After some pleading she agreed to do so with the condition that I alone could enter the room and that everybody else including the Police should go away from the spot. It was agreed to. Suniti got the door unbolted from inside. I entered the room and found her perched on the V.C.'s chair. I persuaded her to leave the room and go her way. However, before leaving she managed to break an earthen flower pot placed outside the room as if to register her visit to the V.C.'s room.

Humour Hammer

(vi) I normally kept long hours in my office as Principal of Shivaji College. It had become almost a habit with me. During my tenure as Dean of Colleges the working hours increased further. Whereas my availability was an assuring feature to different sections of University community, my long hours in office gave me the advantage of maximum interaction with people with varied opinions, which enabled me to develop new insights in university administration. One day when the V.C. (Prof. Baxi) was out of station a group of student leaders came to me and demanded that I get the room of the V.C. opened so that they could paste a poster on his table. That was a strange demand. Instead of directly confronting them I thought of tackling them diplomatically. Expressing my inability in getting the room opened I offered to receive the poster to be handed over to the V.C. on his return or alternatively they could paste the same on my table. But the students were not satisfied and went back giving me five minutes' notice to arrange for the opening of the room.

Hardly five minutes had gone when the students reappeared. They demanded that I should immediately get the room opened or else they would break the furniture of my office. Wishing not to procrastinate the engagement I cautioned the students in a raised voice saying 'dare you break the furniture here'. Upon that their retort, almost in a chorus, though in reduced decibels was 'what will you do if we break the furniture here?' I continued in the same strain 'in that case I would buy new one'. Clueless of how to end the stand off the students burst into a loud laughter and went out of my room saying in my hearing distance, 'it is difficult to hoodwink Dr. Rana, let us not stop here any more, otherwise he will blunt the edge of our agitation with his affable manners.' I was immensely pleased with the turn in the situation. The students went back happy forgetting all about their 'mission'. In the process I learnt that an ugly situation can be turned into a happy one by tactful handling and that the hammer of humour is more effective than the hammer of iron.

Trust Test

(vii) I was made Staff Advisor of DUSU in 1982. DUSU elections, especially of the Executive Committee used to be full of tension. Apprehending violence the authorities of the University made elaborate arrangements including deployment of police on a large scale every year. I had been observing the scene for a number of years and had felt that the event had been hyped out of proportions. When I got the opportunity to handle the event myself I decided to scale down the arrangements and tried to make things more transparent. The extra circle of barricading the venue of the election was dispensed with. But I did not compromise when it came to firm decision making. The out going President of the students' union was placed under police custody immediately when he tried to disrupt the process of counting of votes. The Secretary, a Sikh boy was creating a scene outside the counting hall as he had been denied entry because of his carrying a kirpan. The matter was brought to my notice. I went to the gate outside and asked the student why he was insisting on taking the kirpan inside the hall where counting of votes was going on. He replied that the kirpan was a religious symbol and was not meant to be a weapon of offence. I decided to allow him to carry the kirpan inside the hall on religious ground and at the same time cautioned him that if he misused the kirpan he would harm his own religion. He went in wearing the kirpan round his waist and conducted himself in the most disciplined manner. The student S.Ravinder Pal Singh developed a valued relationship with me for years to come.

Tactful Act

(viii) The result of the election of the Executive Committee of DUSU for 1995-96 had been announced. There was some dissatisfaction among a section of the students having affiliation with a political party over the number of seats won by the different groups. Apprehending trouble I had tucked the folded sheet containing the record of counting and the result safely under my rain coat. I was accompanied by Prof. Rajiv Khanna to reach the residence of the V.C. to submit the record for his signatures. As soon as we walked a few steps towards our cars I was gheraoed by the disgruntled group hurling all sorts of accusations on me. They would not let me go. I requested the Police personnel present not to intervene, as I preferred to handle the students myself. I continued to plead with them very politely and patiently in spite of their shouting provocative slogans. In the mean while the crowd surrounding me had swelled. Taking advantage of the situation I managed to pass on the folded sheet to Prof. Khanna with a signal to quietly escape and reach the V.C. residence. As soon as Prof. Khanna reached a safe distance I changed my tack and tenor. I told the students that they could continue to gherao me for the whole night and that if I chose to leave no one dared to touch me. After waiting for a couple of minutes I made a move towards my car parked a short distance away. No student obstructed me but slogans shouting continued as I moved away from the scene.

Mandal Vandals

(ix) The University had increased the examination fee for various courses in the year 1991. The revision was overdue and was effected after assessing the general feeling in University circles that an upward revision was overdue. No dissenting voice was heard till the DUSU elections were held. Mr. Rajiv Goswami who had received severe burns in his attempt to immolate himself during the anti-reservation agitation near the end of 1990 was elected President of DUSU defeating the candidates of well-established student organizations of the major political parties. These elements were on the lookout for laying a trap for the newly elected President in order that he either joined their respective camp or otherwise did in his programmes. Under this environment he was inspired by some elements to start an agitation against the fee rise. Goswami initially staged a daylong dharna outside Jawahar Vatika. Next day a section of the press insinuated that Rajiv had betrayed the cause of students by lifting the dharna without achieving any concession from the authorities. Peeved at this news Rajiv restaged the dharna combining with hunger strike. Negotiations with Rajiv were continued for a number of days. When an amicable settlement was about to be reached the rival faction organized a parallel dharna.

This competitiveness in agitation though initially bothersome to the administration turned out to be counter-productive for the students. The V.C. Prof. Baxi was clear in his mind that the decision to increase the fees would not be reversed. He made this known to all who were interlocuting in the matter. The only worry of the University administration was the precarious health of Rajiv. He had been under medical treatment for a long time and some of his burn wounds were still to heal. He had to go out to take pain killer shots with regularity. That being winter the risk of infection was always there. So heating arrangements were made and sufficient winter clothes and beddings were provided at the venue where he would spend the night. Still anxiety remained in our hearts about his well-being. One day the V.C. rang me up at 2.00 p.m. in the night informing me that he had received a message that Rajiv was not feeling well and that we have to take him to the hospital. I immediately took out my personal car and reached the V.C.'s house where Prof. Baxi joined me. We both took Rajiv to the University Health Center and got the necessary injection administered. Thereafter we dispatched him to be admitted to Batra hospital under escort of a senior official and a doctor of the Health Center. We had hoped that the agitation would be over as there was none left to continue the hunger strike. To our amazement next morning we found Rajiv on dharna and hunger strike. Evidently some forces were working behind Rajiv to keep the agitation going for meeting their own vested interests. The V.C. continued to be firm in his resolve not to withdraw the increase in examination fees, which had the support of the teaching community in general. The agitation started showing signs of fatigue. Ultimately the issue was resolved after a token reduction of rupees five in the increase. We were happy that the principle of fee-increase was accepted which enabled the University to effect another rise in examination fees a few years later without any hassles.

Legal Eagles

(x) There was a time when admissions to LL.B. course were made separately by each of the three Law Centers on the basis of marks obtained by the candidates in the qualifying examination. There had been reports of large scale use of questionable methods adopted for seeking admission at Law center-II functioning in the evening at Mandir Marg. There were reliable reports of complicity of the Section Officer of the Center in such goings on. The V.C. Prof. Baxi asked me to do something to stop the rot. The first thing I did was to recommend the transfer of the Section Officer, which was put into practice immediately. The next step was to ensure that the cashier accepted the fees of the eligible students only after obtaining the orders of the Professor-in-charge. Original certificates of the qualifying examination in respect of the candidates admitted were to be retained till the admissions were over. In spite of all the precautions having been taken one day some students barged into the office of the Prof.-in-charge and managed to get the fees deposited for a number of candidates. Thereafter those very students managed to remove all other documents in respect of such candidates. Evidently all the cases were of ineligible candidates or of those who did not figure in the merit list. On receiving the report the University cancelled all those admissions and resumed the admissions as per merit on the basis of marks in the qualifying examination.

Law and Order

(xi) I was also entrusted with the responsibility of sorting out the problem of housing Law Center-II. The NDMC wanted the University to vacate the M.B. School building housing the Center in evening shift. After a survey of the building I had personally come to the conclusion that the environment was not congenial for running Law classes there. All kinds of unwanted elements hovered around the place. Teachers felt dissipated to reach there and absenteeism among both students and teachers was rampant. Several teachers practiced law in the courts during the day and would have hardly any energy left to do justice to their teaching work. Mafia groups were freely operating in the Center's premises. Several ills afflicting the Center came to light when a newly appointed Professor-in-charge put a number of conditions before taking charge. The major demand was provision of security on a big scale. The Proctor and I met the DCP (MS. Deol) and discussed with her appropriate police arrangements. The DCP turned out to be a student of the center currently studying for the final year. She personally knew about the conditions at the Center and therefore, was able to bring complete order immediately. We also caused some transfers in the non-teaching staff to break the nexus of the mafia with the administration.

Space Race

In the meanwhile a committee headed by Justice Chinappa had recommended the shifting of the Center to the Campus. But lack of sufficient space to accommodate the office and library was a constraining factor. Even sufficient number of teaching rooms was not available in the law faculty building to run evening classes. So funds were made available from the development fund of the University to construct a few temporary rooms for the purpose. The temporary building was ready within a couple of months and we shifted the Center to the campus of the Law Faculty. The library was accommodated on the first floor of the newly constructed auditorium, which has a story of its own to be recounted separately. The shortfall in teaching rooms was met by arranging some rooms in the Arts Faculty building nearby. After some years a few more temporary rooms were added to cater to the needs of the Center. Later the work of building more area was stalled halfway through due to disagreements among the Center's teachers on the proposed use of the extra space created. I understand the matter was later finally resolved and the building was completed and put to appropriate use.

Hall of Fame

(xii) An elegant two storeyed auditorium with some cubicles on the second floor stands testimony to the untiring spirit of a teacher who did not wait for the financial help or formal approval of the authorities to redeem his pledge made to his students to build an auditorium in the Law Faculty campus. Prof. Mata Deen was the Prof.-in-charge of the Campus Law Center. He motivated the students of his Center to raise voluntarily funds for building an auditorium. With the consent of the students a pro-rata amount was charged from them every year for the purpose of a development fund. Coupons were got printed for raising funds from the public. The coupons were distributed among members of the staff and students after keeping proper record. In the meantime request had been sent to the University administration for according approval for constructing the auditorium. Responding to the enthusiasm of the students and encouraged by the flow of funds Prof. Mata Deen went ahead with the programme of construction without waiting for the formal approval of the University. Needless to say that he had procured the services of accredited architect and structure engineer for the planning of the building. The V.C., Prof. Baxi had laid the foundation stone of the auditorium.

The building was ready in record time. By this time the tenure of Prof. Mata Deen as Prof.-in-charge of the Campus Law Center had ended. His superannuating was approaching near. Some elements hostile to him raised the question of unauthorised construction. Some others questioned the raising of funds without proper permission of the University. A vehement campaign against

Prof. Mata Deen led to the appointment of an Inquiry committee comprising Justice Goswami. Apart from the charges pertaining to the auditorium, Prof. Mata Deen was charged of some irregularity in law admissions. He was indignant over the turn of events. He had thought that he would be rewarded for his selfless work in raising funds and making the dream of an auditorium a reality. In stead, he was being punished. Therefore, throughout the Inquiry he continued to be recalcitrant and did not do enough explaining which did not look difficult from the way he had kept the records of money and material.

In the meanwhile the matter of his re-employment came before the EC, which kept it pending till the report of the Inquiry committee was received, and action taken thereon. I had the satisfaction of motivating him in placing his case patiently and logically before the authority that mattered. The report of the Inquiry committee was examined in light of the replies and material supplied by him to the EC. It turned out that Prof. Mata Deen could not be punished for bona fide actions taken in the interest of the students. His failure to follow due procedure did not warrant penal action against him. The EC rightly decided to drop any further action against Professor Mata Deen. Prof. Mata Deen completed his full term of re-employment and finally retired at the age of 65 years. Later the Ambedkar University, Agra appointed him visiting Professor. Leading a peaceful retired life in Delhi Prof. Mata Deen Passed away some time back.

Unlawful Entry

(xiii) Students of Campus Law Center had been sitting on dharna over some problem of admissions. Their demand could not be acceded to, as the same was not justified. Their leaders had thought of disrupting the examination which was scheduled for 2.3o p.m. that day. They had even invited the DUSU Secretary, Shri Ajay Chauhan to support their agitation. The examinees had gathered in the compound and were keen to take the examination as scheduled. Sufficient number of policemen had been deployed to facilitate unobstructed entry of examinees to the venue. As the time of the commencement of the examination drew near the Secretary of DUSU started exhoring the examinees not to take the examination that day,also assuring that an alternative date would be fixed for the same. By this time I had reached the scene and had assessed the mood of the examinees. They were keen to take the examination. I therefore climbed a raised platform and declared that the examination would not be rescheduled and those who fail to sit for the same would be treated as absent. I had also deputed a few staff members to quietly spread the message among the assembled students. Fifteen minutes before the scheduled time the bell rang and a trickle of students followed to reach the examination rooms on the first floor. Another obstruction, however, had to be tackled. As the students reached near the staircase it was discovered that the gate had been locked and the key was missing. I lost no time in ordering the breaking open of the lock. The act was performed by the ever ready to help Deputy Proctor, Dr. R.S. Chaudhary. The examination passed off smoothly to be followed by more peaceful times.

Abortive Merger

(xiv) The committee headed by Justice Chinappa had inter-alia recommended the merger of the teaching staff of the three law centers. Accordingly the EC passed a resolution, which provided for future recruitment of teachers in a common pool with option to the existing teachers to join the pool. Apportioning of teachers and allotment of teaching work in different centers was to be administered by a committee under the chairmanship of the Dean of the Faculty. This measure was taken with a view to improve the standard of teaching. Before there could be an occasion to implement the decision Prof. Baxi resigned to take up a teaching assignment in England. The ink of the recording of the decision had hardly dried when the faculty members started raising objection against it. The decision was rescinded during the tenure of the next V.C., Prof. V.R.Mehta.

Hearty Matter

(xv) Immediately after I joined as Principal of Shivaji College my priority was improvement of academic standards. One of the measures adopted by the staff council was to stop re-admission of failed students in the same class. Exception to it could be made on the recommendation of the department concerned. One of the failed students of B.Com (Pass) II year in the year 1982, Mr. Rajesh Garg organized an agitation against this policy. Failing in his attempt to enlist enough support of the student community, he resorted to sit in and hunger strike in front of the staff room. Even this gimmick was exposed in a couple of days. One day around 11.00 a.m. when I was sitting in the staff room with some teachers a group of students barged into the staff room and started bolting its doors from inside announcing that I along with the teachers was under gherao. I acted fast and prevented them from bolting the doors assuring at the same time that I would respect their symbolical act and would not leave the room stealthily. Apart from Mr.Garg the group included Mr. Sushil Pandit who had the same year migrated to Ramjas College in B.Com (Honours) III year class. The students used all gimmicks in their pocket but failed to stir me. Though some of my colleagues were impatient to no longer bear with the situation and wanted a show down sooner than was my calculation. I was able to persuade them to wait till 5.00 p.m. by which time the classes would be over and the students not interested in the agitation would have left the college. Our strategy had worked.

The agitating students found themselves isolated by 5.00 p.m. Announcing that it was time for us to leave and therefore no body should venture to stop us, all the teachers present there and I moved towards the door. A feeble attempt by Mr. Garg to stop me was of no avail and soon we all were out of the room. Mr. Pandit, otherwise a very decent student challenged me to enter the College the next day. I accepted the challenge and announced my time of arrival as 9.00 a.m. The next morning I reached the College at 9.00 a.m. and found Mr. Pandit standing outside the gate. He tried to stop me but brushing him aside I entered the college followed by several colleagues who had reached in the meantime. As students of the college were not backing the agitation classes were going on normally. When I was discussing the situation created by outsiders with the teachers in the staff room I was lured into the office room by some miscreants on the pretext of a telephone call to be answered there. As soon as I entered the office a group of outsiders trooped in physically lifting Mr. Rajesh Garg to demonstrate how feeble he had gone because of the hunger strike.

They were menacingly accusing me for bringing about a serious situation and insisted that I should accept their demands otherwise I would come to grief. I was firm and resolute in my stand and refused to oblige them. In the meantime several members of the non-teaching staff of the college who were around and were watching the scene came forward and warned these outsiders to desist from further precipitating the situation and leave the place failing which serious action could be taken against them. Word had also reached the teachers who immediately rallied to ensure that the miscreants caused no harm to my person. Dr. R.D. Mishra had identified one of our own students Mr. Tiwari indulging in indecent behaviour with him. Mr. Tiwari was made to leave the college, though it meant personal efforts on my part to get him migrated to Khalsa College with the extraordinary facility of changing an elective subject in the second year. Our decision not to admit failed students stood the test of nerves and verves.

Practising Principles

Mr. Rajesh Garg as some others passed the examination the next year. Such students were eligible to be readmitted to the next higher class. The teachers in the Commerce department were apprehensive that if admitted Mr. Rajesh Garg could be a menace, especially if elected as a student leader which was a near possibility. I agreed with the teachers but did not want to follow double standards. My stand was that if the norms allowed it Mr. Garg should be admitted without linking the issue with the previous year's agitation. The teachers ultimately agreed with me and Mr. Garg was admitted to the third year of the course. It is a different matter that on subsequently being elected President of the College students Union he indulged in avoidable confrontation with the college administration. But I took his activities in their stride with equanimity of mind. In the heart of his heart he had all respect for me. In fact later when he wanted readmission in B.A. (Pass) course the next year for the purpose of fighting election for DUSU Secretary's post he sought new venues for the purpose, as the norms of Shivaji College did not permit such an admission. On my request Principal Mohan Lal admitted him to P.G.D.A.V. College. Mr. Garg was elected Secretary of DUSU for the year 1983-

84. He has ever remained full of regard for me and I have always valued his attitude towards me personally. I learn that Rajesh was elected member of the Delhi legislative Assembly in the December 2013 election. I wish him well.

Chain Action

(xvi) The category B examinations of the year 1983 were in progress. I took a ten days' break and went to Simla with my family. Dr. S.K Nayyar was looking after the examination work during my absence. As I returned he informed me about the loss of a gold chain of one of the examinees the previous day. While we were discussing the matter the evening shift chaukidar, Shri Gordhan brought a gold chain, which he had found on the verge of a flowerbed just a few minutes back. Obviously it was the same chain, which had been lost by a girl the previous day. Since she had left no address it was apparently difficult to trace her. But I considered it my obligation to trace her and restore the gold chain to her. Instead of immediately lodging a report to the police I moved in the matter systematically. First of all I got the gold chain packed in a sealed packet in the presence of witnesses so that there was no tampering with the original material. Then I located the two rooms where girl students, seven in all had been seated during the examination the previous day. I got their roll numbers noted and arranged to have their residential addresses from the examination branch of the University. A confidential messenger was sent to the first girl's residence where it was learnt that a friend of her had lost her gold chain at the examination center at Shivaji College. On contacting the second girl it became clear that she was the rightful owner of the chain. Her brother who had escorted her to the center gave the same verion. However, to be doubly sure she was asked to come to the College the next day at 5.00 p.m. As soon as she arrived at the gate accompanied by her brother the next day the watchman, Shri Gordhan recognized her as the girl who had made frantic inquiries about her lost chain on the day of her examination. After completing the necessary formalities the chain was restored to its rightful owner. The girl as also her brother was visibly happy and thanked us all present for the interest we had taken in the whole matter.

Dealing with Devil

(xvii) As Principal of Shivaji College I took several measures to streamline the general discipline. These included the posting of a guard at the gate and the cycle stand. One day while Mr. Prithvi Chand and I were having lunch in my room the guard with an injury on his forehead came in and complained about an intruder at the gate. I immediately went out and found the assailant brandishing a knife from across the boundary wall of the College. On my challenging he started moving fast towards the ring road. My reflexes acted sharp. I immediately took out my car and chased him. Shri Prithvi Chand was with me. We spotted him jumping into the compound of Rajdhani College across the ring road. I parked my car at the nearby petrol filling station. In the mean time some teachers and a number of students had followed and joined us. We all jumped into the compound and surrounded the miscreant. We asked him to surrender his weapon and raise his arms as his game was up. He raised his arms swearing that he had thrown the weapon away. We captured him and also recovered the knife from the dump of construction material lying there. The students were furious and started beating him. But I prevailed upon them not to take the law in their own hands. The culprit along with the weapon was handed over to the Police. The incident created an impact on the College community for maintaining solidarity and peaceful environment.

Admission Admonition

(xviii) One of the measures adopted by me to raise academic standards in Shivaji College was to make admissions strictly on the basis of merit. The teachers had extended their full co-operation in the matter. One day during the admissions of 1977 Dr. Ram Singh Chauhan, an old colleague from Khalsa College came to see me in connection with the admission of a student in my college. I expressed my inability to admit the boy, as he did not have the requisite percentage of marks. The initial response of Dr. Chauhan was in disbelief. He thought that I was joking. I requested him to appreciate my position, as I could not depart from the norms evolved in the college with my own initiative. In the mean time I had ordered tea for him. But he refused to have tea with me and instead challenged me with regard to my claim of allowing admissions only on the basis of merit. He also told me that he would have no relations with me in future and left in a huff but not without admonishing me in so many words.

I felt sorry for him. At the same time his conduct set me thinking whether I would be able to always uphold the strict norms of admissions. However, I promised to myself to maintain the tempo built in the very first year of my job of a Principal. Pulls and pressures from influential people in the coming years did not deter me from my resolve to continue the policy. I must acknowledge the co-operation I always received from members of the governing body. Intake of better students year after year gave a fillip to my determination. Several years later I happened to come across Dr. Chauhan in a function. I went up to him and asked whether he was still angry with me. He was very polite with me and said, "Not any more. I have observed that you have been consistent in your admission policy over the years since you had refused to oblige me." I thanked him for that and gave him the credit for stirring me to embark on such a difficult course.

Help Per Rules

(xix) The teacher in-charge of admissions for B.Sc.(General) A course during 1977, Dr. Satya Prakash had miscalculated and declared the cut off percentage at a lower level than required. That resulted in turning up of more students than the vacancies. Even after admitting surplus number of students equal to the number of estimated withdrawals a good number of students were still pressing their claim for admission as they fulfilled the declared criteria. Finding himself in a difficult spot Dr. Satya Prakash declared the admissions closed. Many students went back disappointed and some even disgruntled. I learnt about the matter on my return from a meeting in the University later in the day. I discussed the matter with Dr. Prakash and some other senior teachers in the concerned subjects. All of us were unanimous in our approach to increase the number of seats to form another section of the class and invite those who had been refused admission. Accordingly all such students were informed of our decision to admit them. Letters were sent out to all of them through personal couriers the same day giving two days' time to complete the formalities and pay the fees.

Almost all of the students concerned turned up the very next day- some of them along with their parents. They were visibly pleased with the action of the College in unilaterally reviewing the decision and informing them personally and so promptly. One of the parents handed over to me a letter from the then Chief Executive Councillor, Shri Kedarnath Sahni. Shri Sahni in his letter had requested me to help the students if rules permitted. The same parent reported that Shri Sahni had told them when they met him soon after their wards were refused admission that I would not depart from norms and they should meet me and explain their problem. He further remarked how correct Shri Sahni was. I expressed my regrets for the inconvenience caused to the students and their parents and granted admission to them the same day. Our surplus admissions fitted well in the policy enunciated later that year by the University to admit additional number of students to the extent possible in view of fact that students passing out school in 1977 formed the last batch of 11 years of schooling.

Straight Record

(xx) Unexpectedly Mrs. Indira Gandhi dissolved the Lok Sabha early in 1977 much before the expiry of the extended term and announced fresh elections. The opposition parties were taken by surprise. But the short notice proved a blessing in disguise for them. The much eluding unity under one banner was forged more as a necessity than a matter of conviction or mutual trust. The Janata party was formed by the electoral unity with the symbol of the Lok Dal of Chaudhary Charan Singh. The Janata Party had enlisted the support of several organizations and individuals who had not supported the Emergency. The media was in full support of the party. Statements poured in daily from one or the other organization and groups favouring its. To counter such measures the Congress also embarked on a campaign of publicity through the media. One evening sitting at the dinner table with my family my daughters drew my attention to a news item flashed on the Delhi Doordarshan attributing the signing of a statement by more than two hundred teachers of Delhi University in support of the

Congress. My name was read out among the prominent persons who were reported to have issued the statement. My family members and I knew the news item was factually incorrect in as much the inclusion of my name was concerned. Without losing time I contacted the news editor of Doordarshan and pointed out to him about the lack of authenticity of the news item. He promised to look into the matter.

Within an hour or so I received a telephonic call from a functionary in the office of the All India Congress Committee who knew me personally. He informed me that he gave the news item on the basis of papers given to him by a college principal, whom he named. On being contacted the principal told me that the news item was given by a professor of the University in good faith in the belief that those who believed in the ideology of the Congress would support such a resolution and advance consent could not be obtained for want of time. I found the explanation quite reasonable and left the matter there. It made me a little unhappy later when one of the principals who had been mentioned in the news item contacted me to join him in lodging a complaint with the Shah Commission, which was inquiring into the 'excesses' of Emergency. I told him how I had dealt with the matter to my satisfaction when it had arisen. I wondered how it took the appointment of a commission to awaken his conscience. I curtly told him that I did not agree with his approach in the matter. Perhaps this gentleman was the only one among the 'authors' of the statement who had written to the Shah Commission regarding the matter. But the irony is that he was seen rubbing shoulders with the supporters of the Congress party after it regained power in 1980. This Principal was the same gentleman who was involved in a case of use of unfair means in an examination later in 1989.

Emergency Urgency

(xxi) Related to the days of Emergency is a personal experience I wish to narrate here. As a part of the programme of implementation of family planning the Directorate of education started inducing school teachers having more than two children to go for vasectomy operation. Till the order, given only verbally, was complied with the teachers were asked to report at the zonal offices of the Directorate to listen to homilies from overzealous officials. We had three daughters and a son in our family. We had thought that our family was complete and we had no plan to produce any more children. We also thought that that there were methods other than vasectomy to practice family planning. To go for vasectomy under official fiat did not go well with our psyche. I met the Deputy Director to discuss the matter. Introducing myself as Principal of Shivaji College and told him that going for vasectomy was a serious decision which needed time and planning. He immediately suggested that we could go to the government hospital and mention the name of the wife of the then Chief Executive Councillor, Shri Radha Raman as the motivator and the operation would be done in minutes. Obviously the officer had not followed what I had said to him. On my expressing unwillingness to go for any operation he suggested that in that case we could motivate two other persons to under go the operation and in the same breath volunteered the information that we could easily locate in the hospital premises such persons who were ready to go for operation on payment of a modest sum. I found the latter suggestion innocuous. Next day my wife and I went to Hindu Rao Hospital and without much effort found two volunteers who agreed to go for the desired operation on payment of rupees hundred each. It was not a costly deal to settle a sensitive issue. However, for future we did not forget to maintain the status quo in the number of our children.

Pending Grants

(xxii) Shivaji College had started several honours courses in the late sixties and early seventies. The UGC had sanctioned the required funds for purchase of books. The amounts were spent out of the recurring grants of the College instead of claiming separately as non-recurring grants already approved by the UGC. As the UGC was quite liberal in the matter of release of grants the College did not face any difficulty in managing its expenditure. But the UGC was put to some kind of alert after the change of government in 1977. In 1977-78 it went ahead to finalise the admissible amounts in the maintenance grants and adjusted the excess amounts released over the years. It meant a big drop in the release of recurring grants to the College. Without loosing any further time I took up with the UGC the matter of release of grants sanctioned earlier for the honours courses. I personally met the Secretary Mr. R.K. Chhabra, who promised to get the needful done expeditiously. But unfortunately there was no progress in spite of a chain of lengthy correspondence. The UGC itself was facing a hostile attitude of the then government. The financial situation was getting tight for the College. In fact overdraft was resorted to in one or two cases. On one occasion some of the senior teachers along with me volunteered to wait for the release of their salaries till the required sums were received from the UGC. I requested the University to use its good offices for the release of the grants. A meeting was arranged with Dr. M.L. Mehta, additional Secretary of UGC in the office of the Dean of Colleges, Dr. P.L. Malhotra. I explained how desperate the situation was and candidly put the responsibility for the crisis on the apathy at the level of UGC.

At the end of the discussion it was agreed that Dr. Mehta would dispose of all our files the day after and that to facilitate the work I should bring duplicate copies of the papers already submitted. I took my accountant along with all the papers including the college letter-head and college stamp in case a fresh letter was to be given on the spot. Dr. Mehta had devoted the day available to him in getting all the files of Shivaji College on his table. On the appointed day we sat in Dr. Mehta's room from 10 a.m. to 5 p.m. with a short lunch break. Most of the files were cleared by the evening and the release of grants arranged in a couple of days. I still remember the gracious act on the part of Dr. Mehta. We became good friends and interacted often on several issues in a complimentary spirit for years to come.

Pricipal Bhan

(xxiii) Dr. R.K. Bhan Principal of Shivaji College (1961-64) was to retire some time in the middle of 1964. He had requested the governing body for extension of service. Simultaneously he was trying for this position in a newly opened college of the Delhi administration (later named as first Hastinapur and subsequently Moti Lal Nehru College). Dr. Bhan had inspired a campaign in his support. He managed to get a memoranda signed by a section of teachers of the College. He even tried to vilify a couple of senior teachers who did not call his tune When the matter came up for consideration in the meeting of the governing body I as one of the representatives of the teachers suggested that since the item related to the service of the Principal it would be appropriate if both the teacher representatives abstain from the meeting. The other representative did not agree to this. Both of us participated in the discussions and voted differently. The University representatives remained neutral. The Principal did not get extension of service. However, he was lucky to have got the appointment in the new college. Since Dr.Bhan had a major say in hiring staff in the new college he took away a good number of teachers of Shivaji College along with him.

Taking by the Horns

(xxiv) When Shivaji College was taken over by Delhi Administration and merged with another college already functioning at Karampura, the combined unit became a reasonably big college. The question of discipline was taken up with all earnestness. I happened to be the Proctor of the College. Several teachers and some students had complained of the wayward ways of a first year student of the new college. I called and counseled him to mend his ways .He belonged to a village and understood my language. He thought he could hoodwink me by making tall promises in an ingratiating fashion. In his own rustic way he told me that on my asking he would do even the impossible in the manner of a he-buffalo delivering a calf. I did not feel assured and continued to have a watch on his conduct in the College. His behaviour with fellow students, especially with female students was found lacking in decency. On my recommendation the Principal suspended him from the classes and banned his entry in the college pending inquiry. Matters came to a head when one day he entered one of the class rooms in the College. On being informed I reached the spot and asked him to get out of the room. Finding him stubborn I went to the office to call the police. Sensing that I meant business the boy slipped away. I chased him for some distance outside the College. But dodging me in the zigzag of rows of houses he managed to escape. The police team also arrived speedily and succeeded in tracing him in one of the houses nearby. They arrested and put him behind the bars. The police knew him better. He was suspected to be a carrier of drugs. During the evening the same day an advocate and a member of the Delhi Metropolitan Council met the Principal at his residence taking cudgels on behalf of the boy. They expressed their surprise over my audacity in getting their protégé arrested and passed veiled threats against me. The Principal was candid in warning them against entertaining any thought of harming me as he told them of my background and the support of men and the law that I enjoyed. Thereafter we never heard of whatever happened to the boy. I never saw him crossing my path or be around anywhere near the College again.

Catching a Thief

(xxv) During the days I was Principal Shivaji College I used to carry my lunch in the brief case meant for carrying important papers. The attendant posted outside my room used to take out the lunch box at lunch time and organize things. One day I had put some money in the brief case and locked it. At lunch time I gave the key to the attendant for taking out the lunch box and lay the food on the table. I quickly took my lunch and went to the staff room leaving the key with the attendant. On my return to my room the attendant handed over the key to me and quickly disappeared. His expression of some kind of nervousness raised suspicion in my mind. I immediately checked the briefcase to ensure that the money I had put in it was there. To my surprise the money was missing. The attendant was not around. He was found loitering somewhere in the college building and was brought to me. I straightaway told him that he had taken something from my brief case probably by mistake. If he returned the same within five minutes his act would not be construed as theft. Otherwise the police would be informed of the incident. To facilitate things for the gentleman I moved to the staff room. It did not take him more than a couple of minutes to inform me that my thing has been restored intact and I could go to my room and check the same. I never thought that my hit and trial method would produce the desired result so quickly. As promised I pardoned the attendant. He in turn quenched my curiosity by narrating the details of his abortive operation. He told me that tempted by the wad of currency notes he thought of pocketing it. But fearing that any one could notice his bulging pocket if he kept the money on his person for rest of the day he placed the packet under the carpet below the table right in front of my chair to be retrieved in the evening when he would leave for home. I wondered at his ingeniousness in selecting the hiding place for the booty. It did not take me long to pin him down when sometime later he managed to steal the brand new pair of sports shoes of one of the students of the computer science class. Giving him a third chance for trying his nimble fingers at something more costly or important was not advisable. So I decided not to reappoint him after the expiry of his current temporary tenure.

Prompt Response

(xxvi) Once Dr. Sarup Singh forwarded to me a letter which he had received from one Mrs. Kidwai living with her civil servant husband in Egypt asking me to help her. Mrs Kidwai had in her letter stated that she had written several times to the Registrar of Delhi University requesting for sending her the degree certificate of the examination she had passed some twenty years ago. But she did not receive any reply. She needed the certificate in connection with a job in sight which she wanted to take up urgently. She had been a student of Dr. Sarup Singh but had not been in touch with him for years. She had learnt from a friend that Dr. Sarup Singh later became Vice-Chancellor of The University. She got his address from a friend and wrote the above referred letter to him in the hope that as former V.C. of the University he could help in the matter.She had mentioned all the required particulars in her letter. Treating that letter as an application to the University I got her case processed in the concerned branch. It turned out that her degree had been withheld for want of her not having passed the compulsory test in Hindi. As per the latest rules she was exempted from the same. Her case was processed accordingly and her degree certificate along with an attested copy was sent to her. The whole process took only a couple of days. I also informed Dr. Sarup Singh suitably. A few days later Dr. Sarup Singh forwarded to me her letter of thanks. She had been immensely impressed by the promptness of the University this time. I felt happy that I happened to be an instrument of this make over.

Good Turn Returns

(xxvii) My eldest daughter Nandini was in Lagos, Nigeria during 2004-05, where herb husband Deepesh had been posted temporarily. On her last visit to India this year she narrated an incident. Nandini was attending a party of Indian ladies in lagos. She happened to enter into conversation with the wife of an Indian diplomat. Both introduced themselves to each other. On knowing about Nandini's maiden name Nandini Rana and parental home in Delhi her curiosity increased. She volunteered the information that she knew one Dr.S.S. Rana who was Dean of Colleges in Delhi University. When Nandini told her that Dr. Rana was her father the lady was overwhelmed with emotions. She told Nandini that but for her father's help she would not have been there where she was that day. Explaining, she told Nandini how I had helped her in getting permission as a special case to appear for certain examination when all her previous efforts in this matter had failed. My daughter told me how proud she felt to be my daughter. I thanked God that it fell to my lot to help a person in dire need.

The Shawl Shows

(xxviii) The marriage of my eldest daughter Nandini was solemnised on 5 March 1990.The main function was arranged in the park out side our residence in Ashok Vihar. It had rained the previous day. On the day of the marriage it was cool and pleasant. The function went off quite smoothly. The gathering was impressive. Most of the people I had invited attended it. When the function was near its close and most of the guests had left some one brought to me an unclaimed shawl lying on one of the empty chairs. Frantic enquiries did not result in any one coming forward to claim the shawl. I left the matter there to be taken up the next day. Telephone calls made to several relatives and friends next morning did not bear any result. Desperate as I was to trace the owner of the shawl it struck to my mind to take help of the video recording of the function. I sat with my family members and viewed the recording in several rounds. We short listed a couple of shots in which shawls figured and minutely scanned them. At long last I sighted Mrs. Urmil Sharma, lecturer in English in Shivaji College with the particular shawl placed on her arm. I immediately called at my college and speaking to my Sr. P.A. Mr. G. S. Kalsi I gathered that the shawl belonged to Mrs. Sharma. She had shared the information with Mr. Kalsi in the morning but had hesitated to enquire from me thinking that she should not add a jarring note to the festivities at my home. I spoke to her on phone thanking her of her gracious gesture and arranged to restore the shawl to her. She confided that the shawl had been gifted to her by her sister, only a couple of days ago. She was doubly delighted at the restoration of the valued piece of garment. All in my family felt delighted on the dénouement.

Call of Conference

Delhi University hosted the annual conference of Association of Indian Universities coinciding with the Vice-Chancellors' Conference held in December 1993. The University Grants Commission had sanctioned some funds for the purpose. The estimates of expenditure were far in excess. The Vice-Chancellor Professor Baxi was concerned about raising the enormous funds required for the event. In house discussions were held to explore the avenues of revenue. Disappointed by the dim response from several quarters tapped for the purpose the Vice-Chancellor thought of calling off the event and shared his evaluation of the situation with his team members. I gave my own views regarding the prospects of our success in raising the needed funds through a multi pronged approach.

After some discussion the Vice-Chancellor appointed a committee under my chairmanship to evolve measures and strategy to raise the needed funds. Our committee adopted a three point strategy. Firstly, we published a souvenir which gave us an income of more than ten lakh through advertisements. The amount would have been almost double had we agreed to incorporate in the souvenir advertisements from liquor traders as suggested at a meeting held in the office of the Chief Secretary of Delhi. Secondly, the required transport was met by raising a large fleet of buses and mini buses of various colleges of the University on the basis of meeting the cost of petrol only. Thirdly, the managements of some trust colleges came forward for hosting the major lunch and dinner events. The Shri Ram Group contributed towards meeting the expenditure incurred on the conference insignia crafted on a silken festoon in addition to hosting a dinner for the delegates at the Hotel Samrat. Shri Mahendra Nath Gupta of Daulat Ram College was the host of a dinner in honour of the delegates arranged in the Imperial Hotel. Shri Rajendra Gupta of Shyam lal College came forward to extend a treat at a lavish dinner to the delegates at his residence on Okhla Road. He also bore the cost of the Conference portfolio bag. Shri C.M Chaddha of ARSD College contributed towards the expenditure incurred on lunch at the venue of the Conference.

The University saved roughly rupees three lakhs due to the gracious co-operation and help from the Colleges. The contribution of the students of Lady Shri Ram College came in the form of a simple but artistic design of the insignia of the theme of the Conference viz. the protection of environment. I added a piece from my side by suggesting the theme motto '*sa no bhumi vardhayad wardhamana*' from the hymn of the earth in the Atharva Veda. The University administration was also able to find economical and decent accommodation in hotels and guest houses all over the city. Transport was no problem with a large fleet of buses at our disposal. After meeting all the expenditure on the Conference the University ended up with a surplus of a couple of Lakhs of rupees from the amount raised on the occasion The conference was a grand success.

Rock Show Hard

Shri Daya Kishan Mudgil was working as Director of Physical Education during the tenure of Professor Upendra Baxi as Vice Chancellor. Shri Mudgil was doing a commendable job. He turned the University cricket ground into a fine lush green patch. The Delhi University Students' Union managed toget his permission for staging a Rock Show there. He had hardly realized the implication of this concession. The matter was discussed in a meeting of senior officials and the Vice-Chancellor was advised to ask Shri Mudgil to withdraw the permission. Finding himself in a bind Shri Mudgil turned to me for advice. I asked him if he knew what a rock show was. His reply was that it could be some exhibition of different kinds of rocks. I immediately suggested that in that case his problem was over. He could tell the students' Union that he never realized that they wanted to organize a music concert at the play grounds and that his understanding of the Rock show at the time of granting permission was entirely different. Shri Mudgil used his innocence to his advantage. The permission was withdrawn without attracting the wrath of the members of the Students' Union. The V.C. felt quite happy the way the matter was handled. Shri Mudgil became wiser by miles without covering any distance on his feet. But his non-violent feat in handling a volatile issue remained subject of light jokes among his friends for quite some time. Some years later when the University organized a grand flower show with a section on rocks in the same sports ground old timers did not fail to recall Shri Mudgil's innocence regarding the "Rock Show".

Secular Stance

The Principal of Bhim Rao Ambedkar College had invited me to be the chief guest at the Annual function a certain year. On my arrival at the College I found the Principal a little perturbed. He shared his problem with me in the hope that I might be helpful in resolving the same. The Chairman of the governing body Shri Anand Sarup, a former Secretary of education in the government of India had taken objection to the inclusion of invocation song in praise of goddess Saraswati in the progamme on the plea that it would be against his secular belief to be a witness to a religious prayer at a college function. He did not wish the programme to be altered either and instead desired to leave before the function would start. Seemingly hopeful of my support he leaned towards me and asked if he was wrong. Striking the middle path I conceded that he had a right to hold dear his views in matters of faith, but his leaving before the start of the function would amount to disregarding his duty as chairman. Finding him a bit conciliatory I ventured a solution. I suggested that he could join the function when the prayer song had been over. Both the Principal and the chairman agreed. The function started with the singing of the song of prayer of Saraswati.

The chairman appeared on the dais after the song was over. His fragile secularism remained intact. The programme proceeded as scheduled without any alteration. An interesting instance of secular stance this!

V.C. Material

The Vice-Chancellor, Professor Upendra Baxi wanted me to advise him on the course of action to be followed on the issue of fixation of the salary of Dr. V.R. Mehta, who had been offered the post of Professor by Delhi University. In response to Professor Mehta's demand for a higher basic salary the Registrar's office had written to him quoting certain rule of the University permitting higher start in salary only to the extent of five advance increments. In his subsequent communication addressed to the Vice-Chancellor Professor Mehta had stated that he had been already working as Professor for a long time and that he was not prepared to join Delhi University at a salary lower than what he had demanded. He had further added in his letter that he was Vice-Chancellor material and therefore should be given a commensurate salary.. My suggestion to the V.C. was that Delhi University should not deprive itself of the services of an eminent scholar like Professor Mehta over the question of salary alone. I pointed out a provision in the rules which permitted any higher salary in the grade in an exceptional case. The V.C. agreed with me and ordered accordingly. By the time the final response of the University reached Professor Mehta he had been appointed Vice-Chancellor of Kota Open University in Rajasthan. Professor Mehta's joining Delhi University was delayed by a couple of years though in the capacity as its V.C. Indeed, Professor Mehta was V.C. material as was later seen during his more than five years' stint at the helm of Delhi University. He turned out to be one of the most successful and popular Vice Chancellors of the University.

Baljeets Both

I took my family to Shimla during the summer vacation in 1975 to spend some time in the cool climate there. We stayed with my friend Professor Suraj Bhan , of Kurukshetra University, who as a fellow at the Institute of Advanced Studies had a commodious house allotted to him on the Summer Hill close by. During our stay there I had the opportunity of meeting scholars like the reputed archaeologist Dr. B.B. Lal. I also made use of the Institute's fabulous library.We had the benefit of visiting the Himachal University campus on lunch invitation one day at the house of

Professor Baldev Singh of the Sanskrit department. Our sojourns in the vicinity of Shimla included those to Carnano, Nal Dera, Wild Flower Hall and the Retreat. On the last day of our stay at Shimla we went for a last round of the Ridge. Sitting there on a bench in the after-noon sun my wife mentioned to me her cousin sister Neeru was also in Shimla with her husband on honey moon trip but she was not aware of where the was staying. Telling her half in jest "I would just go and call them here even though I had never met either of 5them" I left heading straight to a crowded spot. Spotting a newly wedded couple I asked the young man if he was from Kurukshetra. He had hardly completed his reply in the affirmative when I directed the next question to the young girl asking if she was Neeru. She said yes in her reply but added with an expression of surprise mixed with happiness," will you please disclose your identity, I am excited, you must be from, my relatives." Enjoying the anonymity in the company of the young couple I escorted them to the corner where my wife, my mother and our children were waiting. Neeru and my wife hugged each other, my mother blessed her. Now things were clear to Neeru's husband, Baljeet. However, he was formally introduced to us. Next day we all left Shimla together in my car. Baljeet drove it. Making a detour of The famous hill Chail we proceeded to Kurukshetra where we had a short break. Leaving Neeru and Baljeet at Kurukshetra we left for Delhi.

Similar incident took places a couple of years later. One day I answered the call bell at my house and opened the door to a tall handsome young man, Whom I had not met before. Wishing me he instantly inquired if his Didi (sister) was at home. I replied confirming that she was indeed at home. But before I could go inside to inform my wife about the visitor his next question nearly stumped me. His question this time was if I had placed him. In the mean time I had gathered my bearings. Leaving some scope for improvement I shot back a question as reply asking him as to when did he return from Meerut. My guess was a hit. He laughed heartily expressing wonder and wanted to know how I recognized him even though we had met for the first time. I replied that it was his deep and sonorous voice like the mellowed roar of a lion resembling a audeograph of the voice of his father, Baljeet Chachaji. He lived in Meerut. The episode greatly impressed Shri Anand Chauhan and he narrated it several times in the family and to friends when introducing me to them. My father-in-law Shri Vimal Dev hastri and Shri Baljit Shastri were life long fast friends. Their children were like brothers and sisters among themselves. I also shared the pool of affinity after my marriage. The bond got further cemented through several interactions when under the leadership and direction of Dr. Ashok Chauhan the family launched the enterprise of promotion of education in the country on a maga scale- setting up schools, colleges and Universities in India and abroad under the umbrella name Amity.

[illegible] peeling out plaster and worn out woodwork of the exteriors [illegible] institutions said the story of financial crunch, which [illegible] was a world wide phenomenon. Education deserves [illegible] everywhere. However, the interiors of the [illegible] institutions we visited were well kept and well furnished. There [illegible] other infrastructure. We found some of the roads [illegible] narrow compelling the authorities to declare them [illegible] one way streets. Parking of vehicles anywhere on road sides [illegible] against payment [illegible]

[illegible] that the time at our disposal was insufficient [illegible] University. Therefore we approached the [illegible] of our date of departure by a couple [illegible] that the earliest possible date could be after [illegible] could not afford to stay back for such a long [illegible] to take the scheduled flight on 17th July. On [illegible] and after standing in queue for checking in [illegible] we came to know from a staffer that the flight [illegible] Delhi had not arrived from New York and [illegible] was rescheduled for the next day.

[illegible] in the nearby Airport Hotel. For us it was a [illegible] experience of stay in a five star hotel in [illegible] was welcome. When I called my family [illegible] change in the flight schedule I learnt [illegible] sons Neeraj and Puneet [illegible] convocation ceremony [illegible] degree at the London School [illegible] about it a little too late [illegible] to meet them [illegible] Chauhan, who [illegible] the airport continued [illegible]

IV

Beyond Borders

Bhutan: Sherubtse College

The Vice-Chancellor, Prof. Moonis Raza deputed me to represent him at the degree distribution function of the Sherubtse College, Bhutan in April 1989. The College had been affiliated to the University of Delhi a couple of years ago after the Parliament had made an amendment in the Delhi University Act incorporating an appropriate provision for the purpose. Initially B.A. (Pass) and B.Com (Pass) courses were started in the College.

Autonomous Status

Grant of autonomous status was a favourite subject of discussion at meetings with the representatives of the College visiting Delhi University. There were elements in the education department of Bhutan who were toying with the idea of seeking affiliation of the College with either some university in Britain or Pakistan or Bangladesh. As there was no provision for grant of autonomous status to any college in faculties other than Technology, Medicine and Fine Arts this matter could not be taken up by the University at its own level. A suitable amendment in the Delhi University Act was a prerequisite to initiate the measure. The teaching community in Delhi University colleges largely perceived autonomous status as a mechanism to de-link the colleges from the University departments. It was therefore not considered expedient to initiate such a move. I was briefed with this background at appropriate level before leaving for Bhutan. At the time of planning my programme of the visit I got valuable assistance from the former Principal of the College, a Canadian missionary, who happened to be in Delhi around that time. The

College authorities had also invited my wife and had arranged our visit in such a way that we first reach Thimpu, the capital of Bhutan, spend a day or two there and from there travel more than seven hundred kilometers west to east to reach the College in Kanglung with two night halts on the way.

Heading for Himalayas

The first Secretary of the Bhutanese Embassy, Mr. Nima Wangdi got the travel documents (there being no Passport or Visa requirement) prepared and saw us off at the IGI airport, New Delhi on 21st April 1989. Accompanied by my wife I left for Bhutan by the afternoon flight of Bhutan Airways. It flew almost parallel to the Himalayan heights after reaching the northernmost point of Indian air space. The weather was fine. The snow-clad peaks of the Himalayas reflected the glory of the sun as if through their mounds of laughter. Peeping through the windows of the aircraft we could have a view of the Mount Everest with the guidance of the crew. It was an amazing scene - a vast expanse of snow like a white sheet rising in humps at places as if hiding some mysteries of nature beneath. Though we watched the scene from the safety and comfort of the aircraft it was no less an exciting experience, at times an intimidating one. The two hour flight landed at Paro airport lying at the bottom of a narrow valley of the same name at a distance of about forty kilometers from Thimpu, the capital city of Bhutan. Mr. Dorji, the liaison officer received us at the airport and escorted us to Thimpu, a modest but neat and clean town. The forty odd kilometers' journey was pleasant and comfortable. On our way we passed through fully blossomed mustard fields across the narrow valley presenting a spectacle of a large yellow scarf slipped from the shoulders of the lofty snowy peak looking over.

Motithang Thimpu

In Thimpu We were lodged in a spacious and luxuriously furnished suite of the Hotel Motithang, the only big hotel in the town After settling down and having hot bath we went out to have a feel of the environs of the hotel. We also made a short trip to the minuscule zoo next to the hotel building The sun had already gone hiding behind the lofty mountain range, slowly giving quarter to the descending darkness of the evening fully abetted by the thick forest around. The nip in the air was biting. It did not take us long to realize that the night was going to be freezing cold. So we hastened back to the hotel. Dinner was served for us in our room. The heaters provided in both the rooms of our suite did not appear to be sufficient to beat the increasing cold as the night got deeper. Layers of heavy woolen blankets were welcome and it was comforting to be deeply enveloped in them. The morning was pleasant with the sun peeping right into our bed room through the large glass window.

Menu Matter

Getting ready early we moved to the dining hall of the hotel for breakfast. There was hardly any vegetarian preparation available among a rich variety of dishes laid for the guests. Even boiled potatoes were fraught with some non-vegetarian fare. My wife managed to extract some vegetable stuff lying at the bottom of a container on the counter. In the mean time our escort, Mr. Dorji joined us. As he saw my wife and myself struggling with the cutlery and a few potato chips in our plates he understood our dilemma. He advised us to go for continental breakfast and concentrate on juices which items were served on order. His advice was well taken and we did full justice to the new menu.

Palace and Places

After breakfast we went round a few places of interest in Thimpu like the Royal Palace, the Government Secretariat called Tashishu Zong and King's Memorial during the forenoon. All these buildings had a distinct architectural peculiarity mixed with religious symbols of the Himalayan Buddhism. In the afternoon we visited the ancient Zhong, the Simtokha about twenty kilometers away, housing the Grammar School. A characteristic feature that I noted in the Zhong was a series of inscriptions in zonkha script engraved on slabs of slate stone placed in small niches all around the building. The Zonkha script had been developed from the Tibetan alphabet, which in turn had been derived some time in the eighth century A.D. from the Indian Brahmi script. It is believed that the Buddhist saint Padmasambhava who toured Bhutan brought with him the script from Tibet. It did not take me long in deciphering the mantra *'Om mani padme hum'* engraved on stone slabs fixed at all possible places in the building especially the niches in the walls. On our way back to Thimpu we could see the palace of the king's four sisters, all of whom were ministers in the king's Council. T.V. had not reached Bhutan by that time. It was perceived as an instrument of cultural pollution for the exclusive culture and traditions of the country. So the government had banned its entry in Bhutan. Even the king did not enjoy the facility. The king had four wives all of whom were sisters. They did not appear in public. However, the king's sisters attended office and appeared in public.

Eastward Hay

The next morning (23 April) we resumed our journey to Kanglung in eastern Bhutan. Our escort, Mr. Dorji had got prepared at his house poories and bhaji sufficient for the day's meals for all of us. Thimpu is situated in central Bhutan. As we proceeded eastward through this region we came across mostly arid hill slopes covered with dry wild grass with very sparsely located spots of habitation at the bottom of the narrow valleys having some green patches of rice fields and other growth. The last post of central Bhutan was at the top of Pelela Pass where we made a brief halt. Snow at the saddle of the pass had melted. However, there were some traces of snow flakes left trapped between trunks of thick forest trees on the slopes struggling to join the stream of the river (chu) below. After a steep downhill journey for several kilometers on a serpentine course we reached a valley where the road ran along a river (chu). On the other side of the road were lush green meadows. We stopped for lunch at a small wayside grassy patch. Some labourers working on the road gathered near us. My wife walked over to them and wanted to converse with them. The language barrier was overcome with the warmth of feelings on either side. Innocent smile of young children and the giggling expressions of their mothers said all. The ladies had plenty of jewelry on their ears and around their necks. By mid day we crossed the Mikka Bridge. We were now traveling through eastern Bhutan abounding in forests witnessing new plantations to supplement the thick forest cover by using the dotted gaps. By the evening we reached Tongsa, the first halting place of our journey. It was a district head quarter with a well-furnished guest house. I was pleasantly surprised to find that the staff had arranged simple north Indian vegetarian food for us. It included rice, chapati, masoor ki dahl and vegetable of potato and cabbage. Getting up in the morning my wife and I ventured on a morning walk to savour the beauty of the sun bathed nature. The sight of the Tongsa Zhong, a huge castle like building perched on the peak of a hillock far away was inviting and intimidating at the same time. Soon we had to cut short our brief outing with the strong chilly wind forcing us to retire to the comfort of our room in the guest house.

Pass after Pass

After breakfast on the morning of 24th April we started on the next lap of our journey. Crossing passes like Thrumsing La and Yota La we passed through cedar forests with a thick growth of greenery on the slops. But the many stumps of cedar trees dotting the slopes told the sad story of the forest cover falling to the axe of the commercial compulsions. Soon we were to pass by the roadside saw mills producing shrilling sounds in the process of slaughtering the giant logs into smaller slabs emitting an aromatic smell to compensate the passers by. The rich fare all along the route presented by the sight of rhododendrons of different hues peeping from the undergrowth on the sideways was a treat to the eyes. Truly this flower is the national flower of Bhutan. Though our vehicle was comfortable the journey seemed endless and was getting tiresome. The monotony was multiplied by the fact that there were hardly any vehicle crossing us or overtaking us on the unending road wending its way, negotiating one hump after another.

Traces of Tour

The only redeeming feature was the remnants of the flowery decorations on arches and gate ways along the route erected in honour of the king who had traveled from west to east on the same road a day earlier. We would stop at some of these spots to observe what arrangements had been made to welcome the king. The tours of the king across the country appeared to be something similar to the dhammayatras of king Ashoka or the modern day Rath Yatras or road shows put up by political parties during election time.One coul;d see the traces of the traditional communication devices used on the halting spots in the form of burnt out fires to produce smoke signals to the next halting place. The town of Wangdi and the river of the same name fell in this sector. On this sector we drove through the beautiful Gyetse Valley. Next was the Takar Valley formed by the river of the same name. Here is a district head quarter located in the Takar Dzong. Rajiv Gandhi is known to have visited this place for a short holiday. By the evening we reached Monghar, our next halt for the night. Accommodation had been reserved for our stay in the royal guest house. But there was no arrangement of food there as normally no soul lived there .Only a watchman manned the building. Mr. Dorji went to the town and brought some rations to be cooked for us. The journey of the last two days had been quite tiring. Luxurious food was far from my thoughts. Any vegetarian preparation would make us happy, I thought. The monotony of the journey and the engulfing unfamiliar silence were disturbing. At that stage my wife and I were in agreement that another trip of that type was ruled out for any of our future plans. But all the monotony and inconvenience of the journey did not prevent my wife from composing and jotting down paeans in praise of the mountain kingdom of Bhutan.

Tashigang

From Monghar, Kanglung was reachable in half a day. We started early on 25th April and reached Tashigang before noon. The king had stayed at the royal guest house here the previous night and had caught an unusually long (4ft.and 2 inches) Sorum fish weighing 25 kilograms from the river close by. It was on display to as a feet of the young and enterprising king. Head quarter town of eastern Bhutan, Tashigang was full of hussle and bussle. Several educational institutions and Government offices were located there. The market place did not look much different from that in any small Indian town. Kanglung was not very far from there. We decided to cut short our stop over and headed for our destination. We reached Kanglung in a couple of hours. Arrangements had been made for our stay in the Officers' Mess of the Dantak, a detachment of the Border Road Organisation of the Government of India. Dr. Pramod Sagar, a teacher from Shivaji College working on deputation in Sherubtse College was very helpful during our stay there. A hearty meal with north Indian aroma at dinner time was a real treat at the end of three days' journey on a seemingly endless road.

Convocation

Next day, April 26 the convocation ceremony of the College was held with all the fervor preceded by traditional religious ceremonies. I distributed the degrees to the graduates on behalf of the V.C. After the convocation I held discussions with the education minister of Bhutan and the College authorities about the possibility of starting some honours courses and introducing Bhutan related courses in history, geography and environment without technically going for autonomous status for the College. The discussions were fruitful, as events of next few years would show. The University of Delhi granted permission to the College to introduce honours courses in English, Commerce, Economics and Geography. Further, courses in history of Bhutan and geography of Bhutan were added as alternatives to some of the existing courses in these subjects. Computer Science was introduced as one of the subjects in B.Sc. (general) course. A separate subject on environment with special reference to Bhutan was added some years later. In view of such developments the question of autonomous status, which had been greatly exercising the mind of the College authorities and the government, receded to the background. There should be no hesitation in admitting that the replicated courses of Delhi colleges taught in the Bhutanese College had some kind of colonial Ssmack. But at the same time it must be said that the College gained enormously and progressed through its affiliation with the University of Delhi. It has ultimately been raised to the status of a University, the first in Bhutan. It still draws faculty from Indian universities, especially the University of Delhi with which it has umbilical relationship.

After the convocation was over community lunch was organized in the sunlit large compound of the college campus followed by a colourful cultural programme presented by the students. Members of the staff as also the guests joined the finale. The Education Minister presided over the function. The same night the Education Minister hosted a dinner at the State Guest House at Tashigang to mark the event of the convocation. Senior government officials had been invited to interact with the college authorities and discuss issues concerning academic growth of the College in an informal manner.

Army Warmth

Our return journey began in the morning on 27th April. Dr. Pramod Sagar accompanied us, as he was to visit Delhi in connection with some College work. On our way back we had our breakfast in the Mess of an Indian detachment stationed a few miles away. The Indian officers and their family members received us warmly and inundated us with their warm hospitality. During conversation with the officers we gathered that another army detachment comprising men and officers hailing from Haryana was camping nearby. I could not resist the temptation of meeting them. As there was no proper road to take our vehicle there we got down from our land cruiser and reached the camouflaged camping site, walking through a rugged pathway. We introduced ourselves to the men working near the commandant's tented office and told them that the purpose of our visit was just to wish them luck in their mission. The officers and men were happily surprised to find visitors from their native area at the most unlikely place. They served us with refreshing cold drinks as the day had turned a little hot. They also took us round showing the non-security areas of their camp. Thereafter we resumed our journey and proceeded on the road down the slopes passing through eastern Bhutan. This part of the country was full of dark green forest lands and lush green paddy fields in the valleys.

Devthang Day

By the evening we reached Devthang, a picturesque mole situated about twenty-five kilometers from the border with India. Arrangements had been made for our night stay in the officers' mess of GREF (of Border Roads Organisation) there. Still we were heading towards Samdrup Jonkhar, the border town so as to be as nearer to our destination Guwahati as possible. We had hardly crossed the Officers' mess when the commandant of the unit Col. Dutta on his evening stroll came our way. As Dr. Pramod Sagar knew him personally we stopped to greet him. Colonel Dutta insisted that we stay for the night in his unit mess at Devathang as originally planned. We agreed and stayed at the army mess. We did not regret having stopped overnight at this beautiful resort. Col. Dutta and other officers were very kind and friendly and made our stay at Devthang most comfortable and memorable.

Bold in Bodoland

The next morning we started for the last lag of our sojourn in Bhutan. In half an hour's time we were in Samdrup Zonkhar, a Bhutanese township located almost on the border with India. Here we had a chance meeting in an army establishment with one Mr. Kenny, an old acquaintance of my wife's family. He was surprised to have been recognized by my wife even after a passage of twenty five years. This chance meeting was equally a surprise for my wife. After spending some time there in doing shopping we resumed our journey. We had now changed to a military vehicle as it was not considered safe to travel in a civilian vehicle through a better part of the road leading to Guwahati infested with Bodo insurgents. For obvious reasons the Bodo insurgents had decided not to come into clash with the Indian army. Luckily no incident happened on the way and crossing our fingers we reached Guwahati safe. From there we took the evening flight for Delhi, which brought us to Palam airport by 10 o'clock in the evening of 28th April 1989.

Spirit of Juice

Our children were preparing for celebration of Silver Jubilee of our marriage on 3rd of May 1989.Among the gifts we received from the Bhuta government was a small carton which I thought contained tins of Juice (as I had given no proof of my drinking preferences). But on our arrival at Delhi airport I noticed the carton was soaked in liquid stuff. On reaching home I discovered a couple of liquor bottles with their contents emptied in the carton. An odd bottle or two retrieved intact were passed on to some connoisseurs of the spirit. However, I valued the lovely gift of a Bhutanese Tankha which I religiously keep on the wall of our drawing room. We still cherish the memories of the warm hospitality extended to us by the Bhutanese officials and the College staff led by its Principal Mr. Zangley.

East-West Best

I made the second trip to Bhutan in 1994 again in connection with the degree distribution function of Sherubtse College. Having grown wiser by the previous experience I chose to travel via Guwahati both ways. My wife had already decided not to repeat the enterprise. But yet another arduous travel was awaiting me to attend to the call of duty. The condition of the road from Guwahati to Samdrup Zonkhar had further worsened from what it was in 1989. Several attempts to repair it through private contractors had proved abortive as the Bodo insurgents would demand heavy sums as protection money as soon as a contractor started work. At last the government decided to give the work to the Border Road Organization, which ultimately ensured the repair of the road. But it was later. My escorts had brought a sturdy vehicle which stood the jerks of the bumpy rugged road. The wit and humour of the two Bhutanese escorts made me forget the discomfort of the tough and rickety journey.

During onward journey the night halt was in the officer's mess of a detachment of the Indian army at Samdrup Zonkhar. It was a well appointed place to stay in comfort. The food was excellent comprising north Indian vegetarian dishes. I skipped my breakfast the next morning with the misconception in my mind that empty stomach I would have no travel sickness. This proved counterproductive. As I went up the heights in the Land Rover Vehicle I developed travel sickness. Intermittent bouts of vomiting almost emptied my stomach and tired me out. But the comfort and hospitality extended to me by the College on my arrival at Kanglung made me forget all the fatigue and discomfort of travel. All arrangements and ceremonies of the convocation were a repeat of those held on the previous occasion except the additional pomp and colours.

Meeting a Contemporary

For a change I found myself in the company of my contemporary in St.Stephen's College, Mr. Pushkar Johri, who as Indian Ambassador to Bhutan was the guest of honour at the function. We had met after about forty years but it did not take us long to recognize each other. Nostalgia overtakes when two old

Stephenians meet. We recounted several events that happened in our days in College. Another company was that of Prof. C.R Babu, (later Pro-Vice-Chancellor of Delhi University), who was there in connection with a workshop on environment. I recall Prof. Babu taking photographs with my camera of all the events almost at a stretch. I also had the opportunity of visiting various departments of the College. There were many improvements both in terms of new buildings and additional equipment in the laboratories. It was a pleasant surprise to see that the ban on Television was no more there. The king had probably realized that keeping his country men insulated from outside influences was no more possible or practicable or even desirable any more. In any case the elite of the country living abroad were already enjoying the facility. The variety entertainment programme presented on the occasion also reflected the new spirit and lighter mood. Modernity had been given a visa to enter Bhutan after all. .But at the same time it treaded with caution. It was a part of the reforms set in by the enlightened king.

Missed the (Air) Bus

Professor Babu and I traveled to Delhi together and went through an exciting episode. It happened like this- As per the entries on our return tickets the departure time of the flight to Delhi was 4.00 p.m. We had reached Guwahati before twelve o'clock. We had ample time at our disposal, which we utilized in visiting the Kamakhya temple, doing some shopping in the city market and having lunch. It was 2.00 p.m. By this time we were left with no work to be done in the city. Thinking that the airport was reachable in only half an hour we lingered on in he city and then traveled at leisurely speed to reach the airport around three o'clock. On entering the departure area we found the check-in counters closed. We did not notice many passengers in the waiting hall either. Such could not be the scene at the airport an hour before a flight's departure. Very soon it dawned on us that something was amiss. On anxious enquiry we came to know to our surprise that the flight had been rescheduled to take off at 2.30 p.m. w.e.f the date of our return journey. We could see the doors closed and the aircraft moving on the runway and ready to take off. On production of our tickets showing departure time as 4.00 p.m.

the duty officer told us that our travel agent was responsible for the confusion.

However, when we disclosed our identity and requested the airport manager to do something for us a window of relief opened. It was agreed that we would be accommodated in a delayed flight arriving from Agartala to take us to Calcutta (Kolkata) from where we could catch another flight waiting to leave for Delhi. The co-operation extended by the airport staff was unbelievable. On arrival of the flight from Agartala we were taken directly to the aircraft and allowed to put our luggage directly in the cabin. Message was passed on to Calcutta airport with the request that the flight to Delhi marked for us should not leave before we board it. A special bus was arranged to ferry us directly to the waiting aircraft and thus save time that would have been taken in checking out and checking in again. The comedy of errors did not end yet. The bus was there ready at the tarmac to ferry us across to the waiting aircraft. But as the bus left leaving us to board the aircraft we were asked to first check out and then check in after obtaining fresh boarding passes. Perhaps it was the right course. We went through the drill quickly and finally boarded the plane. The ground staff helped us immensely. As both of us moved down the aisle to take our seats in the rear we silently and ungrudgingly bore the unpleasant remarks and unwelcome stares of the passengers who had to impatiently wait for considerable time for the flight to take off. We heaved sighs of relief to have been able to reach Delhi the same day as planned originally.

Playing Prank

The drama was still to continue. Another scene was being enacted at Delhi. Whereas I was in the dark about the revised time schedule of the flight my office staff and through them my daughters (my wife and son were out of station on that day) Manjari and Monica had come to know about the change and accordingly arranged to send the staff car to bring me home from the airport as per the new timings. On being told by the airport staff that though my name was in there in the list of passengers, it was not among those who had arrived by the particular flight, the staff car driver informed my daughters about this and returned from the airport disappointed. That piece of information put my daughters at their wit's end. Where could I have disappeared in mid air, they wondered? But their resourcefulness led them to seek the help of the Proctor, Prof. M. Adhikari. They also telephonically informed Shri Pramod Sagar in Bhutan about the 'mishap'. With the efforts of both the colleagues things became clear as to what had exactly happened. The revised programme of my travel was also ascertained. So they were relaxed and waiting for my arrival by the alternative flight. Unaware of the goings on in Delhi due to the change in timings of my flight I planned to play a prank on my daughters who, I had thought, must not be knowing my revised travel programme. Prof. Babu and I took a taxi from the airport to take us home. As soon as some commotion occurred at the gate of our house on my arrival there, my daughters came running towards me in amusement rather than in surprise as they were already in know of what had happened and were expecting me to arrive around that time. Thus my plan to play a prank on my daughters fell flat.

Srilanka :Southwards

It was an interesting coincidence that having visited a country on India's extreme north a year earlier I was called upon to visit a country on India's extreme south. This time I got an opportunity to visit Srilanka in May 1990 as a member of the UGC delegation for the purpose of selecting Srilankan students for admission to Indian Universities under an agreement signed by the two countries. The arrangement was necessitated because of the backlog in university admissions resulting from the closure of educational Institutions during that country's war with Liberation Tigers of Tamil Elam (LTTE). At that time I did not hold a passport. As the intimation for making the visit was received at a short notice I arranged to get a temporary passport issued to officials on government duty. The same was the case of another member of the delegation Shri Hira, a Joint Secretary in the UGC. The other two members of the delegation were Prof. (MS) Bhuvan Chandel of Punjab University and Dr. H. Rao, Secretary, Council of Higher Education, Andhra Pradesh. Mr. Prakash, an IFS officer represented the Ministry of External Affairs. We reached Madras

(Chennai) by a late evening flight from Delhi. Since we were to fly to Colombo early next morning we preferred to stay at a modest hotel near the airport. Later we regretted the decision, as the stay was quite uncomfortable. The hotel rooms were hot and humid with plenty of mosquitoes to disturb our sleep. But the ordeal did not last long as we moved out early in the morning to check in at the Madras (Chennai) airport for taking our flight to Colombo.

Above the Indian Ocean

For some distance our plane flew over the eastern coast. The dark coast line seen from the windows of the aircraft looked like a rusted iron rim of a wheel reminding me of Kalidasa's description of the same in his Raghuvansha, during the aerial journey of Rama and Sita on their return from Lanka. Very soon we were borne above the deep blue Indian Ocean. It did not take long to pass over the strait. Now I could see the lush dark green landscape of western coast of Srilanka. Our flight landed at Colombo airport amid light drizzle. The immigration and custom clearance formalities were gone through with speed with the help of our hosts who took us to the Oberoi Intercontinental hotel where arrangements for our stay had been made.

Modesty Meets Modernity

For me it was the first occasion for staying in a five star hotel. My modest style of living was at odds with the aura and aroma of the place. In fact my first night's sleep was disturbed several times by the need for visiting the bath room at short intervals. When I finally got up in the morning and noticed a thick layer of dew formed on the exterior of the large french window of my room I recalled that fiddling with the temperature control apparatus out of curiosity during the day I had inadvertently turned on the cooling switch of the air-conditioner to the maximum level. The high level of chill thus created in the room was responsible for attracting large amount of vapors outside on the surface of the large glass glazing panel. It soon dawned on me that the chill in the room was also responsible for my frequent visits to the bathroom during the night. In the process I also got to learn how to operate the cordless remote control of an air-conditioner.

Something Fishy

Next day in the morning our first meeting was a curtsey call on the Education Minister. All kinds of snacks were laid for us on the table. They were apparently all non-vegetarian stuff. On being told that I was a vegetarian our host served me with sandwiches, which in the very first bite betrayed their contents inside contained fish (some thing fishy!). I was later told that in Srilanka they do not consider fish food as non-vegetarian. I can't say if it was so. Then we had a session of interaction with the chairman of the UGC and his colleagues. We brought enough homework to be completed in internal meetings of the group at our hotel. In the evening we were guests of the Indian High Commissioner at dinner. Next evening we attended an At-home party hosted by the President Mr. Jayawardane. On another evening the Deputy High Commissioner organized a dinner in our honour. The Vice-Chancellor of Colombo University entertained us at lunch in a five star hotel. The next evening meant for a long cultural programme presented at a seaside five star hotel Samudra culminated in a lavish (but of very little use for me) dinner. Almost every dish had fish as one of its components. I had to be content with some vegetarian sea food and some preparations of potatoes. For me it turned out to be a fine starved dinner in place of a five starred dinner. Never the less, the cultural function arranged in the court of the hotel by the sea side was quite a reward. Music and dance needed no language to enthrall the mixed audience.

Heritage Haven

The progress of our work being ahead of the clock, a short break for holiday was desired. Our hosts organized for us a three-day trip to Central Srilanka. On the first day of our trip we traveled to Anuradhapur, an important archaeological site in South Asia. The complex extending over several square kilo meters included the remains of the ancient capital city of Anuradhapur, a series of large Buddhist Stupas of solid brickwork, the Mihintale dam (Mahendra Tal, named after king Ashoka's son), the temple of Buddha with the sacred peepal tree unbelievably spread widely in all directions indicating an eternal character through its inherited genetic uniqueness. Our team also visited a site museum where newly discovered antiquities were on display. We also had chance to meet Professor Gunaratane currently supervising the excavations. The day was hectic but quite rewarding, particularly for me as my academic interest converged with what was going on in the areas shown to us. It was incidentally the festival time and the time for worship. Visitors thronged the Budhist temple for the evening prayers and lit small lamps on all kinds of hangings and platforms. It was a Deepawali like scene sans the crackers. Our night stay was in a neat and well-maintained government guest house with air-conditioned rooms. I however, could not relish the food served there as it had an excessive mix of hot red chilies.

High on Rock

Our first halt of the next day was at an ancient site where we saw a huge tall statue of Buddha in standing posture installed in a specially carved in cave on the steep face of a hill. It was an archaeological site with contemporary looks due to the fact of its having been turned into a place of worship by monks. We got a taste of the hot temper of one of the monks there. Impressed by the hugeness of the statue of Buddha Dr.Rao wanted to get himself photographed standing by the side of the statue. He perched himself at a height touching the limbs of Buddha in the process. This act of Dr. Rao incensed one of the monks who shouted in rage at Dr. Rao, gesticulating menacingly at him. One of the UGC officers escorting us intervened and tactfully silenced the monk. Nearby was a large water reservoir (Weva-Vapi?)to serve as a source for irrigation channels. Lush green paddy fields and dark green groves of coconut trees abounded the place.

Lion Hill

On the next lap of our journey we traveled through rugged dusty roads and dark green plantain groves to reach Sihgiri (Singha Giri), another place of interest for tourists. The site is dominated by a huge steep rock hill with its spacious top emerging in the middle into a smaller rock taking the shape of a lion (Singha). Even the cantours of the front legs and paws of the lion could be figured out cearly. On the western concave face of the hill are paintings in the style of the Ajanta caves reachable through a man-made steel staircase hinged to the face of the rock wide enough to accommodate the two way movement of tourists in single file. There are many short inscriptions engraved in Mauryan Brahmi script on the face of the steep rock. The staircase though safe gives a feeling of being precariously placed for those who venture to climb it for the first time. I noted many among the visitors not opting for the climb. I was fortunate to have reached the top and to have seen the Lion on the rock or the Rock Lion if one chooses to call it so. At the foot of the hill did a water storage and supply system comprise cascading large water reservoirs developed in ancient times to cope with the requirement of water to the habitat at the foot of the hill and nearby area. It could be described as a marvel of engineering skills in the days of yore. The weather was hot and humid. A relaxing cup of coffee with vegetarian snacks was a reward at a makeshift restaurant with thatched roof by the side of a water body.

Kandy Candour

It was evening time when we arrived at Kandy, at one time the capital of Srilanka. The Chairman of the UGC had his home there. He had invited us for the night's stay with him. He had reached Kandy ahead of us and received us at his magnificent house located on the top of a hillock. The place was cool and pleasant. A light drizzle added to the flavour of the weather. Incidentally the day was also the day for the sighting of the holy relic of the golden tooth of Buddha. Taking advantage of our presence in Kandy we visited the famous shrine and witnessed the holy relic and the religious fanfare, which was quite impressive. At dinner the Chairman introduced us to his mother who was from Punjab in India. She had married the father of the UGC chairman when both were in London pursuing their studies for the profession of medicine. She received us affectionately and recounted with nostalgia some incidents of her life in India. Dinner included several north Indian vegetarian dishes free from any dose of red chilies. For me it turned out to be a real treat. Next day we returned to Colombo enjoying on the way the ravishing natural beauty of the landscape, its flora and fauna.

Reservation Calculus

We finalised the list of students to be admitted in accordance with the reservation policy of Srilanka government. To begin with it appeared to be a cumbersome process as there were numerous reserved categories and sub categories with varying percentages determined on the basis of population of a particular group. The categories included groups on the basis of language, region and religion, each element interspersed into another for further categorization. But it turned out to be quite workable as we progressed in our calculations. The list turned out to be not unwieldy since we had selected only those who were eligible for admission to the relevant courses in Indian universities.

Bonding Ashore

During our stay in Colombo we experienced an emotional encounter quite unexpectedly. A couple of days after our settling down to our work we started getting request from some security employees of the Indian High Commission deputed for our protection in the city for a meeting with us. As we had been going through a hectic programme on each day it did not materialize till the day before our departure for India. In the evening two members of the staff came to our hotel and requested us to have breakfast with them the next morning. They also introduced themselves to us informing that they belonged to a village in Sonepat district of Haryana and that guessing from my name and manner of conversation they had guessed that I too belonged to Haryana. The invitation was irresistible for the reason of its inspiration. We joined them at breakfast the next morning. It was drizzling outside and we were savouring steaming halwa and hot poorie bhaji prepared in desi ghee in their modest but neat and clean quarters. Our hosts told us that they had been posted in the Indian High Commission in Srilanka during the deployment of IPKF there and hoped to continue there for some more time. All the members of the delegation were moved at the gesture of these patriots.

Flight Alights

After breakfast our group devoted an hour's time to photography session at the Gall Road, Port area and the Parliament area. Our hosts escorted us to the airport well before the departure time of our flight to Madras (Chennai). After waiting for some time in the waiting hall we came to know that the flight was delayed and might not leave that day. Fortunately our escorts had not yet left the airport building. We came out and told them about the new situation. With their intervention and help we were taken to the transit hotel a few kilometers away and rooms allotted for our stay. After finishing dinner we had hardly settled for the night's rest when a message came that after all the delayed flight was ready to leave in an hour's time. We immediately packed up and reached the airport to catch the flight.

Chennai Chance

On reaching Madras (Chennai) international terminal we shifted to the domestic terminal to take the afternoon flight to Delhi. Waiting there in the hall we met Mr. Subrahamanya Swami who was to board a flight to Delhi. A few minutes later we noticed sudden commotion inside the terminal. Police personnel were giving anxious looks at people around. In a couple of minutes Shri Rajiv Gandhi surrounded by party workers appeared. We moved closer and greeted him introducing ourselves. He reciprocated asking us how we were in Madras. We told him about our mission and then he proceeded to reach the V.I.P. lounge. We did not find him among the passengers in our flight. Apparently he had left by an earlier flight. I guess the Chennai visit of Dr. Swami was not unconnected with Rajiv Gandhi's visit. We returned to Delhi by the early evening flight carrying sweet memories of the visit. It is sad that Shri Rajiv Gandhi's sojourn in Tamil Nadu the next year during election campaign turned out to be the last journey of his life. He was killed by a suicide bomber in SriPerumbudur on 20 May 1991.

Australian Auspices

Some Persons of Indian origin living in Australia were associated with the organizing of the World Sanskrit Conference at Melbourne in Australia during early January 1994. My wife's sister's family also lives in Melbourne, .My brother-in-law, Dr. Naunihal Singh sent us the registration forms. My wife and I both got registered as delegates and also sent our respective papers to be presented at the Conference, which were accepted.

Singapore Airlines

The University sanctioned to me one-way travel grant with permission to fly by any airline. Singapore Airlines being the most suitable we decided to fly with them. The travel agent gave us 9% rebate, which I proportionately surrendered to the University for adjustment at the time of settlement of my account. Our travel plan included a 12 hours' break at Singapore on onward journey with a provision for free city tour and a day's break with free hotel accommodation on return journey and free food coupons @ $ 16/- per day on each occasion. We could hardly utilize the coupons in full, as our requirement of food was meagre. Flying by Singapore Airlines was a enjoyable experience. Food, service and passenger care was of highest quality in addition to the comfortable seating and entertainment facilities. My wife and I both hardly fitted into the category of fliers who take maximum advantage of the hospitality of the Airline. However, we were lucky to have Indian vegetarian food. All this comfort and luxury by our standard turned out to be compensation for the bit of hassle that we had to face at Delhi airport.

Clear Unclear

Everything had gone smooth till we reported at the immigration counter. After a patient wait at the counter we were awakened as if from a slumber when the official checking the papers informed that my wife could not travel to Australia as her passport carried the stamp ECR (Emigration Clearance Required). My initial remonstrations with the official did not help. My son- in- law Deepesh who had accompanied my daughter Nandini to see us off at the airport intervened a bit sternly and introducing us to the official and impressing upon him of the urgency of the travel of my wife to Australia appealed to him to relent. In the mean time the senior officer standing nearby who was watching the situation quietly came forward and told the official handling our papers that according to the latest rules the ECR stamp was not relevant and therefore my wife was entitled to travel to Australia. The official tried to hide his discomfiture by posing as if he was doing us a favour by finally interpreting the rules to my wife's advantage. We did not grudge him the fidgeting and proceeded further thanking him any way but not without profusely complementing the senior official for the decisiveness he had shown. As another kind gesture he allowed my daughter and my son-in-law to enjoy the comfort of the V.I.P. lounge along with us at the departure terminal. We boarded the plane for the 9.00 p.m. flight looking forward to the Singapore Airlines experience.

Fabulous Place

Our flight landed at Singapore airport around six o'clock in the morning. The extensive Terminal-I meant for flights of Singapore Airlines looked highly impressive, a city in itself, most spacious, luxurious and glamorous in all respects. The moving ramp across the length of the terminal was a unique feature making things quite easy for the passengers. An electric train connects it with Terminal-II meant for flights of other airlines. The flight from Singapore to Melbourne was of eight hours' duration but clockwise it showed ten hours due to our eastward course. Our flight to Melbourne was to depart at 8.30 p.m. We had the whole day to ourselves. We spent the better part of the day going round the terminal. I was highly impressed by the standard of the bathrooms and the level of their maintenance. It is rightly said about the bathrooms of Singapore airport that they are matchless in the world of airports. Each unit of bathrooms has an attendant. There was a signage at each bathroom unit displaying the checklist for maintenance of various items showing the time of the service done along with the name and signature of the attendant concerned. We had our breakfast and lunch in a Restaurant in the terminal building against the coupons issued to us by the Airline. We joined the city tour group in a bus at 3.00 p.m. Before leaving the terminal our passports were deposited with the immigration department at the terminal since we had only single entry visa to be kept spare for our stop over for a day in the city on return journey. We were taken around a few places including the Museum and the market place and the Indian bazaar. The distinctive feature of Singapore was high rise buildings, flyovers and the Metro Railway. The roads were clean and well maintained. We had our dinner again at the same place but could eat very little accustomed as we were to the Indian food, which we did not find at the terminal Restaurant. Our flight for Melbourne took off on time in the evening.

Melbourne Morn

It took eight flying hours to reach Melbourne but the clock time was two hours ahead.

It was past six in the morning of 30 December 1993 when our plane landed. Immigration check was not cumbersome. The staff there allowed us all the eatables we had carried from Delhi. These included sweets and pickles of different sorts. We had faithfully declared all that we had carried. My wife's sister Pratibhaji and her husband Dr. Naunihal Singh received us at the Melbourne airport. They lived some sixty miles away from the airport. As we drove through a freeway, it took us hardly an hour to reach our destination, Glen Waverly.

The conference was to start a couple of days later. We settled down comfortably and did some sightseeing in Melbourne including the Hare Krishna temple and other places of interest before the opening of the Conference. Melbourne is a city of gardens and perhaps one of the most beautiful cities of the world as they say. The most enjoyable occasion was a trip to the Phillip Island and the Queen's Cliff reachable by a steamer after a journey of nearly sixty miles by car. Equally memorable was the picnic organized by some members of the Indian community in the Botanical gardens by the side of the river Yarra in Melbourne. The variety of tasty Indian food brought by members provided a rich assortment for the occasion. I still remember the tasty dish of *kheer* prepared especially for the occasion at the Restaurant of one of the members.

Conference Time

The Conference was a successful event. Sanskritists from all over the world, largely from India had gathered to share their intellectual outputs. Both my wife and I presented our respective papers at the Conference. My friend Dr.(Mrs.)Yajna Seni Popat from Germany had come to cover the conference as a Sanskrit journalist of Deutsche Welle. Another friend Dr.(Mrs.) T.S. Rukmini from Canada was also there. One evening during the Conference days a programme of Indian dances and other cultural items was presented by a group of Australian artists for the benefit of the delegates. Indian snacks like samosas and jalebees were served as refreshments on the occasion. A tour of the Vine Yards of Melbourne arranged by the organizers of the Conference did not attract many members. So was the case of the many wine bottles waiting on the table to seduce at least some of the Sanskritists. In the poetic symposium organized on the last day of the conference I presented my parody-*gatam tava shrutam mayaa, na hi shrutam tava aagatam* on a lapsed grant from the University Grants Commission.

Seek and Hide

On conclusion of the Conference on 16 January my friend Dr. Popat shifted to Dr. Singh's house as she had to stay in Melbourne for two more days before leaving for Germany on 18 January. My wife made a programme of shopping with her in down town. Dr. N. Singh dropped both of them at the Museum Station in the city. I traveled separately and was to join them later at an appointed time. It was decided that we meet at the exit gate of Museum station of the under ground Metro Railway. I reached the spot on Elizabeth Street outside the Museum station with which I was conversant having traveled on an earlier trip. When the two ladies did not turn up there for long after the decided time I moved to look up for them at the steps of the Museum building which was on the opposite side. I had not realized that there was another exit of the Museum station on the Swangston Street right in front of the Museum. I did not find the ladies there as they had moved to the exit point on Elizabeth street from where I had already moved to search for them on the other side. In the mean time I called at the residence of Dr. Singh to find out if any clue could be had of the riddle. I gathered from Reshma the daughter of Dr. Singh that my wife and our friend were equally puzzled at the rigmarole and were frantically looking for me. Having failed to trace them I left for Dr. Singh's residence. I reached there ahead of the ladies only to go back to the terminal station to take them home from there. It took me some time to convince the two that the confusion happened due to the misunderstanding of the point of meeting and that I had not fashioned the episode deliberately. Had they called Dr. Singh's residence once again they would have got information about where I would be waiting for them.

Canberra Confusion

Taking queue from some other delegates my wife and I modified our plans for our return journey to India. It was decided that we take our return flight from Sydney in place of Melbourne. We had invitation from Mr. Agarwal of Canberra to stay with him for a day. Arrangements were in place for our stay in Sydney also. Accordingly Singapore Airlines were approached to alter our Travel schedule, which they did promptly and now we could board from Sydney. We left Melbourne by a night bus and reached Canberra early next morning. Having failed to trace our host Mr.Agarwal, we stayed in a motel near the bus station. We could contact him only after a long hide and seek game played with us by the two small chits of paper containing his residential and office telephone numbers separately. I was calling him at his office when he had not reached there and at his residence when he had left for his office In any case we wanted to make the best use of the day and visited the new Parliament building, the Science Center and the High Court, commuting all distances on foot throughout. Canberra is a city of spaces and sunshine. We had no regrets for having taken a break in our journey there. Just as we were to return to our motel, we thought of making the last effort to trace Mr. Agarwal. The right chit emerged from nowhere from my papers and I called him up at his office. He was disappointed to know how we missed to call him right earlier. He reached the place from where we had called him. He took us round some places and then to his magnificent villa where we had dinner with his family. His wife was kind and warm hearted lady. His son was very supportive in dropping us at the motel late at night and arranging things for us for our timely reporting at the bus station the next morning.

Sharmas of Sydney

In Sydney our host was Dr. Chitra Sharma, a lecturer in Delhi University, who was on long leave and was living in her sister's house in Sydney. We visited a few spots, the most impressive being the opera house and the harbour bridge area. The architectural design of the opera house was unique. It presented the scene of dolphins emerging out of the sea in great strides. The Lotus Temple of the Bahai faith in New Delhi has similar elements of architecture.

We found the city most magnificent though a little crowded in the business districts.We experienced traveling in a double Decker Metro Railway. After a day's stay in Sydney we left for Singapore. Mrs. Chitra's husband, Mr. Sharma had arranged a friend's car to drop us at the airport. He stood by us till we proceeded for security check. I was impressed with the hospitality extended by the couple whom we had not even met earlier. Dr. Rakesh Saxena of ARSD College had telephonically introduced me to Dr. Chitra. Sydney airport has the architectural design similar to that of Indira Gandhi International Airport, New Delhi. The commercial area and the boarding lounge were quite impressive. We also had the pleasant experience of receiving unsolicited help from the ground crew in carrying our hand baggage to the cabin.

VIP Wait

There was a day's break in our journey at Singapore. The airline had arranged for our stay in a five star hotel in the city. We reached the hotel by ten o'clock of the night. By that time Deepesh and Nandini had returned to Jakarta after their short stay in India. We talked to them on phone. It was a pity that we did not think of rescheduling our travel plan so as to meet them in Jakarta. After all Jakarta was only a couple of hours' flight away from Singapore. The hotel room was well appointed. However, our dream of burying ourselves in the soap foam bubbles in the bath tub could not be realized as we did not know how to prepare it, though the material was lying there. We had a sound sleep at night. The next morning after taking breakfast we went to the famous shop of Mustafa for doing some shopping. On our return to the hotel we found a message from the Singapore airlines asking us to report for check-in two hours in advance of the time already given for reasons of security. Taking the message seriously we reported at the airport at 4.00 p.m. in place of 6.00 p.m. Luggage of each and every passenger was being checked manually even after x-ray screening. Later we came to know that the Prime Minister of Singapore was traveling to Delhi by the same flight. That explained the extra security precautions. In many countries the heads of government do not travel in the normal flights of their airlines. The Prime Minister of Singapore was perhaps the most democratic autocrat. He has taken his country to great heights of development.

We don't find any contradiction in his roles. After all, democracy can not be confined to a monolithic concept. History is full of examples of democracies allowing participation and consultation of the widest number but in different ways.

Hungary : Budapest

The 1997 session of the International Congress of Asian and North African Studies was scheduled to be held from 6th to 12th July at Budapest, Hungary. My paper had been accepted for presentation at the conference. So I decided to attend the conference. I was sanctioned 50% of the air fare by the University and the department of Culture of the Ministry of Human Resource development granted the remaining 50%. Thus assured of the financial support I decided to extend my programme to cover England and Germany also. But due to shortage of time I could not arrange Visa for a stop over in Germany. Dr. Rakesh Saxena of ARSD College and I chalked out our travel schedule together. We landed at Frankfurt airport by an Air India flight at 7.00 a.m., from where we were to catch a connecting flight to Budapest scheduled for 9.00 a.m. Following the signages meant to guide transit passengers we reached the check-in area meant for our flight. The counter did not open even till fifteen minutes were left for the departure time. We started making anxious enquiries. To our dismay people around were generally unhelpful. Was it a language problem? We conversed in English. As time passed, our anxiety increased. We did not know what to do. It occurred to me that I should make use of my knowledge of German, howsoever meagre. With a little effort I was able to convey our dilemma to a lady who very kindly escorted us to the concerned counter. The assistant there made us feel comfortable and issued the boarding passes in due course of time. We boarded the flight which took us to Budapest in an hour's time.

At Budapest airport we were received by the organizers of the conference who had already arranged for our transportation to the hostel where we were to be lodged. The weather was pleasant with light drizzle cooling the not so hot European summer. Three of us- Prof. Harnam Singh Shan from Punjab, Shri Rakesh Saxena and I were lodged in a three seated room in a multi-storey hostel.

Gas connection had been provided in the lobby on each of the floors. We made optimum use of the facility to make our own breakfast during our stay in the hostel. The conference was held in the Economics University of Budapest. The number of delegates ran into several hundred with India contributing a good number. I presented my paper 'Indian Epigraphical Studies in the Twentieth Century' in one of the sessions.

Twin City

Budapest is a twin city of Buda and Pest situated on either side of the river Danube. A chain of bridges spanning the Danube connects the twin cities. The Metro Rail subway of two levels below the river further removes the twin ness. Traveling frequently along its bank during our stay there we witnessed the mood of the river changing from a placidly flowing calm stream to a menacingly swelling mass of water intimidating even the steadiest steamer. A day's sight seeing trip along the Danube turned out to be memorable. The Indian ambassador was kind enough to entertain the Indian delegates at dinner one evening. On another evening an Indian restaurant owner gave a dinner party in down town to the delegates from India. On yet another evening all the delegates were guests of the Hungarian President. The last party was a farewell party at lunch. It was a lavish and longish event. Champaign and all kinds of wines were in liberal supply. But most of the delegates from India being teetotaler concentrated on the vegetarian stuff and soft drinks and of course cans of different flavours of juice.

Lost and Found

I must mention an incident that occurred at Budapest. Mr. Rakesh and I had wanted to visit Austria during the conference days but we did not possess a Visa for the purpose. Since we had double entry visa for Hungary it was not difficult to obtain Visa from the Austrian Embassy in Budapest. We went to the Indian Embassy to seek help in getting Visa. The First Secretary, Mr. Das arranged things and we could go and complete the formalities at Austrian Embassy for the purpose. As we came out of the Indian Embassy I discovered that my small pouch containing travelers' cheques worth several hundred US dollars and some documents was missing. I suspected that somebody had picked my pocket during my travel in bus or tramway earlier in the morning. Several such incidents had reportedly occurred involving conference delegates during the last couple of days. We cancelled our programme of visiting the Austrian Embassy and went back to our hostel room to ascertain whether I had left the pouch behind in my room. All search in the room turned out to be fruitless. Disappointed as I was, I went to the telephone booth on the ground floor to report the loss of the traveler's cheques to the City Bank. In the mean time Mr. Rakesh Saxena started making enquiries about the whereabouts of the nearest police station for the purpose of reporting about the loss of travelers' cheques. Some students who were playing table tennis in the same hall over heard the anxious enquiry being made by Mr. Saxena. On being told that the matter was the loss of a green pouch containing US dollars, they revealed that a pouch of the same description had been found lying on the board near the public telephone booth by the lady attendant working at the reception. The lady had gone out for lunch. We waited till she returned. By this time I vividly recalled how I had placed the pouch on the board while looking through the telephone book to locate a certain telephone number and how I had forgotten to pick up the same while leaving the place in a hurry to reach the Indian Embassy. After verification the lady returned the pouch to me. The contents of the pouch were found intact. I thanked her for being so alert and honest. Did the mix up in my memory had something to do with the phenomenon of jet lag?

Left Hand Drive

I found the city transport system in Budapest quite impressive and efficient. The buses were sleek and comfortable. The tramway worked very well within the older parts of the city. The underground Metro trains were found to be the best mode of travel. There were no conductors in any of the systems. They worked mainly on trust and the efficiency of the checking mechanism evolved to book the defaulters. It took me some time to adjust to the right hand drive system in Budapest when riding a bus or crossing a street.

Country Side

We made a day's trip to the popular tourist spot Shensken, which was reachable from Budapest by the metro rail, which ran under ground for some distance in the city and Emerged over the ground on reaching the country side. Shensken is a terminal halt. It attracts large number of tourists daily. The neat and clean eateries offered a varied fare to choose from. Salad in its different combinations was the most popular item. The shopping arcade on the river front was a favourite haunt for tourists. The deep and swollen Danube majestically flew furiously carrying vast mass of waters to be delivered to some promised land. We enjoyed watching the country side scene from the running train. Unbridled horses and dark maroon cattle grazing in the vast pastures, farmers relaxing in the courtyards of their hutments presented a familiar scene of the countryside anywhere.

United Kingdom : London

Dr. Rakesh Saxena and I had planned to visit London on our return journey from Hungary to India and had chalked out our flight schedule accordingly. We were to fly to London by British Airways on 13th July 1997. Mr. Atul Chauhan, son of Dr. Ashok Chauhan was to receive us at London (Heathrow) airport. On reaching Budapest airport we learnt that British Airways had been grounded due to strike by their staff. After some wait an alternative flight of Hungarian Airways was arranged for passengers flying to London. The timing remained more or less the same as scheduled for the original flight. Coming out of the Heathrow airport terminal at London we looked for Mr. Chauhan but he was nowhere there. When contacted on telephone he told us that on making enquiry he had learnt that British Airways flights had been cancelled that day and that he had no clue of our revised travel programme. He offered to reach the airport immediately and escort us to his place (Oxford Street) where we were to stay during our sojourn in London. Though we were new to London we preferred to reach his place on our own. We had heard that the London Metro Rail system was the best in the world. .Mr. Atul gave us tips about routes to be taken and trains to be changed. We reached Central Point Metro station at Oxford Street changing trains at two points without any hassles. Coming out of the Metro station I rang up Mr. Atul Chauhan from a nearby telephone booth. Within minutes he was there to receive us. His apartment was in the same tower, which stood majestically over the Metro station on Oxford Street. The building also served as a reference point for us like a lighthouse showing way to ships at sea for the days we were in London.

Tour Bus

Our halt at London was of four days. One whole day was set apart for local sightseeing. We purchased a full day travel as you please ticket of the circular tourist bus. A tourist guide explained the important landmarks along the route. One could break journey, visit any place of interest and again board another bus of the concerned company. This way we were able to see the area around the Buckingham Palace, the two houses of Parliament, Ten Downing Street (Prime Minister's official residence), the Big Ben Tower, London School of Economics, India House, the Tower Bridge, the Thames riverside, Trafalgar square, the Hyde Park, Madam Tussad's Wax Museum etc. The museum housing wax models of people and events brought before our eyes vivid pictures of the waxing times. The eloquently lifelike models included those of Indira Gandhi, Narasimha Rao, Rajiv Gandhi, Benazir Bhutto. Diana formed part of the group of the royalty but was placed a little distance away from other members of the family, indicating her estrangement with Prince Charles. The latest addition from India is the model of the celebrated cinema star Mr. Amitabh Bachchan.

Broad Abroad

At the time of our visit to London Professor Indra Nath Choudhury was the Director of Nehru Center there. He invited us to a lecture by Professor Harish Chaturvedi of Delhi University. As his wife (Professor Usha) was away in India at that time Professor Choudhury took personal pains to get a dainty Indian meal prepared for us at his house. It is said that a visit to London was incomplete without a visit to the South Hall. We had kept this in mind and took the first opportunity to make a round of the South Hall. The sight out on the roads was like the one in New Delhi's Ajmal Khan Road, the difference being more orderly traffic and lesser number of people on the street. Mr. Atul Chauhan did not miss the opportunity to do some shopping of provisions for an Indian meal. Such stuff was foreign to Oxford Street where he lived. So he got the feeling of having collected some kind of booty. A Pakistani taxi man took us from South Hall to the nearest Metro station from where we could catch a train for Oxford Street. He entered into a friendly conversation with us and even offered us a free ride, which of course, we politely declined. As is well known, Asians abroad huddle together and have no divisive vibes. How one wishes we, heterogeneous Indians were deported to a foreign land together to learn our lessons in homogeneity.

London University

The University of London was next on our itinerary. It was at a walkable distance from Oxford Street. Mr.Atul Chauhan had fixed an appointment with the Head of the department of South Asian studies in the London School of Oriental and African Studies. Our interaction with members of the staff there was quite rewarding as we exchanged views on several topics of mutual interest. I presented to the University library a copy each of the books, Sarup Singh: A Living Legend, A Study of Skanda Cult, and Man Aangan (a collection of poems in Hindi by my wife Chander Prabha). Later we went to the University cafeteria to have lunch. This was the place where Dr. Sarup Singh had once missed his lunch one day some forty five years ago for want of money due to delayed receipt of remittance from home. He had preferred to feign bad stomach to borrowing from a colleague. Dr. Sarup Singh had a hearty laugh when on my return I narrated the episode to him.

Road to Oxford

Mr. Sinha, a family friend of the Chauhans took us to Oxford in his car. The drive of about two hours was very pleasant. The country side with its vast expanses of green fields and thick groves on either side of the wide and well paved road added to the joy of a smooth ride. We found the University town neat and clean. We visited the Institute of Oriental Studies where I presented a copy each of my book '*A Study of Skanda Cult*' my wife's book 'anubhutiyon al chhin' to the librarian. Then we visited the Boden Library and had discussions with some members present there.

The peeling off plaster and worn out woodwork of the exteriors of some institutions said the story of financial crunch, which I thought was a world wide phenomenon. Education deserves greater inputs every where. However, the interiors of the institutions we visited were well kept and well furnished. There was no dearth of other infrastructure. We found some of the roads in oxford quite narrow compelling the authorities to declare them as one way streets. Parking of vehicles any where on road sides was allowed only against payment.

Desired Delay

We had realized that the time at our disposal was insufficient for a visit to CambridgeUniversity. Therefore we approached the Air India Office for extension of our date of departure by a couple of days. We were told that the earliest possible date could be after two weeks. As we could not afford to stay back for such a long period we decided to take the scheduled flight on 17th July. On reaching the airport and after standing in queue for checking in for quite some time we came to know from a staffer that the flight, which was to take us to Delhi had not arrived from New York and that the same was rescheduled for the next day.

Stay, don't Pay

We were lodged in the nearby Airport Hotel. For us it was a pleasant surprise. The experience of stay in a five star hotel in London without any cost was welcome. When I called my family on phone to inform about the change in the flight schedule I learnt that Beena (Nandini's sister-in-law), her sons Neeraj and Puneet were also in London in connection with the convocation ceremony of Neeraj. He was to receive his MBA degree at the London School of Economics. It was a pity to have learnt about it a little too late, as I could not leave the hotel to visit the city to meet them. However, I spoke to them on telephone. Mr. Atul Chauhan, who had very supportively come to see us off at the airport continued to give us company at the airport hotel for most of the day. My stay at the hotel was the result of another hassle in the chain of such happenings during my travels. Should I call it jinx or bonus? I think it is better to say with Shakespeare that 'all is well that ends well'. We flew to Delhi by the Air India flight the next morning. The parting gift from the Heathrow airport was the cash refund of the tax I had paid on the few purchases made during my stay in London.Dr. Rakesh did not fail to mention that whereas he was put to some personal frisking and scrutiny of his belongings I was spared all that screening. My hunch was that it was the case of random selection, nothing beyond.

Japan : Tokyo : Degree of Hospitality

Delhi University had conferred the honorary degree of D.Litt on Daisaku Ikeda among others as a part of the Platinum Jubilee celebrations of the University in 1998. Due to preoccupation Ikeda had not attended the convocation. However, he had expressed the desire to receive the degree personally from the Vice-Chancellor and had invited him to visit Japan with a small delegation to accompany him on the occasion. The Vice-chancellor, Prof. V.R.Mehta accepted the invitation and included me as a member of the delegation. The other members apart from Mrs. Mehta were the P.V.C., Prof. Abad Ahmad, the Registrar, Mr. K.K.Panda and Dean Planning, Prof. Neelmegham. The delegation reached Tokyo on 5th January 1999. The day's programme included visits to some Soka Gakai institutions and a meeting with Ikeda. I had not fully grasped the personality of Ikeda at the time I was preparing a convocation citation for him on the basis of available information. He was no moron serious looking philosopher. On the contrary I found him pleasant and friendly with a tinge of informality in every interaction we had with him. King Ashoka was the common subject between him and me. He evinced extra interest in having conversation with me when I told him about my teaching Ashoka's inscriptions to the M.A. students in Delhi University. At times he would address me as Ashoka. He specially commended to me to have a closer look at the Ashoka section in the museum he had created in his university at Tokyo.

Rising to the Occasion

The degree awarding ceremony was to open with the Delhi University invocation song from the Rigveda (sangacchadhvam samvadadhvam etc.). The Vice-Chancellor and other members of the delegation desired that I should do the invocation. I remembered the text of the invocation but not wanting to take any chance of a mix up of words I arranged to have a copy of the text from Delhi University by fax. I rehearsed the singing of the invocation several times. I can hardly sing, but as God had willed the invocation song came perfect on the hour of reckoning. Every body in the delegation was happy and I felt relieved that I could rise to the occasion. The ceremony was held in an impressively large auditorium and it was attended by people equal to the number of seats-no seat remaining vacant and no person standing for want of a seat. Everybody entering the hall was required to remove the footwear and put on neat slippers kept especially for the purpose at the entrance. Amazing co-ordination this! Next day's programme included a meeting with the Mayor of Tokyo. He was a member of the Soka Gakai International headed by Ikeda. Lunch in an Indian Restaurant (Tajmahal) and a shopping trip to down town were other preoccupations of the day. Peeping through the window of my 31st floor hotel room I could see a jungle of concrete all around with no ground surface visible. The same jungle with transparent glazing of houses lit up at night presenting a panorama of a fairyland. The weather being cold and windy we could hardly venture out of our rooms or the air-conditioned van when visiting places. The team of our guides and interpreters was very helpful and polite. Without their help and guidance the vegetarian members of our delegation would not have picked up the right kind of food items at the hotel.

Hiroshima Heroes

On the morning of 7th January we flew to Hiroshima, the first victim of atomic destruction during the Second World War. The way our travel schedule was handled at the airport made it clear to me that the Soka institution had a wide network in different offices. Its members worked like committed cadres. Our flight landed at Hiroshima amid light drizzle. From the airport we were directly taken to a Soka center in Hiroshima where our delegation was received with traditional hospitality by the director of the center . Arrangements had already been made for our comfortable stay at the best hotel of Hiroshima located on one side of the memorial park. My room was number eleven on the 31st floor. The next day began with the laying of wreathes at the martyrs' memorial at the site where the atom bomb had been dropped. We were told by the guide that the bomb was dropped to explode a little higher than the ground level so as to create maximum impact. The partially damaged dome (the steel frame had not melted) of a building (the municipal headquarters serving as the Japanese war office during the war time) stood in silent eloquence of the story of devastation brought about by the atomic holocaust and also of the resolve to stand up against all odds. The audio-video hall and the Museum at the site of the memorial brought alive the drama of destruction enacted more than half a century back.

The Director of the Museum at the Memorial site happened to be none other than the son of one of the martyrs in the atomic ravage. This gentle man, a small kid then had been saved as he lived with his mother far away from Hiroshima. His father was a station Master with the Hiroshima Railway and was on duty when the tragedy befell him and others in the city. Presspersons covering our visit asked the Vice-Chancellor several inconvenient questions regarding our country's atomic policy and our support to the war effort of the British government. But Prof. Mehta handled such questions with aplomb of a veteran political scientist that he is.

Our programme also included a meeting with the Mayor of Hiroshima. We did some shopping in a multi-storey department store near our hotel and had our lunch in an Indian restaurant. The Indian delicacies were far superior to what I had experienced in good restaurants in Delhi. After taking a round of the city in our van we bade goodbye to Hiroshima and made for the airport to catch the flight for Narita airport, Tokyo. I could not fail to notice the small crowd, which had gathered at the Hiroshima airport to bid us farewell. Apparently our hosts had drawn these people, mostly poor women and children from their institutions meant for the education and development of the deprived sections. But we did not miss the richness of the warmth of their feelings.

Mount Fuji

On our flight to Narita we witnessed the majestic snow covered crater-like peak of the Mount Fuji. It appeared as if the fire emitting mountain had taken to snow eating in a big way. Hence the lofty white calmness. Arrangements had been made for our stay for the night at the airport hotel at Narita. A flight of the Japan Airlines, Nippon brought us back to New Delhi on the 9th of January 1999. Earlier there was an hour's break at Bangkok airport where special arrangements had been made for the members of the delegation in the VIP lounge. The tour had been hassle free, may be, by the punyas of some members of the delegation or because of the Japanese way of doing things.

USA : Daughter's Call

It was July of 2009. My eldest daughter Nandini had shifted residence from Doha to Houston in USA. Her husband Deepesh had bought a spacious house in the high end area of Woodland in Houston. My son- in- law Deepesh was to join back the family after completing the tenure of his assignment in Doha in June next year .My elder grand daughter Nikita had moved out to join her College in Austin. My daughter and her younger daughter Dakshina were left to occupy the big house giving them a feeling of living in a vacuum. It was also the time around when a a few incidents of dacoity had taken place targeting houses of Indians in the neighbourhood. The Indian community in the township was in panic as, irrespective of their possessions, they were perceived to be goldmines. My son-in-law rushed back to Houston and rented a flat in a gated community nearby which was quite secure .My daughter talked to me on phone one day. Her voice was chocked describing the situation at her place. I could feel her distress. Without much deliberation I offered to join her leaving all my commitments in Delhi. It came as a pleasant surprise to her and proved catalytic in her regaining emotional stability. Deepesh sent papers of sponsorship which helped me in getting US visa in less than a month's time. I was in Houston on 23 October. I had not cared to nurse my hand injured badly in a freaky blast of a dud cracker which I was trying to handle on Diwali night for some fun for my grand children. I travelled by Qattar Airways with half a day's stop over and change at Doha. The air port terminal at Doha was spick and span. Waiting there for several hours was not tiring or boring. The disciplined queuing up of passengers for the flood of flights departing one after another, the rigorous procedure for security check and the quiet and manners of the helping staff were the hall marks of the efficiency of the airlines.

Long Haul

The journey from Delhi to Doha was only of three hours. But what awaited me to reach Houston was a long haul. I knew the flight would be of sixteen hours, With my right hsnd in bandage I managed all my chores during the flight without difficulty. One thing that I could not manage was sleep. Choicest Hindi movies, songs or ghazals played on the sea tpanel or the sumptuous food served intermittently would not attract the angel that it was. The aircraft icon displayed on the panel screen to indicate the progress of the flight appeared to be falling back even though moving forward, in the manner of a spider struggling to climb higher and higher with determination. Not exactly an ordeal but in deed, a long wait for a person under taking such a journey for the first time. No doubt it was an experience of its kind. It did end and ended well. Luggage collected and soon I was before the immigration official at Houston airport. The gentleman did not ask many questions. I was required to fill some forms. Noticing my right hand in bandage he filled up the same for me and further offered to wave off the requirement of putting my signature on it. But I managed to meet the requirement with my left hand. In fact my left hand had turned right since the time its counterpart got injured. My daughter, her husband deepesh and both my grand daughters were there at the arrival terminal to receive me. I forgot all the inconveniences of the journey and felt cozy in the company of my own children. All that was stranger and unfamiliar went into the backyard of my mind. I made light of the anxious questions they asked about my bandaged hand. After about an hour's drive we were at my daughter's house. Assured of the restored morale of the family my son- in – law went back to rejoin his duty in Doha. But before that he drove nearly eight hundred miles in one day to drop Nikita at her college in Austin.

Health Hassles

I had taken sufficient amount of medicines including the routine ones for my heart problem and those required to treat the burns on my right hand. On the third day after reaching Houston Nandini while changing the dressing on my hand noted some signs of infection on the wounds. She showed my hand to Deepesh on skype for guidance, He advjsed her to contact a friend of his who would take me to a doctor who saw patients having no insurance cover. She lost no time and drove sixty miles to take me to the doctor .It was for the first time that Nandini drove some miles on the highway- a difficult task indeed. My driving skills backed by an international driving license obtained in advance of my U S visit did not come handy because of the injury. The doctor had charged exorbitantly as I was uninsured person. But he pre3scried the right medicine and precautions for progressive healing However another episode of sustaining injury on my left thumb in the course of handing the car door one day left me a little disheartened. In between, my blood pressure also rose higher than normal quite often. Nandini shared my health problems with her friend, Mrs. Reddy from Andhra whose husband's elder brother was a cardiologist. Deepesh took me to his clinic one day. Dr. Reddy got the required tests done. His assessment was that my health parameters were right and that I should not worry much about fluctuations in blood pressure unless there was some discomfort. This gave me renewed self confidence as far as health question was concerned.

Losing Track

Deepesh made frequent visits to his home in Houston. Some he combined with his official tours. In such cases his company arranged conveyance to and from the airport. Incase of of personal visits Nandini used to pick him up from and dropped at the airport. On one of the early latter occasions Deepesh forgot to carry his mobile phone while leaving for the airport to catch a flight for Doha. We had gone more than half way when Deepesh realized what had happened. He decided to first reach the airport and check in and then wait for Nandini making s dash to home to collect his mobile phone and take a chance to reach back in time and deliver the same to him. It was indeed a tall order but drove fast and reached the terminal to find Deepesh waiting at the gate. Deepesh was visibly relieved at the retrieval. The phone contained all his business contacts.

It was late evening by the time we resumed our return journey. Somewhere midway Nandini lost track of the way back home as it was her first drive to the airport. Several loops of the parts of the route made and repeated payments made at the same toll gates bore no solution to as we again and again came to the same spot. Getting down and searching for help was not advisable at late hours. The GIS system of the car could also not be worked to help. A visit to a night store near the high way also proved futile. .At last we reached the portals of an Inn where the Pakistani manager gave us proper guidance to put ourselves on the right road. Our ordeal was soon over. Nandini got her bearings right At last we reached home late at night.

Harsh Kumar

Shri Harsh Kumar originally from Uttar Pradesh lived in Houston at a place some sixty miles away from Woodlands. He had become a good acquaintance after meeting me several times at Maharaja Surajmal educational complex at Janakpuri. He also invited us at several events of his upcoming American school at gurgaon. I thought of visiting him while I was at Houston. But unfortunately I had forgotten to take his contact details from his India station. The telephone number noted in my diary turned out to be the old one. It was through the efforts of Shri S. P. Singh that I could get the address of shri Harsh Kumar. I wrote him a letter with the request to contact me at the given number. He responded promptly on receiving my letter. He invited me to be his guest for a couple of days. I was waitng for the week end when Deepesh could drop me at Shri Harsh kumar's place. But before that Shri Harsh Kumar came over one day to pick me up. He was accompanied by his octogenarian father who lived in another city with his younger son in the north and had come to see Shri Harsh Kumar. Two more guests from India were already there – The sister and brother -in – law of Shri Harsh Kumar. The four of us made a compact group and had long chats. Shri Harsh Kumar was in a big estate and could be described as mansion for the royals even by American standards. He was basically a finance wizard and ran several enterprises. He also ran a chain of schools at the junior level..I stayed there fir three days. On the fourth day Shri Harsh Kumar dropped me at woodlands. Still remember the warm hospitality extended to me.

Out and In

Dakshina's tutor for mathematics had fixed the local council library as the venue for the class. Nandini and I found the one hour wait in the well appointed library quite rewarding. I got the opportunity to read some good books there. Some times Nandini would borrow some book of my liking on loan from there. Whenever Deepesh came for a holiday from Doha he would take us all to some Indian restaurant for eating. In his absence Nandini and her two daughter would take me out for local sight seeing or to different malls to make one or the other purchase. Woodlands was a sort of self contained sub city. One day we went to see the beautiful neighbourhood of Springs where my daughter's family had previously lived.Their house had its backyard facing a big golf course. The place looked like a green colour sheet hiding underneath humped objects here and there.

False Alarm

In addition to other possible security arrangements Deepesh had got a burgler alarm system installed in his house. It was directly linked with the police control room. Any false alarm ending in a visit by the police entailed some payment except the limited initial freak calls. The first such free call had already been exhausted soon after installation. On another day the bell of the alarm time clock placed near the entrance rang just when Nandini applied the key into the door to open it on our return from the market.She took it for the burglar alarm. In panic she moved away into the open. The next door neighbor who was around came forward to help. We three of us opened the door and went in cautiously to check if any thing was wrong inside. Nothing wrong except that the time keeping clock alarm was still on and was responsible for the mix up. It was another learning experience for us.

Consumer is King

I invariably accompanied Nandini whenever she made a trip to the market or drop her younger to school or pick her up. This helped me to familiarize with the American conditions. The local shopping complexes with wide compounds had enormous parking areas and were located off the main roads to be approached through connecting roads. The main halls run by corporate had all the departments under one roof. On the sides were located individual shops catering to specialized services.

Visiting the Malls for shopping was both a learnin policeg and recreational experience.. The wares spread out in various departments under one roof gave one the feeling of welcome and freedom of choice. Trust ruled and CCTVs at vantage points took care of the odd transgression. Stores used marketing strategies to attract maximum number of customers.. Sometimes one would advertise slashing of rates at throw away prices without disclosing the number of articles only to attract a glut of early birds keeping a night vigil of a sort. Those disappointed among the throngs willy nilly settled for buying articles at normal rates, as returning empty handed wo'nt justify the long journeys undertaken at some cost. Some made even the reluctant buyers feel comfortable by offers of buy back at par or replacement of goods within a specified period. American economy being consumer centric therefore he is treated like a king.

Full Filling

Automation and time saving are two among the features of American life. One day my daughter Wanted to get gas (we say petrol) for her car. She drove a few kilometers towards the market place sand stopped at a filling station. There were several points but there was no attendant around. As I was about to ask my daughter she told me that there was a self service system in place and that she was to swap her company card and enter the needed quantity and then proceed to manage the rather heavy nosel herself. I could see the procedure was simple and quick. The gas filled, my daughter moved the car to another corner of the filling station.

Swash Wash

It was now the car washing service point where Nandini stopped the car. On the driver's side was a machine where she entered digits meant for the type of service required to be done. A green light showed on the door in front and soon the car was inside a small room steadily parked with both of us inside it. And in seconds. Strong splashing jets opened from different directions. The car had a real swash wash with sponging levers working in tandem. The driers were not to be left behind to do their bit. The red light on the exit turned green now and Nandini drove the car to emerge on a service road leading to the main road. It was a few minutes job done with precision and speed. No waiting rooms or endless wait involved No human hands or errors.

Return Home

One day I sustained an injury on my left thumb in a repeat freaky accident. That put me off considerably though Deepesh immediately got me some really effective first aid. Getting into any health related problem for an uninsured person was a sure invitation to financial problem. So I got my return ticket preponed by a few days. Deepesh linked it with his own journey upto Doha after a short holiday. I felt assured and relaxed to have travelled together wth him on the major part of the travel We were together in the plane whe it was fifteenth of January, Birthday of Deepesh. I wished him many happy returns of the day. It was a nice feeling to have wished at such heights and with all warmth. I stayed at the Doha airport for a couple of ours and took a flight for New Delhi to reach there the early hours of sixteenth of January 2010. As I came out of the airport terminal it was thick fog enveloping everything and biting cold reaching the bones to strike hard. The burn injury on my hand has almost cured and my mind cured of the feeling of not having seen what America was like.

Trip not Made

It was one day during the period when Professor Gangrade was officiating as Vice- Chancellor that the head of the department of Slavonic Studies met with me and asked me for my consent to let him include my name among a delegation slated to visit The then Soviet Union as guests of that Government for about ten days. the Professor had not been feeling happy with my stand on certain issues brought by him before the University Bodies. Thinking that his invitation might be an attempt to bring me round to his point of view, I straight away expressed my unwillingness to accept the proposal. The delegation did visit the Soviet Union. It had a couple of Principals as also the Director of South Campus, Professor Abad Ahmad. On return of the delegation Professor Ahmad told me that by not joining the delegation I had not missed much. This removed the iota of feeling of having missed a trip to Russia. Subsequent developments proved my decision was right. The Professor ran into several controversies including the one relating to the above said trip. Later when a clear headed lady became head of the same department she succeeded in getting several issues of her department resolved. My role was constructive and transparent as ever before.

The professor was happy over the turn things had taken and came over to me one day to thank me for my co-operation. Musing he asked me how was the lady able to persuade me where he had failed. I told him that whereas the lady acted like a head of department, he tended to behave like a husband. He could not agree more. The lady happened to be his wife.

V

Law and Practice

South Campus

South Campus of the University is an example of practice preceding law. The Campus is both a territorial entity and an academic entity but we find no mention of it in the Delhi University Act. Bits and pieces incorporated in the various provisions of the University's Statutes and Ordinances give an idea of some aspects of the Campus. When in 1989 the Vice-Chancellor, Professor Moonis Raza brought a draft Ordinance concerning all aspects of the Campus there was vehement opposition to it from the teaching fraternity all over the University. Nevertheless the Campus has made rapid progress and has developed into a popular hub of teaching and research especially in the area of Applied Sciences.

Autonomous Colleges

On the other hand law enacted in advance for two important reforms in the University could not be translated into practice. One was the amendment in the Delhi University Act making a provision for declaring colleges conducting courses in the Faculties of Medicine, Technology, Music and Fine Arts, as autonomous colleges. During the tenure of Professor Yash Pal as Chairman of the UGC granting autonomous status to colleges was a favourite agenda. But Delhi University could not be persuaded even in a limited way to opt for the scheme. The experiment made in large number of colleges, especially in government colleges in Rajasthan leaving a few cases did not prove successful. It may be mentioned here that at the relevant point of time a former student of professor Yashpal was the Chief Secretary of Rajasthan. Even the author of the scheme Professor Yash Pal himself is reported to have later admitted in private that the scheme was a non starter. In the Delhi College of Engineering the teachers had all along wanted autonomous status without loosing any of the privileges that were available to them as government servants. So, progress on that path continued to be stinted. However, tracks changed with the shifting of the College to its new spacious campus at Badli. Its state of the art laboratories, modern academic and residential buildings combined with commodious hostels both for boys and girls greatly contributed in melting the resistance among a large section of teachers in the College who wished to cling on to the old campus at Kashmiri Gate. The Delhi government gave a pleasant surprise to the College community by raising its status to that of a University by the name Delhi Technical University (DTU). However, the loss of the brand DCE (Delhi College of Engineering) left the student community a confused lot for some time at least. The University was of course able to sort out the initial glitches amid a fierce agitation launched by the students.

An old off shoot of the Delhi College of Engineering, however, innovated in charting out a course ultimately leading to its autonomous status or at least to remain free from the red tape of bureaucracy. The College currently known as Netaji Subhash Institute of Technology was founded in the early 1980s to be managed by a Board of Governors as a registered Society headed by the Lieutenant Governor of Delhi. For this College also autonomous status has remained a mirage so far. Otherwise, the Institution in its new campus at Dwarka is doing well as center of excellence in technical education.

College Councils

The second reform was the amendment in 1972 of the University Act incorporating a provision for the creation of one or more College Councils for two or more colleges. Follow up action was taken by the University by enacting appropriate Statute. The Teaching community of the University was highly incensed over the issue. They saw in the measure an attempt to delink the colleges from the University departments. There was a strong agitation against the innovation. The then Vice Chancellor, Professor Sarup Singh sensing the general mood proceeded to repeal the Statute.

In the process he incurred the displeasure of the then Minister of education Professor Nur-ul-Husan for not consulting him before acting in the matter. Professor Sarup Singh on his part did not fail to express his grievance in the former not consulting him at the time of going for the enabling amendment in the Delhi University Act in the first place.

Recognition of Teachers

As per provisions of the Act and Statutes of the University every college teacher must be recognized as teacher of the University. Such recognition is accorded by the Executive Council on the recommendation of a selection committee prescribed in Statute19. A practice had developed over long years to process the cases of recognition by circulation of papers among the members of the relevant selection committee. This system had been working satisfactorily till the mid nineties though there had been inordinate delay in some cases of the faculty of Medical Sciences. Some people approached the Vice-Chancellor Professor Mehta to find a remedy for the delay. The new Registrar in his enthusiasm obtained legal advice from the University's Senior Counsel to the effect that the cases of recognition should be considered by the selection committee in a meeting and not by circulation of papers. The Vice-Chancellor approved the advice and sent the file to me for follow up action.

I met the Vice-Chancellor and explained to him the problems that would arise in the new system. Convening of meetings of the selection committees would not only be financially unviable it would be almost impossible to complete the schedule of meetings required for the enormous volume of cases every year. As members of the selection committees the V.C./P.V.C. would be hardly left with any time for other business. The V.C. immediately realized the impracticability of the new system and asked me to find a way out after discussing the matter with the Senior Counsel. I suggested that the old system be continued with the proviso that a meeting be held in case any member of a selection committee insisted for the same. The Senior Counsel agreed to the suggestion. The V.C. felt relieved that the remedy sought to cure the system was gracefully abandoned before it could worsen the situation. I believe the provision was there to serve as a final filter to ensure that no prescribed norm had been violated at the time of initial appointment before the seal of the University recognition was put on a teacher to be called a teacher opf the University.

Alumni Association

The Alumni Association of the University elects every five years ten persons from among its members for membership of the University Court. The rules under the relevant Statute provided for election by postal ballots. The electoral list revealed a pattern showing the residential addresses of large chunks of members as one and the same. A kind of syndicate had been created by vested interests to manage the election of members of a few selected families. The list had become obsolete in as much as many members were not even alive. With the growing awareness among new members about the prevailing pattern a need was felt to reform the system. Accordingly Statute 45 and the election rules were amended during the tenure of Professor V.R. Mehta. Shri J.C Kochar and I drafted the amendments, which provided for five yearly renewal of membership of the Alumni Association and for an option to vote by postal ballot only to those members who resided outside Delhi. Other members would be required to vote at polling center to be set up by the University in Delhi. The new system was put into operation in January 2003 when the five-yearly election was due. But as the number of validly nominated candidates after withdrawal was equal to the number of seats (ten) no election took place and the intricacies involved in the new system could not be tested. This unique unanimity among the aspirants, who mostly were former activists of the University, was not surprising as these elements had perfected this art for years on. There was informal testing of their comparative strength and contrived withdrawals were obtained. Perhaps the coming years await a real contest some day.

Home for Homeopathy

The biannual election of 26 teachers to the Academic Council would bring into focus several difficulties faced by the teachers of the Delhi College of Engineering. Their retirement age at fifty-eight as compared to sixty with a provision for extension of five years for teachers of non-government colleges was perceived to be discriminatory. A demand was raised for the application of Ordinance XII (meant for teachers of non government colleges) to these teachers without realizing that they were already governed by the government service rules. There could not be a dual set of rules for them. As such no action was taken towards meeting the demand.

However, when the Nehru Homeopathic College run by the Delhi Government sought affiliation with Delhi University the elected teacher representatives stood in the way vehemently pressing for the application of Ordinance XII in case of the teachers of the College as one of the conditions. Such a condition could not be met with on technical grounds. So the matter kept hanging. After I became Dean of Colleges the Principal met me and pleaded for the affiliation of his college with the University. I studied the previous papers on the subject and the provisions of the rules and regulations of the University and the rules of the government. I came to the conclusion that Ordinance XII could not be made applicable to the teachers of the college, as it was a college maintained by the government. At the same time I thought it was a pity that a professional college was being deprived of the privileges of the University of Delhi. I personally discussed the matter with various teacher representatives and explained the paradox in their stand. Happily every body agreed with my point of view. The Academic Council and the Executive Council accorded affiliation to the college after following the prescribed procedure of an inspection committee. A new chapter was added to the academic variety in Delhi University. Ultimately other follow up actions have been taken and now the University has department and faculty of Homeopathic Medicine.

College of Education

Shri V.K. Kapoor, later Lt. Governor of Delhi was the Chief Secretary of Delhi in 1989. He had a proposal to convert the State Council of Educational Research and Training (SCERT) into a college of Education affiliated to Delhi University. He discussed the matter in a meeting where the Dean of the faculty of Education, Professor Krishan Kumar and I were present. Professor Kumar was not sanguine about the proposal. He had his own reservations on the issue of the SCERT being converted into a college of Education. On my plea that the University should support a full-fledged independent college adhering to the Statutes and Ordinances of the University, he agreed to the idea in principle and offered to place the matter for consideration of his colleagues in the Faculty. However, he insisted that the Delhi government should first make available to the University its annual man power requirements in the area of school teaching.

The matter dragged on for quite some time and was taken up seriously some time later on Professor V.K. Sabharwal taking over as Dean of the Faculty of Education. The Delhi government sent a revised proposal for opening a college of Education in east Delhi. The inspection committee headed by me visited the proposed site at the Bhai Parmanand Polytechnic in east Delhi. Shri Sahib Singh Verma, the then Education Minister of Delhi was personally present to impress upon the need to open a college of Education. On the recommendation of the Committee the Academic Council and the Executive Council gave approval for the opening of what is now the Maharshi Valmiki College of Education with an annual intake of one hundred students for the B. Ed. course to begin with. The step came as a big relief to the aspirants for teachers' education in Delhi. A superannuated Professor of the faculty of education, Dr. R.P. Sharma shouldered the responsibility of organizing the College as Officer on Special Duty for a couple of years. After a couple of years a regular Principal was appointed. The College has played an important role in meeting the ever increasing demand for teacher education in Delhi.

Reluctant Client

Professor Mehta's tenure of five years as Vice-Chancellor was to expire on 17 March 2000. The process of appointment of the new V.C. had been initiated quite in advance of the completion of the tenure of the incumbent but it appeared that a decision was unlikely to be made by that date. The question whether Professor Mehta could continue in office till the appointment of a new V.C. not withstanding the expiry of his tenure of five years had been widely debated among the University community. Some believed that Professor Mehta should demit office at the end of his tenure of five years. Case of Prof. R.C. Mehrotra was cited where a letter from the ministry of Human resource Development pointing out the statutory position presented before the Executive Council did not help. I was one of those whose reading of Statute 10 supported the continuation of Professor Mehta as V.C. till the appointment of a new V.C. but not for more than a year. In fact I shared my interpretation of Statute X with Professor Mehta much before his term was to expire. He had made it clear to me that he was not interested in continuing beyond the term of five years even if asked by the Government. Nevertheless the members of the team of the V.C met him to know if he was ready to continue. On his unequivocal refusal they decided to organize a function to bid farewell to Professor Mehta on the last working day of his tenure. Taking queue from this decision several associations organized functions to bid farewell to Professor Mehta. The function organized on 17th March at Shankar Lal Auditorium was a grand finale to the chain of functions. Such a function in honour of a retiring V.C. had not been witnessed in the past as old timers said.

A couple of hours after the function was over Professor Mehta called me on phone and told me that the Government wanted him to continue till the appointment of a new V.C and that he was not prepared to retract from his already declared stand. He was kind enough to ask for my advice in the situation. I reminded him of my interpretation of the relevant provision of Statute 10 offered to him a couple of days ago and added that at that stage he should continue in his post as the same was in accordance with the provision of Statute 10. Finding him still reluctant I suggested that he should tell the government to make a written request to him failing which he could demit office forthwith. Professor Mehta agreed with me and told the Ministry officials accordingly. The Ministry wrote back requesting him to continue in office till the appointment of a new V.C, which it added was likely to take place in a few days' time. Professor Mehta had no better alternative than condescending to continue as V.C. for about two months.

I had the satisfaction of having offered a correct interpretation of Statute 10. Professor Mehta, however, felt amply perturbed at the turn of events. He occasionally attended his office at the North Campus and mostly functioned either from South Campus or his residence at DLF City, Gurgaon. The sad part of this otherwise normal development was the twist given to it by a couple of persons enjoying personal proximity to Professor Mehta. One of them, a young and otherwise dynamic Professor was reported to have gone to the extent of describing the graceful and dignified function held on the 17 March 2000 to bid farewell to Professor Mehta as rape performed on the Vice-Chancellor by his team mates. It is a different matter that Professor Mehta knew his team mates and their feelings for him better than this gentleman could imagine. But nevertheless such indiscreet utterances must have disturbed the core of his heart immensely. This gentleman Professor had on different occasions earlier inadvertently created several controversies to resolve which the Vice-chancellor had to spend enough of his energies.

Say in Selection

There was a case of ascertaining the validity of the recommendation of a selection committee for appointment of lecturers in Sri Aurobindo College (Evening) pending for decision by the University. The V.C., Professor Moonis Raza brought the matter for discussion in the team meeting on the morning of the very day of my joining duty as Dean of Colleges (28th October 1988). The V.C. explained the case to the members of his team and posed the question whether the majority recommendation of the selection committee was valid in spite of the fact that the dissenting minority included the two experts of the University. He asked for my opinion on the issue. I replied that all members of the committee had equal weight and a majority decision was a valid decision. I also cited a similar case dealt with by me as Principal Shivaji College a couple of years back. The V.C. as also the other members of the team agreed with me.

On reaching my office I found among files pending disposal a similar case processed by my predecessor for placing before the EC for rejection of the majority decision of the selection committee on the ground of the two University experts not agreeing with the decision. The case related to the placement of two teachers of economics in the selection grade in Satyawati College. I also noted that the opinion of the Senior Counsel of the University had been obtained in the matter. Since I held a different view on the subject I sought the permission of the Vice-Chancellor to re-examine the case in consultation with the Senior Counsel. I framed a number of questions that would have arisen if the advice given by the Senior Counsel were to be implemented. I also gave my interpretation on the issue. The Senior Counsel, after examination of the arguments adduced by me agreed that the majority decision was valid decision. He cited several Supreme Court rulings in his revised advice. His regret was that earlier the case had not been placed before him with full facts. My office processed the case in light of the new interpretation and the University approved the placement of the concerned teachers in the selection grade.

Another instance of a similar nature arose years later in Ramjas College when the Head of the department of Economics and the second expert did not agree with the majority opinion in the selection committee. However, the appointment was made on the basis of the recommendation of the majority of the members of the selection committee. The head of the department took the position that he and his other colleagues would not attend meetings of the selection committees in any of the colleges in future unless a decision clarifying the role of the University head of department was clearly taken. The case was referred to the Senior Counsel who gave a well-argued opinion on the question stating that the head of the department or for that matter any other member of the selection committee enjoyed no special weightage in the decision-making. A letter was sent to the head of the department along with a copy of the legal opinion with the request to continue to perform the statutory duty of participating in the selection process. This settled the matter and mercifully the work of selection of teachers in the concerned department did not suffer any more. But it should go to the credit of the then Head of the Department that he accepted the clarification with grace and fully co-operated for the future.

Private Affair

One of the matters that kept coming up before the University during my tenure as Dean of Colleges was the demand for granting affiliation to private self-financing institutions. The Priyadarshini College of Computer Technology functioned for some time without affiliation to any university. Delhi University regretted its inability to grant affiliation as it was at that point of time not in favour of introducing the dual fee structure. Tired of promises made by the management from time to time the students filed (most likely inspired by the management itself) a writ in the Delhi High Court for affiliation of the College with Delhi University. The University defended its policy of not granting affiliation to self-financing institutions. The Court at one stage wanted the management to have discussions with the officials of the University. A meeting was arranged in the University, where Mr. Siddique the chairman of the Priyadarshini College, the Registrar and I were present. The chairman started aggressively dropping names during the course of discussions. The Registrar and I made it very clear that we could not be influenced by the contacts of the chairman and that no amount of pressure brought upon by him was going to be of any help. The outcome of the meeting was submitted to the Court. Finally the High Court dismissed the writ upholding the position taken by the University.

The question of affiliation of private self financing colleges cropped up again when the Bharati Vidyapeeth, Pune sought affiliation of its MBA programme with Delhi University. The P.V.C. Professor Abad Ahmed and I defended the policy of the University at a meeting in the Ministry of Education. Both of us explained to the officials in the ministry how proposed affiliation would open floodgates of requests by private trusts outside Delhi and in Delhi for affiliation of private institutions. The matter stood there as far as the University of Delhi was concerned. But the Ministry perhaps had its own compulsions and went to the extreme option of allowing affiliation of the Bharati Vidyapeeth with the Poona University by a special order as per provisions of the Delhi University Act.

Indraprastha University

In the meanwhile several other trusts were pressing the Ministry to use their good offices to have affiliation with Delhi University for their self-financing courses. The Ansal group wanted affiliation of their college of architecture. The A.P.J. Society was seeking affiliation for different graduate programmes in applied sciences. The then Minister of Human Resource Development, Shri Arjun Singh discussed the issue in a meeting with the Vice-Chancellors of Central Universities located in Delhi and pleaded for finding a solution to the problem. None of the existing universities in Delhi was willing to accord affiliation to the self financing institutions being proposed by private trusts. After extensive discussions a consensus emerged for asking the UGC to appoint a committee to examine the issue along with the possibility of opening a new University in Delhi for granting affiliation to privately funded self-financing institutions located in the National Capital Region. Accordingly the UGC appointed a committee headed by Professor Bipin Chandra of the Jawahar Lal Nehru University, New Delhi. On the suggestion of our Vice-chancellor Professor Upendra Baxi I was also made a member of the committee. The committee held a couple of quick meetings and gave a report for establishment of a central university in Delhi with the national capital region as its territorial jurisdiction. The concept was of an affiliating university performing its academic functions through panels of fellows drawn from the faculties of reputed universities in the country. The affiliated institutions were conceived as autonomous bodies having powers and responsibilities matching their role.

The recommendations of the committee were accepted by the UGC and the central government. A suitable bill was also drafted and perhaps also approved by the Cabinet for introduction in the Parliament. At this stage the matter was put in cold storage. It was sometime later in 1997 when the government of Delhi took initiative to set up a state university in Delhi that some of the features of an affiliating university as recommended by the committee were incorporated in the draft of the legislation. Such an initiative was triggered at a meeting of the Vice-chancellor Professor V.R. Mehta with the Chief Minister of Delhi, Shri Madan Lal Khurana. I was also present in the meeting. When the chief minister pressed hard for opening of new colleges in Delhi under the University of Delhi the V.C. strongly resisted the move and in stead suggested that the Delhi government should think of opening a new affiliating university to take care of the increasing demand, especially in professional and technical areas. It was pointed out that several trusts were ready to take up the responsibility to open self financing colleges. The Chief Minister appeared to be convinced of our argument.

The Indraprastha University ultimately came into existence in1998. Several privately managed self-financing professional and technical colleges were opened in the very first year. The number grew fast in the years that followed. In 1999, the tercentenary year of Guru Gobind Singh, the name of the University was expanded as Guru Gobind Singh Indraprastha University. It is a happy coincidence for me that I happened to be associated with the setting up of three institutions by the Surajmal Memorial Education Society in affiliation to this University viz Maharaja Surajmal Institute (1999), Maharaja Surajmal Institute of Technology (2001) and Maharaja Surajmal Institute of Pharmacy (2003) in Janakpuri New Delhi. Functioning under the over all guidance of Shri Ram Niwas Mirdha in the formative years the Institutions have already earned a name in quality education and good management practices, and rank quite high in academic standards in the GGSIP University.

Astute Statute

I got to establish a personal equation with Professor K.K. Agarwal, the first Vice-Chancellor of the newly established GGSIP University during the process of opening three Institutions by the Surajmal Memorial Education Society referred above. His term of appointment was to end on 31 October 2003. The Statutes of the University provided for the procedure for the appointment of the Vice-Chancellor. The Lt. Governor was the appointing authority proceeding on the recommendation of a selection committee which in turn was aided by a search committee. The term of the Vice-Chancellor was five years but he was eligible for reappointment. However, he could not continue in office after attaining the age of sixty five years. Within these provisions Professor Agarwal was eligible for reappointment. As his term came towards the end speculations with regard to his successor started in the University circles. Every one including Professor Agarwal interested in the matter was focused on the process of the two tier committees. My understanding of the relevant statute of the GGSIP University in relation to the procedure to be followed if the incumbent Vice-Chancellor was to be reappointed was entirely different from what the general perception was. Discussing the issue one day with Professor Agarwal I pointed out to him that if the Lt. Governor wanted to reappoint him the normal procedure of the search committee and the selection committee was not called for and that the procedure was to be set in motion only when the Lt. Governor had arrived at the decision not to reappoint the incumbent Vice-chancellor. On professor Agarwal's request I prepared a detailed note explaining the import of the relevant statutes in support of the view taken by me. Professor Agarwal was surprised but happy to know about the true meaning of the statutes. What followed is history now. Professor Agarwal got appointed for the second term though amid tense moments of suspense till the last. He got another chance for serving the University, which he had been nurturing like his own child. It is learnt that the procedure adopted in this appointment had been unsuccessfully challenged in the Delhi High Court and is now pending in an appeal in the Supreme Court.

Stale Stay

The Delhi Gurudwara Prabandhak Committee (DGPC) nominates the governing bodies of several Sikh educational institutions including the three colleges affiliated to the Delhi University. The group, which came to power in the 1984 elections of the DGPC made a move to replace the personnel of the governing bodies of the educational institutions controlled by it. However, the opposite group approached the court and obtained a stay on the issue. As the membership of the nominees of the DGPC is approved by the Executive Council for a term of one year the stay should have been applicable for that period only. But somehow the University administration had been taking the view that the stay was applicable till the original writ was decided one way or the other.

When I joined as Dean of Colleges in October 1988 the officials of the DGPC met me and desired that I process their request for approval of fresh nominees in light of the rules. My own understanding of the law was that the stay order became in fructuous after the end of the tenure of nomination of the members. I discussed the matter with the Vice-Chancellor who advised me to seek legal opinion in the matter. The Senior Counsel of the University, Shri P.P. Rao after a detailed examination of the case opined that the stay applied to the period of the tenure of the members of the governing bodies and advised that the proposal of the DGPC for approval of the fresh nominees be placed before the Executive Council which was competent to approve the new set of persons. Accordingly the matter was placed before the Executive Council, which approved the newly proposed names. Immediately after the names were conveyed to the respective colleges the rival group moved the Delhi High Court and obtained stay of the operation of the University's approval. The case lingered in the High Court for a number of years but ultimately the stay was lifted and fresh nominations were considered and approved by the University every year for the future.

Added Years

As per provisions of the statute 28 of Delhi University a period upto five years can be added to the length of service of a teacher who entered service at an age of more than twenty-five years for the purpose of determining superannuating pension. The provision had also been incorporated in the recruiting rules contained in Ordinance XXIV. The system had been working smoothly since 1973. But sometime in the mid nineties the Finance Officer, Mr. Nim took the stand that the provision was not applicable to teachers who did not possess a Ph.D. degree. I held the view that the provision was applicable to all category of teachers entitled to pension. The Treasurer of the University also shared my view. But the Finance Officer continued to be rigid in his approach to the question. Several teachers kept waiting for the settlement of their cases for fixation of pension. After several rounds of discussions with the finance officer it was agreed to place the issue before the Executive Council for clarification. The Executive Council ultimately decided to rule that the provision was applicable to all teachers. The pending cases were expeditiously processed. However, later on the facility was again restricted to those teachers who had a research degree.

Government Provident Fund

Section 46 of the Delhi University Act makes it incumbent on the University to constitute a provident fund and provides that the provisions of the Provident Fund Act 1925, shall apply to such fund as if it were a Government Provident Fund. The same applies to a provident fund constituted by a college if the rules of the Fund have been approved by the Central Government. The University and the colleges have been administering the respective provident funds for decades. The investments of the funds had been made in government securities and in the nationalised banks. Some time in 1980s the Government had also permitted the investment with the Unit Trust of India (UTI). Logically and in terms of the provisions of the University statutes the University and the colleges apportioned interest to the account holders on the deposits in accordance with the interest earned. At one time it went up to 14%. The Government however, had a different pattern of investment for the General Provident fund accumulations and as such declared the interest rate on a fixed rate of 12% which later went on changing down wards. The University and the colleges allocated interest at a higher rate in accordance with the interest earned through prudent investments.

Surprisingly in mid 1990s,(perhaps on the insinuations made by the then Finance Officer of the University) some over enthusiastic Officers in the Ministry of Human Resource Development took the view that the University or the colleges could not allocate interest to the subscribers at rates higher than those declared by the Government for its employees on the specious plea of the government having jurisdiction over all matters of these funds for their being deemed as Government Provident Funds. These Officers paid little heed to the pleas of the University that these funds were given the technical name of Government Provident Funds only for the purpose of application of the provisions of the Provident Fund of India Act 1925 (in the matter of settling issues relating to these funds in courts of law). A queer situation was created when the investment of these funds earned interest more than what was enough for allocation on the rates decided upon by the Government of India. The unallocated amounts out of the earnings were nobody's money. When queried on this aspect the Ministry officials are reported to have given the answer that the unallocated amounts could be kept in suspense account. It was a strange reply, indeed. Such could not be the intention of any law (that certain money can perpetually be put recurrently in a suspense account). The subscribers on whose behalf the interest was earned were entitled to the earnings and the same should have been allocated to their accounts.

The University after some resistance acquiesced under the weight of the powers that be. It is a pity that there is so much disregard of law in most enlightened places. But as poetic justice would demand the issue is no more quite relevant in view of the rate of interest in financial institutions having been lowered to a great extent. Even with the most prudent investment the return hardly reaches anywhere near 12 % figure. In another related matter the University had to struggle hard in convincing the office of the Provident Fund Commissioner of India that its Fund being treated at par with a 'Government Provident Fund' was exempted from condition of depositing its amounts with their office.

But the same matter regarding the deposit of the amounts of provident fund with the Commissioner's office kept hanging for getting an exemption on a permanent basis. At one stage the commissioner's office went to the extent of issuing distress warrants for extracting the deposits from the University and the colleges. The Commissioner's office insisted on a periodical renewal of the exemptions. As of now there appears to be an interesting situation of thaw.

Taxing Property: Canine Concern

Another matter which the officialdom in the Municipal Corporation brought to a sharp pitch was the demand for property tax from the University and the colleges. What triggered the event is both amusing and painful. It happened sometime in the mid 1980s. Shri Madan Mohan formerly Controller of Examinations of the University had earned a name for himself in running the examinations of the University with marked efficiency. Later on becoming the Registrar of the University he worked hard to bring all round improvement in the administration. As one of the measures to enforce discipline he prohibited the entry of all animals including pet dogs into the University gardens. This directly hit the then Assessor of property tax who lived in Kamla Nagar close by. He used to bring his pet dog along on his morning walks in the University gardens. The officer was highly peeved at a perceived insult. The ban on the entry of a canine in the manicured gardens of the University was to open the gates for the flood of fury from some one dry to depth. He perhaps delved deep into the ocean of arsenal and managed to discover a weapon to hit the University hard. He fired a missile in the form of a distress warrant for attachment of the University bank accounts for default of payment of several Lacs of Rupees as property tax. The University had to run for cover to get a stay order from the Delhi High Court.

In course of time many colleges met the same fate at the hands of the municipal administration. However, judicial intervention gave them some relief. I myself as Principal of Shivaji College tackled this issue by adopting a multi pronged strategy. I made immediate payment of the minor taxes like fire tax and scavenging tax, sought exemption of education cess on the plea of the College itself imparting education and pleaded exemption from payment of general tax in accordance with the circulars issued by the Municipal Corporation from time to time in terms of the exemption rule 15. Ironically I received enough assistance in the matter from non else than the same officer who had fired the first shot in the matter against the University. I happened to meet him in the Chamber of the Chairman of the Standing Committee of the Municipal Corporation where I had gone to take up the case of my College. The Chairman, Shri Deep Chand Sharma was kind to me and instructed the officer to deal with the case of my College sympathetically and not to cause any distress to the College by sending any more distress warrant. The cases kept on hanging in the courts and with an arbitrator in case of the University. I believe with the introduction of the Unit Area Method for determining property tax and more transparent rules of exemption there are no hassles now.

Abortive Ordinance

Ordinance XII of the University provides for the re-employment of distinguished teachers including Principals upto the age of sixty-five years. Whereas almost every teacher got re-employment, Principals in many colleges faced opposition to their getting re-employment. Sometimes they became victims of party politics at the level of governing bodies, especially in the colleges maintained by the Delhi Administration. One of the earliest such cases was that of Shri O.P. Dogra of Rajdhani College. Shri Dogra was known to have affiliation with the Rashtriya Svayamsevak Sangh (RSS). Congressmen nominated by the Government of Delhi dominated the governing body of the College. Convinced that Shri Dogra was being denied re-employment on political considerations the University authorities amended the relevant parts of the Ordinance to the effect that a distinguished teacher, including principal of a college will be treated as re-employed unless denied re-employment with the approval of the Vice-Chancellor. Prima facie it took away the power of the Governing Body to re appoint an employee. Not unexpectedly, therefore the Visitor (the President of India) in exercise of his power under sub section (5) of Section 31 of the Delhi University Act suspended the operation of the Ordinance till he had the opportunity to disallow the same. In the mean time the Ordinance was placed before the University Court which had the power to cancel it. The Court (largely comprising the university community) predictably approved the amendment in the Ordinance. It did not take long for the Visitor to order disallowance of the Ordinance.

Net of NET

The UGC regulation prescribing minimum eligibility conditions for the post of lecturer inter -alia included the clearing of the National Eligibility Test (NET) conducted by the UGC. But Delhi University did not adopt the same in its eligibility conditions. The situation continued for quite sometime and the UGC did not call the University in question. The UGC however, made its stand clear when the matter went to the Delhi High Court in a writ petition filed by one Mr. Raj Singh of MD University Rohtak. Mr. Raj Singh had passed his M.Com Examination from the M.D University in first division with first position in order of merit. He had cleared the NET also. He felt aggrieved on his non-inclusion in the list of candidates called for interview in a certain college in Delhi University and therefore, moved the High Court.

After extensive hearings the High Court gave its verdict declaring that the UGC regulation was mandatory and the University of Delhi was bound to follow the same.

Even at this stage the UGC was ready to consider a via media to accommodate Delhi University's stand if it agreed to call for interview all candidate who had cleared the NET. I was privy to this approach when I happened to broach the issue with the then Chairman of the UGC, Professor Rama Reddy in a meeting on some other matter. I suggested to the V.C. to open discussions with the UGC to deal with the difficulties arising out of the eligibility condition stipulated in the new regulation. Also the Senior Counsel of the University commended such an approach. But the Vice-Chancellor decided to go in appeal before the Supreme Court to have the matter settled finally, one way or the other. The Supreme Court upheld the power of the UGC to issue regulations on the Subject. At the same time it gave helpful explanations relating to the consequences, which would flow from the non-compliance of the UGC regulation by any college or the University, the highlight being the stoppage of grants. The Supreme Court delivered the Judgment on the Special Leave Petition in the first week of September 1994. The Vice-Chancellor had already resigned on 16th August 1994, nine months before the expiry of his tenure.

The UGC had been giving exemptions from the condition of qualifying in the NET to those who held a Ph.D degree or an M. Phil degree on year to year basis after intermittent periods. In this way the UGC policy was proving to be only a hold on operation temporarily. Or was it a crowd control measure in the job market in the university system, not in any way related to the functions of the apex academic body? Or is it the case of a money spinning machine fully justifying its continued relevance for the otherwise cash starved University Grants Commission? It is believed that the six monthly test fetches more than rupees twenty thousand thousands as entrance fee per annum. The latest heard on the subject is that the UGC has decided to exempt from this condition all those who hold a Ph.D. degree or an M. Phil degree earned before certain year. In service candidates wishing to shift to another institution continue to enjoy the benefit of exemption as before. I believe that man power planning and induction be better left to the university system which has diverse parameters across the country. Both authority and accountability should lie there. There is already a committee appointed by the UGC to look into the problems connected with NET and suggest measures to deal with the same. At present the measure is mired in several controversies and differences on its basic concept and method of delivery. The switch over to total objective type test has not been matched with theappropriate follow up action in revising the syllabus accordingly, at least in some subjects.The biggest anomaly is the year to year variation in percentage of marks fixed for threshold of clearing the Test. Let us hope the committee finds early answers to such questions.

Campus of Open Learning

The School of Correspondence Courses and continuing Education was initially set up in 1966 as Directorate of Correspondence Courses as a wing directly under the administration of the University. The teachers were designated as assistant directors. In due course of time the teachers wanted the status of a college for the Directorate and the designations of teachers like lecturer reader etc. for themselves. The University went ahead with the changes as desired and gave the Directorate the status and trappings of a college to be maintained by the University. A separate Ordinance-XX-4 was enacted for the purpose. The speedy and phenomenal growth of numbers –both of teachers and students over the years led to problems of various kinds. Academic content gradually depleted. Even though the School was geared to distance education mode the occasional contact programme was made more intensive as it meant extra income to the teachers and other staff. Expansion programmes were more focused in creating additional facility in terms of building and other infrastructure for holding more and more regular classes round the year in the name of contact programme.

Gradually the School tended to turn into another regular college with unmanageable numbers thronging the place, thus serving more as a rendezvous for different sorts of elements who have hardly any thing to do with studies. The scene further created the related problems of hawkers squatting all over the place on the road in front of the School. The situation was controlled and ably managed by the Principal, Shri Ruddar Datt for a number of years. But things started deteriorating after his retirement. No Principal could be appointed for a number of years on the specious alibi of structural reforms offered by the teachers of the School.. The Acting Principal, though an able and sincere person was continuously destabilised by various elements in the school and outside. The teachers focused on raising new and newer demands to improve their own prospects of promotion. The old theme of setting up a separate faculty of distance education was taken up with renewed vigour during the tenure of Professor Baxi, which however, could be translated into necessary legislation during the term of Professor V.R. Mehta. I had my own views on the matter, which I continued to share with the four Vice-Chancellors I worked with. I would like to mention here my thoughts in the matter.

Open and Shut

Per say I had no objection to innovations in and diversification of courses in the School of Correspondence Courses. I was also not averse to creating a department or a faculty of distance education catering to the subjects dealing with teaching and training or research in academic field of distance education. At no stage such a proposal was formulated or even mooted. The existing teaching staff engaged in the work of delivering the conventional courses through the correspondence mode would not be interested in such an innovation as they would have no academic presence there. Therefore the thrust on their part was on getting the existing conventional subjects (already under the jurisdiction of several existing faculties) clubbed under the jurisdiction of a separate new department and faculty of open learning. Hardly any body among the teachers realised that such a step would result into the paradox of parallel faculties for various courses. For example the subjects like English, Hindi etc. of the B.A. pass course in the School would fall in the jurisdiction of the Faculty of Arts and also the Faculty of Distance Education, a dichotomous situation indeed. Similar would be the situation regarding subjects like History and Political Science etc. in the faculty of Social Sciences and Commerce in the

Faculty of Commerce and Business. Further the concept of Campus of Open Learning has more to do with geographical location of programmes and administrative convenience. The South Campus is serving that purpose without any statutory legislation.

Some amendments to the statutes and ordinances of the University were carried out towards the end of Professor Mehta's tenure. Though I had my disagreement with the measures taken by him I refrained from expressing the same formally after expressing them personally to the Vice-Chancellor for whom I had great regard. He had his own compulsions and responsibilities as head of the University. The Campus of Open Learning along with the Department and Faculty of Distance Education, could not be put into place for want of approval by the Visitor of the Statutes concerned before Professor Mehta demitted office. It is learnt that the approval of the Visitor was later obtained but the University is faced with several problems in the full implementation of the decision. To my mind grave consequences would follow when the implementation takes place. Firstly the employees of the School will be amalgamated with the general pool of the University employees. Their inter se seniority would pose intractable problems. Secondly the teachers already designated or promoted, as Readers of the School would lay their claim for promotion as Professors of the University which privilege they do not enjoy at present. In case the privilege is granted to them it will set a chain reaction leading to a demand for similar treatment given to the teachers of other University maintained colleges.

As of now the latest is that the University first appointed an Officer on special Duty as head of the School. Now finally a Director of the Campus of Open Learning has been appointed. But it is not understood what academic uniqueness has taken place since the new avatara of the School. There are a few more points concerning the Dean of campus of open Learning (DCOL) that need attention. This official has not been given a place among members of the University Court. Further he has not been included in the order of precedence of officials who would officiate in case of a casual vacancy in the office of the Vice-Chancellor etc. As per the existing Statute the Registrar would officiate as Vice-

Chancellor even if the DCOL is holding his office. How can the DCOL take orders from the Registrar who according to the scheme of things in the University must take precedence after the DCOL?

Grade of Readers

Public interest litigation in the Delhi High Court pertaining to the long drawn strike by the Delhi University Teachers' Association during 1982-83 resulted in the introduction of the nomenclature Readers' Grade in place of the well known appropriate name 'Selection Grade'. The promotion scheme introduced in 1983 accordingly provided for the promotion of University lecturers to the post of Reader whereas lecturers in colleges to Lecturer in Reader's Grade. With the introduction of revised pay scales w.e.f.1.1.86 the concept of promotion of college lecturers to the post of Reader was also introduced. However, the selection committee for recommending promotion to the post of Reader in colleges was University based. In practice no teacher cared to apply for promotion as Reader as the procedure was perceived to be not only cumbersome but also a road leading to uncertain destination. More over there were several hundred teachers who had been promoted as Lecturers in Reader's Grade under the 1983 scheme. They raised the question of their being re-designated as Readers. The DUTA under the leadership of Dr. M.M.P. Singh had softened the attitude of Professor Moonis Raza. When his term was about to end he asked me if the University could re-designate the concerned teachers as Readers. I explained to him the then existing provisions, which allowed the recognition of college teachers as Readers through the system of processing a case by a selection committee prescribed for each subject. I suggested that the teachers desirous of having their cases considered could apply for the same. But this system was not acceptable to the teachers. The matter remained where it was.

It was during the tenure of Professor Baxi that the scheme of re-designation of teachers as Readers was put in place after making a suitable provision in the ordinances of the University. Since the number involved in the exercise was rather large the mode of all the eligible candidates together appearing before the respective selection committee was adopted. Wherever Principals insisted on individual interview of a candidate the representatives of DUTA created hurdles. Since the nominee of the Vice-Chancellor was from among his team members the process moved slowly, though steadily. In a time of a year or so several hundred lecturers in the Reader's grade were re-designated as Readers. But the EC made it clear in a resolution that teaching experience, as Reader of this category of teachers shall be counted with effect from 1.1.1986 or the date of eligibility which ever was later. The DUTA demanded that these Readers be recognized as Readers of the University without going through the procedure prescribed under the Statutes, which the University was not ready to concede. However, the Executive Council agreed that such cases of re-designation could be reported to it for record. The Ministry of Human Resource Development had objected to the University giving promotion as Readers to those teachers who did not hold a Ph.D. degree. The University strictly followed the criteria in cases of promotion for future, but old cases were not re-opened.

Service Shock

The Principal of Shivaji College was left with no alternative but to terminate the services of Dr. Mohammad Khan Durrani, a lecturer in Sanskrit before the completion of his period of probation in July 1968. Though there were serious charges of misconduct against him but the same were not brought to bear on the case for the reason of saving the future career of Dr. Durrani. Moreover no inquiry was required for termination of service of a teacher during probation. He approached the then President of India (Dr. Zakir Hussain), the Prime Minister, Mrs. Indira Gandhi and the leader in the opposition, Shri Atal Behari Vajpai (later Prime Minister of India). The College received communications from all the above quarters pleading the case of Dr. Durrani. In his separate representations to these dignitaries Dr. Durrani had laid ample emphasis on the fact of his being a Muslim scholar of Sanskrit with a Ph.D. on the comparative study of the Bhagavad Gita and the Quran. In fact the Secretary to the President, Dr. Nagendra Singh in his letter addressed to the Chairman of the Governing Body, Shri Ram Niwas Mirdha had mentioned that the President had desired that the faults of Dr. Durrani should be overlooked, as he was a Muslim scholar of Sanskrit. However, the College knew better and kept the action already taken against him unaltered.

Dr. Durrani filed a Civil Writ Petition in the Delhi High Court seeking reinstatement by setting aside the termination order which according to him was illegal. The Principal discussed with me the contents of the writ petition in light of a judgement delivered by a single judge bench of the same court in the matter of Shri Chetan Mohan Gupta v/s Deshbandhu College. Both of us were of the view that the case had been decided in favour of the petitioner Chetan Mohan Gupta due to the brilliant pleadings by his lawyer, Shri Roshan Lal Tandon and the failure of the College lawyer to citing the University laws in their true import. The Principal deputed me to meet Shri Tandon and ask him if he could represent the College in the case. I met Shri Tandon and showed to him the copy of the writ petition. His initial response was that of summary dismissal. He mentioned about his winning a case on the same issue pleading for the petitioner only a couple of days ago. Case against Shivaji College also would meet the same fate, he said and added asking why should he take up a case already doomed to fall. But when I mentioned the points lost sight of by the responding lawyer in that particular case he became attentive and heard me patiently. I explained to him all the strong points of the case from the side of the College. Ultimately Shri Tandon agreed to plead the case. In a meeting with the Principal next time the matter was settled appointing Shri Tandon as the lawyer to defend the case of the College in the Delhi High Court.

The petition was heard for the first time by a single judge Bench comprising justice Hardayal Hardy. Taking the innocence of the petitioner for granted justice Hardy started blaming the College and made some very harsh observations against the College. administration, especially the Principal. He wanted to see the face of the Principal, who, as he put it could not tolerate a Muslim teacher in his College. He further observed that the brief was stinking and that he was going to take the College administration to task. This was too much for Mr. Tandon to swallow. He offered to withdraw from pleading the case if his Lordship had already made up his mind as to the merits of the case without hearing the concerned parties. He further raised the technical point of his incompetence in hearing the writ as single judge in view of an earlier single judge bench judgment on the issue. According to him a division bench or full bench should hear the case. Caught unaware in the tracks Justice Hardy retracted from his aggressive posture and sheepishly concurred with the view expressed by Mr. Tandon and ordered accordingly.

On Contract

Attention of the DUTA activists had riveted to the proceedings of the case in the High Court from the very beginning. Shri S.S. Goel a lecturer in Ramjas College who was present on the first days' hearing of the case brought news of cheers for the teachers on the basis of his impression formed of observations made by Justice Hardy at the first hearing. The division bench included among others Justice Deshpande who had given the judgment in the case of Chetan Mohan Gupta v/s Deshbandhu College a few months back. The case assumed high academic dimensions. Shri Roshan Lal Tandon took the Bench to the depths of fundamentals of the law of the land and the Act, Statutes and Ordinances of the University. The true nature of the appointment of teachers in the University and its colleges was sought to be examined in depth.Mr.Tandun submitted that ut was contractual. The status of subordinate legislation in relation to the applicability of article 311 of the Indian constitution in the instant case was sought to be determined.

Devil's Advocate

Every time the case came up for hearing the Principal would take me along for discussing matters with the lawyer the previous evening or so. Quite often I alone would meet the lawyer. As the case progressed, Shri Tandon would aggressively discuss several points with me. I would respond equally strongly with the strength of the knowledge of the University laws. In the process of dealing with inconvenient questions during these sessions of discussions I started feeling let down. One day I kept back myself from the briefings which the Principal alone attended. On being enquired about my absence the Principal divulged what I had been feeling about the attitude of the lawyer towards me. Mr. Tandon had a hearty laugh and told the Principal that he, posing as the devil's advocate had built up the edifice of the case of the College mainly on the strength of the response elicited by putting offensive questions to me. Immediate arrangement was made to bring me to the lawyer's chamber. The Principal apprised me of what had happened. I joined the briefing session and continued to do so several times going solo till the case was won for the College. Aggressive questioning of the lawyer did not irritate me any more. In the process I got to understand the meaning of the word 'Devil's Advocate' quite well.

Case Cash

The day the judgment of the case was to be delivered the Principal was away in Chandigarh. On receiving the information from Shri Tandon the previous evening I reached the Court well in time. The operative part of the judgment was read out in the open court. The writ of Dr. Durrani was dismissed. Shri Tandon congratulated me saying that the victory of the College was solely due to my contributions. I complemented Shri Tandon for his brilliant advocacy of the case. I felt happy over the right choice of advocate. Had he not turned the tables in our favour? After the judgment was delivered he took me to the lawyers' common room making me pay modest tips to his staff on the way. Refreshments were offered my behalf to all present in the common room. I had not taken any receipt for the money spent by me so far. I knew it could not be reimbursed to me. As my purse containing a meagre sum of about two hundred rupees got nearly emptied I made a signal to Shri Tandon indicating my inability to commit any further expenditure. He smiled and said that the ritual was over.

I had traveled to and from the court on my own two-wheeler. The P.A. to the Principal asked me to prepare a fictitious bill of taxi fare both ways and thus recover the mount spent by me. It was not acceptable to me. I dropped the matter there. Next year when I became Bursar of the College, the P.A. wanted to oblige me by offering to prepare a fictitious taxi bill to reimburse the expenditure incurred by me. This time I not only refused the offer but also warned him not to think in terms of such malpractices in financial matters, which I as Bursar was determined to prevent from taking place. Later when I became Principal of the same college I felt happy and proud that I had left no skeletons in my cupboard to haunt me when I sat in the Principal's chair.

As they were

Leaving the detailed analysis of the judgment for a separate exercise I would like to mention here the main features. The judgment was in two parts- part A dealing with the legality of the action taken by the College against Dr. Durrani and part B dealing with the law in its academic import and the necessity to bring in parliamentary legislation to provide statutory security of service for the teachers. Part A related to three issues viz. (i) Was the termination of service of Dr. Durrani in accordance with the rules? (ii) Was there any mala fide on the part of Mr. S.S. Rana, a teacher in the College and the Principal responsible for the termination? (iii) Assuming that the college had erred and had illegally terminated the service of Dr. Durrani, was there provision under the existing laws of the University to reinstate him? Having answered all the three of the above four questions in the negative the Court under Part B proceeded to examine the fourth question. The Court's finding was that the Ordinances of the University providing for the service conditions of teachers came under the category of subordinate legislation and therefore not enforceable by a writ of mandamus. The Court suggested that the service conditions should be made statutory by the enactment of a law by Parliament. As per the law that stood at the time of the judgment the service of teachers was contractual. Reinstatement could not be claimed under the provisions of article 311 of the Indian Constitution. At best damages could be claimed under the civil law for any illegal termination in violation of the terms of the contract.

This conclusion by the court came both as a revelation and a shock to the teaching fraternity. An immediate fall out of the judgement was a campaign launched by DUTA demanding statutory security of service for teachers. But ultimately when the government proposed a suitable amendment in the Delhi University Act in 1975 the DUTA back tracked and opposed the proposed amendment, which formed part of a comprehensive package of amendments in the Act. Discerning minds interpreted the provisions of the proposed statutory security regimen as a facilitating procedure for the dismissal of teachers not necessarily the derelict ones. The bill lapsed and with it ended the demand for statutory security of service. I always held the view that the exiting provisions eminently suited all concerned, the administration as well as the teachers.

Anachronisms in the Act

The Delhi University Act was first enacted in 1922 notified on 1st May of the same year. Under the Act the University was conceived as a residential unitary University. The Act has undergone many changes over the last more than ninety years. Major structural changes were effected through the amendment Act of 1952 in order to bring the University in tune with the spirit of an independent sovereign India. By that time the size of the University had not grown considerably. So the basic structure of the University was left unaltered. Subsequent amendments were made in response to the immediate needs of the University. During my tenure of about twelve years as Dean of Colleges of the University I observed that the provisions of the Act at several places were either anachronistic or contradictory to actual practice in several matters. I on my part had pointed out this situation to my Vice-Chancellors. But as the obsolete provisions still lingering were innocuous it was not considered prudent to open a Pandora's Box. I would like to mention here the context of the desired amendments.

(i) Unitary University

The genesis of the setting up of the University of Delhi can be traced to the deliberations of the Sadler Commission appointed in 1917 to look into the problems faced by the Calcutta University, one of them being its unwieldy size. The Commission found the affiliating model of universities unsatisfactory. One of the major recommendations of the Commission was for setting up of teaching, residential universities on the model of Oxford and Cambridge Universities. At that point of time Delhi had four colleges viz. St. Stephen's College (1881), Hindu College (1899) and Lady Hardinge Medical College for Women (1916) and Ramjas

College (1917) affiliated to the Punjab University. The University of Delhi was established in 1922 as a Unitary, teaching and residential university. Of the above four colleges Lady Hardinge College, for certain reasons continued to be affiliated with the Punjab University, the other three became constituent colleges of the University of Delhi. The partition of India in 1947 brought to Delhi nearly five lakh people. To meet the increasing demand several colleges were opened. To accommodate the new requirements the University Act and statutes were amended. However, the basic feature of a Unitary, Residential and teaching university was left untouched.

Today the University combines all the above original features with the features of an affiliating and examining university.

(ii) Compulsory Residence

The Delhi University Act (section 33) makes it compulsory for all students except those who pursue a course of study by correspondence to be residents in a College or a Hall or under such conditions as may be prescribed by the ordinances. Over the years the situation has reversed. Whereas it is impossible to think of giving residential accommodation to all students the provision still stands for compulsory residence of students in a college. What saves the situation is the authority given to the University in making an Ordinance to take care of the paradox. But to date no such ordinance has been put in place. It is sheer convention that prevails.

(iii) The Chief Rector

As per existing provision of the Delhi University Act (sub section (10 of section 7-B) the Chief Commissioner of Delhi is the Chief Rector of the university. The post has since been renamed as Lieutenant Governor. But no consequential amendment has been made in the Delhi University Act. Further whatever circumstances necessitated the provision originally, at present it looks quite anachronistic without any function having been assigned to it. However , it may be pointed out that in the order of precedence in the procession of the dignitaries at the convocation of the university the Rector finds a suitable place. Equally redundant is the provision in the Act (sub section (2) of section 7-B for appointment of Rectors. In my memory no Rector has been appointed at least in the fifties and later.

(iv) University and Undergraduate Courses

In the early phase of the establishment of the University it was empowered by the Act to run and administer courses at the post graduate level only. The running of undergraduate courses was in the domain of the colleges. Thus when the University wanted to run under graduate courses in highly specialized fields like Anthropology and Geology directly at the University a via media was found to conform to the provision in the Act. The students were first admitted to some colleges (for Anthropology Hansraj College, and for Geology Miranda House) and instructions including practicals were conducted at the respective departments of the University. In 1994 the department of education in the University decided to run B. El Ed. course, directly in the department. .It was pointed out that the B. El Ed being an undergraduate course should be located in the colleges. Ultimately the course was started in a couple of colleges and is doing well. Though, LLB is a bachelor's degree it is enumerated among post graduate courses under Ordinance 2. Hence there is no problem in its being run directly by the University department of Law. Similar is the position regarding the B. Ed programme which again is listed as a postgraduate course. The University, it may be seen has made a distinction between a master's programme and a postgraduate programme.

(v) Dilution to Deletion

Clause (2) of Statute 30 of the Statutes of the University makes it obligatory that the selection committee for appointments of teachers in a college shall include at least the Principal, one of the representatives of the university on the governing body and an expert nominated by the Academic Council. This Provision of the Statute had been taken note of in framing the relevant ordinance. In case of appointment of teachers, the constitution of the committee given in the relevant ordinance provided for the inclusion of the nominee of the Academic Council, namely the Head of the department. Per say the head of the department was just one member of the committee with no special power. In fact if one were to go by the explanation offered in the document on conditions of government grant to colleges, the head of the department was expected to play an advisory role and had no veto power. However, with the growth in number of colleges particularly those sponsored by the Delhi administration and the emergence of eminent persons as heads of various departments brought about a situation in which the scales of power got heavily tilted in favour of the head of the department. In some cases the candidates queued at the office (or residence) of the head of department for getting an appointment in one or the other college. Except in cases where the Principal was equally eminent and powerful the head of department determined the out come of selections. In the case of a selection in a minority college the head of a department insisted that he would attend the selection committee meeting only if a certain candidate was appointed. The college did not give such an assurance and the head of the department did not agree to attend the meeting. Without the head of the department the requirement of quorum could not be met. Disappointed with the attitude of the head of the department the college wrote to the University requesting for a solution of the problem. The University added a proviso whereby the requirement of quorum was complete if either the head of the department or one of the university representatives on the governing body of the college was present. This solved a technical problem but in the process created a paradox of the university department going unrepresented in the selection process.

The University made amends rather soon. Another member was added to the selection committee as nominee of the Academic Council to be appointed by the governing body out of a panel of experts in the subject prepared by the Academic Council, quite a circuitous way to select an expert. Evidently a better drafting of the ordinance was possible. The amended provision was also faulted by a section of the Teachers' Association on the ground that it did not faithfully answer the requirement of the Statute. The situation came about due to the change in the language of the item of the relevant clause in the ordinances concerning the inclusion of the head of the department, who came to be listed as an independent entity and not as a nominee of the Academic Council. During my tenure as Dean of Colleges this aspect remained a hot subject of debate raised by one section of teachers. The University ultimately put the record straight and appropriately amended the relevant provision to literally answer the provision of the Statute. The new administration made drastic changes in the selection committee on the lines suggested by the UGC. A lot of confusion prevailed on the issue for some time at least. I am not sure what is best. One thing is sure, the scales have drastically changed. Finally the Governing Body, the appointing authority has been marginalized in the constitution of the selection committee. The University component now dominates leading to the building of new pressures on the administration. And the latest is the amendment of the provision of the statute itself to conform to the composition of the selection committee prescribed by the UGC.

University Court Unwieldy

With the passage of time the size of the University Court had grown enormously with the phenomenal increase of the ex-Officio members like Professors and Principals. The external members feeling utterly outnumbered by internal members started a campaign for proportionate increase in their category. Probably the underlying reason was the election by the Court of several categories of external members as also four members of the Executive Council. In the current scheme of things the internal members decided the fate of the candidates. The Court at its meeting in 1977 appointed a committee to examine the question of rationalization of the membership of the Court and submit its report. The Committee was reconstituted every time a new Vice-Chancellor took over. There was hardly any progress in the deliberations of the committee as the external members were unilaterally demanding increase in the number in their respective constituencies proportionately in accordance with the original ratio without deeply going into the rationale for a greater participation of the internal members. The stalemate continued and no report had been produced by the committee till I relinquished the post of Dean of Colleges in August 2000. I need to mention that I continued to be one of the members of the committee all through the years. I hope the committee does not survive any more.

The Court, How Supreme

The University Court is listed as one of the Authorities of the University under section18 of the Delhi University Act, which describes it as the supreme authority of the University. The expression "supreme authority" has been taken too literally by many people, especially the external members. So, invariably at all annual meetings some of these members have tended to assert their "supreme" status by virtue of their membership of the University Court. Sometimes attempts would be made to bring in impromptu resolutions to decide upon any policy matter regardless of the jurisdiction of the Court. Therefore it may be worthwhile to examine the jurisdiction and actual powers of the University Court and to see how supreme it really was.

1. The Annual report as also the Annual statement of accounts including the income and expenditure statement are placed before the Court. The court is not empowered to approve or disapprove the same. However, it can pass resolutions with regard to the accounts and the Annual report. The same would be considered by the Executive Council

2. The University Court elects the following:

(i) four persons from among its members, to be members of the Executive Council for a term of three years.

(ii) the Treasurer of the University from a panel of three persons received from the office of the Auditor and Comptroller General of India.

(iii) two persons from among its members to be members of the finance Committee for a period of three years.

(iv) ten persons from among the members of the Alumni Association to the membership of the court for a period of five years.

3. Every Ordinance made by the Executive Council is placed before the Court at the next annual meeting of the Court. The Court has the power to cancel any Ordinance passed by the Executive

council. It is this power of rejecting (by two third majority) which can be counted among the attributes of a "supreme" Body.

4. The statutes can be amended or new statutes can be made by the Executive Council. Prior approval of the Visitor is required before the statute is made effective. The Court has no role in the matter except the privilege of being consulted if the amendment or the new statute concerns with the status, powers or constitution of the Court. It may be noted that in this context the Academic Council has been given a stronger position. Making of Similar statutes concerning the Academic Council requires its prior concurrence. There is vital difference between consultation and concurrence. So the Court could be compared to the monarchy of England or our own Presidency as far as the description "supreme" goes.

5. The Court has the power to review the acts of the Executive Council and the Academic council but not in cases where these Bodies have acted in accordance with the power conferred upon them under the Act, the Statutes or the Ordinances. There is hardly any possibility of a situation arising when the court may be called upon to exercise such power. Further the Court has residual powers otherwise not provided for by the Act, or the statutes. This power is also notional as the Executive Council is free to enact a new Statute to take care of any such lacuna.

6. The Court has been given an adjudicating power to decide on any appeal of an authority or Board against the decision of the Executive Council in making directions for amending or annulling any regulation made by such authority or board.(proviso to sub section 3. of section 32. of the Act.)

7. As per item (x) of Statute 8 the power of the Academic Council to fix the time, mode and conditions of competition for fellowship, scholarships and other prizes is subject to any conditions accepted by the Court. The possibility of any of the situations arising is almost nil in view of the fact that the V.C.is the chairman of the E.C. and has the right to attend meetings of other authorities of the Univesiry any conflict in this behalf can be resolved before it could reach the University Court.

Suspension to Recompense

A large number of university and college teachers, especially in Delhi were interned in prisons during the internal emergency declared in 1975 on various charges. The government of the day feared that if not detained these elements could be threat to national security and law and order. Since these teachers were per force kept away from their normal duties the problem of the payment of their salaries crept up. Some of them applied for whatever leave was due in their account. That also got exhausted soon. The service rules provided in ordinances XI and XII contained no provision to deal with the new situation. The University, after obtaining legal advice, enacted a special temporary ordinance XIII providing for the suspension of college and University teachers detained during the period of emergency. The mechanism came handy in making payment of salaries to the teachers to the admissible limits. However, the ordinance was to automatically expire as soon as the emergency was to end. Since suspension was no punishment in law the measure was taken in good spirit by all concerned. As a bonus the teachers also got entitled to earned leave at the rate of one day for a service period of thirty days with effect from 1975. There was some relief given for the period of previous service rendered by each teacher- One third of the total period of half pay leave accumulated by a teacher was converted into earned leave. This way the unfortunate episode of detention of teachers had a silver lining or some bonus to offer.

Experiences in Selection Committees:

(i) A meeting of the selection committee for recommending candidate for appointment of lecturer in Sanskrit in Sri Aurobindo College was held in July 1975. An influential Delhi politician had reportedly brought pressure on the Chairman of the governing body to ensure the appointment of his sister whom he had managed to get appointed on ad-hoc basis in the same college a few days ago. He also approached the head of the department for help. The head of department was hesitant in view of the prima facie weak case of the candidate as she had .barely 50% marks in the M.A. examination as against many candidates having first class with a Ph.D. degree. But at the same time he did not want to displease the politician by saying no. He was indeed on the horns of a dilemma. To avoid an odd situation for himself he deputed me to represent him in the selection committee, reportedly promising to the politician to speak to me for helping the particular candidate. The head of the department, however, advised that I should go to the meeting with an open mind. With this advice in mind I attended the meeting of the selection committee. The politician's sister did not perform well in the interview. There were several other candidates who had fared well and had good academic record. The Chairman and the Principal suggested that the committee should recommend the name of the sister of the politician. I however, pointed out that it would be doing gross injustice to other candidates and expressed my inability to agree to their suggestion. After prolonged discussion the committee decided not to recommend any name. The post was subsequently re-advertised and selection was made of a suitable candidate.

(ii) It did not take long for the same politician to surface again on the eve of a selection to be made in Vivekanand College. By this time the criteria for calling candidates for interview had been revised. As per revised norms fifteen candidates could be invited for one post. The head of department working under pressure of the politician mentioned above included the name of his sister among the candidates to be called for interview in violation of the latest norms. He also gave a date for holding interviews. Then on the eleventh hour he 'fell ill' and went on four days' leave giving charge of the department to me with the instruction that I should attend the selection committee meeting already fixed. The Principal got to know of this arrangement. She pprehended that I had been brought in to help the sister of the politician. She met me at the residence of a senior educationist whom I held in high esteem and posed her problem to me. I allayed her fears by assuring her that I would be fair and advised her in writing to call the prescribed number of candidates strictly in order of merit. All the candidates, including the sister of the politician, wrongly included in the original list were excluded. Subsequently the selection was made purely on the basis of merit. A feeble attempt on the part of the Principal to project another politically connected candidate for the top slot was aborted by my discreet intervention.

(iii) The politician referred to above was intent as if to do a hat trick in his abortive attempts to get his sister appointed as lecturer. This time (1976) it was in Kalindi College. I was the head of department at the time. I had finalized a list of candidates as per the prevailing norms and sent the list to the Principal. The Principal presumably under pressure from the chairman included the name of the sister of the politician among the candidates called for interview and wrote to me for my concurrence. I wrote back saying that the Principal had the discretion to call any candidate for interview with the approval of the Chairman, but she must have taken into consideration the University norms in this behalf. The Dean of Colleges, Sardar Mohinder Singh instructed the University representative, Professor R. K. Dasgupta to attend the meeting and not to allow the candidate concerned to be interviewed as she had been called for interview in violation of University norms. The Dean of Colleges also spoke to me on the same lines. I assured him that I would handle the issue in the best possible manner and in my own way. It appeared to me that he had spoken to the Principal also. Professor Dasgupta did not attend the meeting, leaving his part of the job to me. As I entered the venue of the meeting the glum faced Principal told me that the chairman was not ready to interview any candidate if the sister of the politician was excluded from the list. As if by reflex action I said that I was there to honour the stand already taken by the chairman. The chairman had not expected such a response from me. Soon we went ahead with the interviews and completed the job in a smooth way. Before other members could give their assessment of the candidates the chairman promptly took the name of the sister of the politician for inclusion at number one position. All other members of the committee disagreed with him. I tried my best to persuade him to go for the best candidate. He was quite frank and said that he personally was in agreement with other members but he was under pressure from certain elements. On his suggestion the meeting was adjourned to be held at the Principal's residence the next day. He promised that he would co-operate with other members and that he only needed time to convince the people who had put pressure on him for selecting a particular candidate. When the committee met the next day the attitude of the chairman was entirely different. He insisted that the other members were free to state their choice he would put his vote of dissent. No amount of pleading with him succeeded in changing his stand and we ended up with a fractured recommendation. The majority recommendation should have been implemented. But the chairman prevailed upon the governing body members to have the recommendations rejected and get the post re-advertised. Before the selection was organized again I had left the department to take over as Principal of Shivaji College. But again the head of the department who succeeded me ensured that the selection was made on the basis of merit.

(iv) Interviews were held for one permanent and one temporary post in the department of political science in Shivaji College soetime in the last week of September 1980. There were three internal candidates-Chandresh Kaushish, Veena Kukreja and VPS Malik. The department's assessment was that having put in the longest and quite satisfactory service in the College Chandresh should be given preference, other things being equal. For reasons best known to him the Chairman, a retired Professor of the University chose to combine with the University nominees, who ignoring the comparatively better performance of Chandresh favoured the appointment of Veena. The teacher in-charge of the department and I expressed our disagreement with the other three members quite firmly. We offered to record our vote of dissent. At this stage the Chairman adjourned the meeting to be held later. After a couple of days I received from the Chairman a notice of the adjourned meeting to be held at the Arts Faculty building in the room of the University representative. I considered it an unusual move on the part of the Chairman. In any case, I did not make it a point of grievance and decided to attend the meeting. All other members were duly informed.

However, the teaching staff of the College, especially of the department of political science was not reconciled with the attitude of the Chairman. The teacher in-charge gave me in writing that the department had reassessed its needs of staff at the start of the second term and that they no more required a permanent post and that filling a temporary post will suffice. I wrote to the Chairman to take into account this revised requirement while making selections. The informal talks before the start of the meeting were cordial. The Chairman perhaps had made a strategy of his own without taking me into confidence. At the very out set he proposed that VPS Malik should be appointed against the temporary post. All the members agreed and this part was over after all members signed the minutes accordingly. Then the head of the department suggested a panel placing Veena at number one and Chandresh at number two for the permanent post. I reminded the Chairman about my letter wherein I had mentioned that the permanent post be not filled in view of the reduced work load. He was not ready to listen to me. The two University nominees went ahead and put on record their panel. Thereafter I recorded my observations made in my letter to the Chairman and further recorded that even if the post were to be filled the panel should have the name of Chandresh at number one. The teacher in-charge recorded her concurrence with my view. The Chairman signed after recording the words 'subject to the remarks of the Principal and the teacher in-charge.' Obviously the Chairman had not understood the implications of his remarks. Technically and on paper he was with me. I took charge of the papers and thanked the members for taking a decision at last. The next morning I issued appointment letter to V.P.S Malik against the temporary vacancy with the written permission of the Chairman. Since there was divided opinion on the second post I offered to place the matter before the governing body in its next meeting. The Chairman concurred.

In the next governing body meeting the chairmen put himself in an embarrassing position by challenging my interpretation of the minutes of the selection committee. I placed the minutes on the table of the meeting and also read them out for the benefit of all members present. The Chairman was completely isolated. One of the members, a very eminent former Professor of the University who agreed with my interpretation asked the Chairman what was his interest in appointing a person when the College could do without one. The matter ended there. The permanent post remained vacant for the time being. In the re-shuffle of governing body personnel the next year, the name of the Chairman did not figure in the list of any of the Colleges. He was reported to have attributed this omission to my influence in the right quarters, which was far from the truth.

(v) Interviews were fixed for filling up a post of lecturer in Hindi in Shivaji College in 1984. MS Sunita Chaudhary, whose name had been forwarded by the previous head of department worked against that post on ad-hoc basis. Shri Bhagwat Singh Bhalla, a seasoned political leader was the Chairman. The head of the department was an old colleague with whom I had long association. He happened to meet me a day before the date of interview outside the office of the Registrar. The interview was to be held the next day. He asked me in an informal way as to what I was going to do the next day. My reply was that how could I say anything in anticipation of the interview. Then in a patronising manner he added that he was not going to appoint Sunita, come what may . I reminded him that it was the prerogative of the selection committee to make selection and not the monopoly of the head of the department and further added that the Principal, not the head of the department issued appointment letters. Then I advised him to come to the selection committee with an open mind. We dispersed to meet the next day in the committee.

After the interviews were over the Chairman asked the head of the department and the second university expert to short list the candidates to be ranked later. In this process both the University nominees included the name of Sunita among the three probable candidates. The Chairman suggested that Sunita be placed at number one. The teacher in-charge and I agreed with him. The head of department insisted that another girl, a daughter of his colleague in the department should be number one and Sunita could be placed at number two. While discussions were on the head of the department committed the indiscretion of taking the Chairman outside the meeting room and insinuating before him regarding my motive in supporting Sunita's case and also a few things about my village connection. Shri Bhalla himself from village background did not relish the insinuations, as he told me later. He clinched the matter by taking votes.

Three members recommended the selection of Sunita. The head of the department and another expert recorded their dissent on the ground that a candidate with only M.Phil degree was selected whereas candidates with Ph.D. degree were available. But the head of department did not mention any such candidate. The majority decision was implemented with the direction of the Chairman. The head of the department complained to the Vice-Chancellor who asked me about the episode when we happened to meet at a function a few days later. I narrated to him the incident in all its details. He felt satisfied with my explanation and the matter ended there. The coincidence of my appointment as OSD Examinations a couple of days later left the same head of department non-plus. He shared his enigma with the then Registrar Shri Madan Mohan.

(vi) A lady teacher, Dr. Geeta Malhotra had been working against a leave vacancy in the department of Botany for a number of years. She was a candidate for a permanent post interview for which were held. Her work was satisfactory and the colleagues in the department had also requested me to help her. She did well in the interview and I thought that the head of department would have no objection in giving her a chance against the permanent vacancy. But for some unknown reasons the Head, with whom I had good personal relations was not ready to agree on her name. Interestingly he had not suggested any alternative name. He only emphasized to consider her for permanent appointment next year. On my repeated pleadings he put forward a strange condition. He said that he would agree to recommend her name but in that case I should be prepared to end my friendship with him . With due apology to my friend I accepted the condition and the lady was unanimously selected for permanent appointment. Every teacher who came to know of my stand congratulated me on my espousal of the cause of a deserving teacher. My response was that I only did my duty. Later one day I happened to meet this friend of mine at a function in the University. I profusely apologised to him for extracting his consent for the selection of the lady at the cost of our friendship. But I was happy and proud of his friendship when he told me that his esteem for me had risen higher after the episode in the selection committee. My principled stand for safeguarding the interest of a teacher even at the stake of his friendship had impressed him all the more as he put it.

Consistent Stand

With the revision of the pay scale of college teachers, w. e f. January 1973, the government had abolished the provision for placement of twenty five percent of permanent lecturers in the selection grade. The cut off date however, was kept as September 1974 when the new pay scales were announced. On taking over as Principal of Shivaji College I got fresh calculations made to ensure that the permissible number of teachers had been placed in the senior scale. Against ninety permanent posts of teachers placement of only twenty two teachers had been made. It was permissible under the rules to count as one any fraction above .5. So it was confirmed that a vacancy was available. As the placement was to be done on the basis of seniority specifically prescribed by the University in this behalf there was no difficulty in identifying the candidate for the purpose. Dr. K.K. Malik happened to be the teacher concerned. I wrote to the Chairman of the Governing Body giving all details including the relevant provisions of rules and sought his permission to send the case of Dr. Malik for approval of the University. The approval was received in course of time.

Again with the permission of the Chairman I placed Dr. Malik in the selection grade. A teacher, who had been staking his claim on untenable grounds to the placement throughout the period Dr. Malik's case was under process, approached the Chairman through another teacher who was an activist of a particular political party. It was imputed that I had not cared for the relevant rules with a motive to help Dr. Malik on consideration of caste. In an attempt to cloud the Chairman's judgment the complainant alleged that I had affiliations with a political party in the opposition at that particular point of time (1977). I learnt later from the Chairman that he dismissed the complaint instantly telling both the teachers that he had full knowledge of all aspects of the case and that the Principal had kept him posted with full information on the subject. Moreover, the University had at its level examined the case before giving approval to the proposal of the College. As regards my political affiliation the Chairman made it clear that he could not be prejudiced against any person on that basis.

Punishment Pruned

Dr. S.C. Bhatia lecturer in English in Atma Ram Sanatan Dharam College New Delhi shot into prominence during the early eighties. The Vice-Chancellor Professor Gurbaksh Singh appointed him first as Director of the newly created Directorate of Adult and continuing Education. After some time the Directorate was converted into a Department and Dr. Bhatia appointed as Head of the Department. He was slated to be the Dean of the Faculty of Social Sciences in due course of time in a system of rotation. He was simultaneously given the assignment of the University's (Press) Information Officer. The public perception was that Dr. Bhatia enjoyed enormous powers due to his proximity to the then Chairperson of the UGC, Mrs. Madhuri Shah. Incidentally Dr Bhatia's wife who taught English at Laxmibai College, Delhi hailed from Gujarat. Mrs. Madhuri Shah herself was a Gujarati. People tend to discover connections in strange ways. Dr. Bhatia though soft spoken came to acquire a reputation for having his own way in his functioning as Head of the Department. His junior colleagues projected themselves as objects of pity by colleagues in other Departments. A mute resentment continued to build up in the recesses of their hearts. Dr. Bhatia enjoyed the support of the next Vice-Chancellor, Professor Moonis Raza in recognition of his commendable work in the Department. An Inquiry into the allegations made by some female members of staff of the Department conducted by a committee constituted of a Professor of Sociology and a Principal of a Womens' college found the allegations baseless.

Dr. Bhatia's victory brought war to his door. The embittered staff members first used the media to build hype against Dr. Bhatia. Then they literally descended on the new Vice-Chancellor, Prof. Upendra Baxi. Madhu Kishwar, editor of Manushi gave the matter an extensive coverage and sought strict action against Dr. Bhatia. Professor Baxi was placed in a very difficult situation. He was a kind person and meant no harm to any colleague. But it was becoming increasingly difficult for him to stage a defence of Dr. Bhatia who had failed to mend his fences. I used my good offices in securing the resignation of Dr. Bhatia as Head of the Department in the hope that he would have lesser pressure to handle. But that was a belated step and did not satisfy his colleagues. They were after his scalp. With persistent pressure they succeeded in getting a fresh Inquiry Committee constituted under the chairmanship of Justice (retired) Wad. The Inquiry Committee indicted Dr. Bhatia and in the process cast aspersions on the previous Inquiry as also on some former functionaries of the University. Most of the findings of the committee were unanimously rejected by the Executive Council. However, the substantial finding against Professor Bhatia was accepted by majority vote.

Professor Baxi had resigned by the time the report of the Inquiry committee could be fully considered by the Executive Council. It fell to the lot of the P.V.C. Professor A.L. Nagar to deal with the matter. Luckily the issue was settled in the very first meeting he presided over as Acting Vice-Chancellor. The only issue that needed to be debated was regarding the quantum of punishment. The majority of the members had proposed dismissal whereas some members joined me in modifying the punishment to reduction in rank from Professor to Reader. The argument was adduced by some members that Ordinance XI dealing with the matter did not provide for punishment other than dismissal/ termination of service. The argument on the other side advanced by the Visitor's nominee, Dr. Padmanabhan was that an Authority empowered to impose a higher penalty was within its legitimate right to award a lower penalty. This view was strongly supported by several members who had earlier stood for the penalty of dismissal. Shri Sudhanshu Mittal, an elected member played crucial role in this change of stance. After some discussion the Council unanimously decided to award the lower punishment of reduction in rank from Professor to Reader without any reduction in salary. The decision brought no financial disadvantage to Dr. Bhatia. However, he suffered in terms of personal prestige. The second best happened for him.

I had known Professor Bhatia for a short time only, neither was he a personal friend. One image of his that dominated all other impressions about him in my mind was his devoted service to his wife who was in her advanced stage of pregnancy during their journey in the train from Delhi to Poona. It was June of the year

1978. I was traveling with my family in the same compartment of the train. It was heartening to see him getting down almost at each station and arranging a slab of ice to be placed near his wife to give her some comfort in the scorching heat in the compartment. We were nor known to each other at that time.

Kashmiri Cause

Militancy engulfed Kashmir Valley in 1989. It peaked in a year's time. Normal life was disturbed. The militants targeted educational institutions. Terrorist attacks on the Pandit community continuing for quite sometime forced them to leave the Valley. Delhi attracted a large number of Kashmiri Pandits. Their children had to leave their studies mid session. Many of them could not even collect their certificates from the educational institutions attended by them for future reference. The government of India put in place several measures to ameliorate the sufferings of the hapless community. The problem of admissions of their wards was referred to the University for finding some solution. The Vice-Chancellor, Professor Baxi appointed a committee headed by me to look into the matter and make recommendations for the consideration of the Academic Council. The committee recommended enactment of an interim Ordinance regulating the admission and results of the displaced Kashmiri students. The proposed Ordinance had very radical and unconventional provisions. In my presentation of the recommendations in the first instance I had only explained the technical part.

The debate in the initial stages appeared to go a different way, contrary to what had been recommended by the committee. Apprehending that the proposal might fall I stood up to plead for the acceptance of the recommendations. I made a highly emotional speech referring briefly to the intricacy of the Kashmir problem and the Indian psyche on the issue. I appealed to the members to see the issue beyond mere technicalities and reminded them how the University system had risen to the occasion at the time of partition of India. The Kashmir problem, as it had developed over more than forty years could not be solved by the armed forces alone I stated. As I had visited the Valley only the previous year I was able to give a graphic picture of the plight of the general public, especially the members of the Pandit community. One or two more helpful interventions and summing up by the Vice-Chancellor had a salutary effect. The house was metamorphed. The proposed Ordinance was passed unanimously. Apart from facilitating admissions of wards of the displaced persons the Ordinance contained provisions by which a student's eligibility was determined on the basis of third year result of Delhi University examination alone or in combination with the results of either or both of the results of first and second year examination of the Kashmir University. Even after the expiry of the special Ordinance the University continued to make special arrangements for admission of the wards of the Kashmiri migrants to different colleges for a number of years.

Admissions to professional courses in Medicine and Engineering were differently dealt with giving some relief to the affected students.

Ambedkar Center

Ambedkar Center for Biomedical research (ACBR) conceived by Dr. Ramesh Chandra, a dynamic teacher working as Reader in the Chemistry department of the University. The Center was put on paper during the tenure of Vice-Chancellor Upendra Baxi. The then Prime Minister Chandra Shekhar laid the foundation stone in a small courtyard in the vicinity of the Chemistry department. Dr. Ramesh Chandra became its de facto Director (the post was created subsequently and approved by the UGC). The Center got the premises vacated by the University Instrumentation Center, which moved to its spacious new building. It started functioning during the tenure of Vice-Chancellor V.R. Mehta. Dr. Ramesh Chandra rose to the position of Professor in the Chemistry department. He performed the duties of the Director of the Center as an additional charge. Professor Gurbax Singh, the former Vice-Chancellor of the University was the first chairman of the governing Body of the Center. After his death the then Governor of West Bengal Professor Kidwai held the responsibility.

After some time Professor Ramesh Chandra was appointed Vice-Chancellor of Bundelkhand University. He wanted to retain the charge of the Center while keeping his lien on the post of professor. The Vice-Chancellor asked for my opinion in the matter. I was of the view that Professor Ramesh Chandra was performing the duties of the Director of the Center as a professor of the University. Since he would be on leave and lien from that post possibly he was not entitled to hold the additional charge of Director. My logic was 'if the root goes the stem does not survive'. However, Professor Ramesh Chandra continued to have direct control of the Center by names like 'founder Director' during his tenure as Vice-Chancellor of Bundelkhand University, though there was a teacher on deputation who was designated as Acting Director.

In 2005 Professor Ramesh Chandra had to leave Bundelkhand University mid term after the Chancellor summarily removed him from his post. I had happened to visit Bundelkhand University in 2004 to conduct a viva-voce examination of a candidate for the Ph.D. degree. I was amazed to see the development work done by Professor Ramesh Chandra-both in terms of creating infrastructure and ensuring academic expansion at an exceptionally fast pace. I do not know what led to his dismissal. But I am sure of one thing. Professor Chandra thrived in controversies. He combined in himself the extremes of politeness and abrasiveness, to be doled out selectively though. I never suspected him of indulging in defalcation of money. No doubt he had contempt for financial procedures, which in his opinion were hindrance to development. To me personally he was always courteous. I regret his having landed himself in the unfortunate situation He was back in the University and I thought he must have got wiser by the unfortunate episode at Jhansi.There were some hassles before he was allowed to rejoin his post of Professor in Delhi University. He was not given the responsibility of the Director of the Center. Dr.(Mrs.) Daman Saluja, a senior teacher at the center was given the charge to carry out the functions of the Director. But controversies pursued the Professor like his own shadow. Before he could vindicate his position regarding his role in Bundelkhand University through a Court intervention, he was placed under suspension by the University of Delhi for an alleged misdemeanor. Finally he is back in the Department of Chemistry through a verdict of the Supreme Court.

Haggling for Hegemony

Intrigued by the hegemony of certain individuals in getting elected to the Academic Council and the Executive Council the elected teachers brought an impromptu resolution in the Academic Council restricting the membership of elected members to two terms. The administration headed by the Vice-Chancellor Professor Gurbaksh Singh lapped it up as a fortuous opportunity. The resolution was passed unanimously. Later a similar resolution was passed by the Executive Council. Soon suitable amendments were made in the relevant Statutes Thus ended the hegemony of a couple of individuals who managed to get elected to the respective Councils term after term and became some centers of power browbeating the administration on different issues. The measure resulted in opening the avenues for the entry of fresh blood in the forums of academic and administrative decision making. In subsequent years attempts made for a review of the decision did not succeed for lack of support among the teaching community and due to the firmness of the successive administrations. One must however, admire the tenacity of one affected individual who found alternative route to occupy membership of the second Council and another University forum on being rendered ineligible for one council, though after a lapse of several years on his final retirement from service. But his personalized style of functioning and policy of running with the hare and hunting with the hounds rendered his participation unconstructive and ineffective. I don't regret having helped him in receiving favours from the University during my tenure as Dean of Colleges as my sins have been amply atoned by my receiving from him brickbats after my retirement while he remained member of the decision making body of the University. The happy thing is that he did not succeed in doing damage to my image in the University.

I would like to mention that what had been achieved by the above referred amendment would have been frittered away but for a timely action on a discrepancy that had crept in the concerned statute at the time of incorporating an amendment in some other context. I had noticed the same coincidently and immediately brought it to the notice of the university administration.

Grants and Grace

(i) The Delhi University committee headed by the Pro-Vice-chancellor Professor A.L. Nagar was to appear before the review Committee of the UGC for presentation of the proposals for grant during the ensuing five year plan. Professor Neelamegham, the Dean Planning had thoroughly prepared the proposals and rehearsed the power point presentation with members of the University committee. I was also a member of the Committee along with eminent professors like Andre Betei and Mohan Ram. As soon as Professor Neelamegham started the presentation, the chairman of the UGC committee, a retired Vice-Chancellor of Punjab University got impatient and made certain remarks uncharitable to the Delhi University. Professor Neelamegham and other members of the committee kept their cool and adjusted the presentation as the chairman thought fit and gave necessary clarifications where required. The irritation of the chairman was uncalled for. But he crossed all limits of propriety when the Pro-Vice-chancellor was explaining the need of funds for setting up a transformer for supply of electricity at the South Campus.The chairman got agitated and made a snubbing remark that it was not the job of the UGC to supply electricity and that we better approach the Electricity Board for the purpose. At this stage thumping the desk I stood up and protested against the treatment he was giving to our Pro-Vice-Chancellor and other members of the committee. I explained that our proposal was for funds for the purpose of setting up a transformer for proper supply of electricity and that we were not asking the UGC committee to give us an electricity connection. The chairman regretted his remarks and requested Professor Nagar to resume his presentation. Rest of the proceedings went off very cordially with the chairman listening to us patiently. I rose again and very politely dispelled the fallacies about Delhi University expressed by the chairman earlier. All the exercise of the presentation not withstanding the UGC committee spelt out a certain predetermined amount as grant for the plan period. An interesting sidelight of the exercise was that Prof. V.R. Mehta, a member of the UGC committee on the occasion became the next Vice-Chancellor of Delhi University. This being in the knowledge of the chairman a certain amount of grace was expected of him.

(ii) Wiser by the above episode I played a crucial role as a member of similar UGC committees in the years to come in the institutions getting their due. A few instances come to my mind.

(a) The UGC Review committee for northern region was in session for three days at Gaziabad in connection with the allocation of development grants for the ninth plan period. Hundreds of colleges from western Uttar Pradesh turned up to present their cases. Many of the colleges had no clue of how to supply the required information and to formulate their proposals. The chairman in his interaction with them was quite harsh to them and at one point had gone to the length of humiliating a couple of Principals. The Secretary of education of Uttar Pradesh was a mute spectator of the goings on but appeared to be visibly upset. The Joint Secretary of UGC was equally concerned over the uncalled for remarks of the chairman but kept quite in deference to the seniority of the latter. I thought it fit to intervene at that stage. I pointed out to the chairman that he alone was taking a stance to which the other members may not agree. Therefore he should give chance to other members to have their say. I also pointed out that it was also the function of the committee to help the colleges to put their cases properly and enable them to take advantage of the UGC scheme of grants. The chairman got mellowed by my intervention. Soon lunch was called. The chairman excused himself from better part of the proceedings in the afternoon as he was to visit some relative in New Delhi. The rest of the members conducted the proceedings in a cordial atmosphere and disposed off a good number of cases by lending a helping hand where ever needed. We reported the progress and the methodology adopted to the chairman on his joining us towards the evening. He felt quite relaxed and him self maintained the same tempo during the next two days. The Joint secretary of UGC was relieved that her assignment was completed reasonably well. The Secretary education of UP was happy that a good number of colleges would receive development grants-many of them for the first time.

(b) My experience as a member of the UGC committee at Benaras Hindu University, Varanasi was pleasant and quite satisfying. The committee had gone there to determine the grants for colleges of eastern Uttar Pradesh. The committee reached

Varanasi after facing a small hassle at the airport. The luggage of the Joint Secretary had been loaded in the flight for Bhuvaneshvara by some mistake on the part of the airport staff at Delhi. The V.C.of BHU, Dr. Simhadri and Dr. Mandan Mishra, V.C of Sanskrit University had reached by the same flight. Both of them intervened and got a handsome allowance for the Joint Secretary to enable her to be ready for her work from the next day. It was a bonus for her as her luggage was also retrieved and handed over to her before the end of her stay at Varanasi. Guarded by armed police BHU gave the look of a fort. The compound of the VC's house was protected with a wire net to obviate chances of any miscreant forcing his way in. I was highly impressed by his polite but firm refusal for a favour sought by an influential politician in a telephonic conversation. The conversation had gone on for quite some time but the V.C. did not relent nor was his patience exhausted. The committee was escorted to the venue of the meeting under heavy police protection on each of the three days. The proceedings, however, went off smoothly. The members of the committee formed three sub groups and did a thorough job of the work assigned to it. The UGC scheme of disbursing development g rants in a face to face interaction appeared to me to be the ideal one.

(c) During the UGC committee's visit to the Baba Sahib Ambedkar University at Aurangabad and the Barkatullah University at Bhopal I witnessed an interesting phenomenon. Where as the conventional departments were generally on their way of decline the self financing departments and courses run by them were doing fine. The teaching faculty for these departments was hired on contractual basis largely from among students who had done their post graduation from the same place a while ago. This amounted to exploitation of their own product but such staff-mostly females did not appear to have any grudge. Perhaps they had realized that their entry in the departments had taken place without any competition and that the hope of regular appointment was kept alive. The core staff in most cases was drawn from the conventional departments. Evidently this component was highly motivated and made a success of the experiment.

I was also highly impressed by the 'earn while you learn' programme of the university at Aurangabad. The University had vast fertile lands harnessed for productive use with participation of students who received appropriate remuneration commensurate with their share of the work. There were workshops for cottage industry products on similar lines. It is Needless to say that the university had in some measure translated the ideas of Gandhi ji. At Bhopal the then Chief Minister Shri Digvijay Singh took personal trouble to interact with the UGC team at a dinner organized by him. The then Governor of the state Dr. Bhai Mahavir with whom I had long association as colleague in Delhi University invited the committee members for tea at the Raj Bhavan. During discussions he emphasized on the need for central funds for the universities of the state.

(d) I got to learn a lot about the working of institutions and universities across the country during the visits of different committees of the UGC on different occasions. Rohilkhand University Bareilly had college like the Bareilly College which in size matched some universities in the country. Indore University had colleges most of which were managed by very rich private trusts, especially those of the Gujarati trading community. At Nalanda the Buddhist Institution, a deemed university was the venue for inter-action for grants for the tenth plan period with colleges for eastern UP. I was highly impressed with the state of the art library of the Buddhist Institute at Nalanda. The electronic section was indeed well stocked and well maintained. I had also opportunities of meeting some very distinguished academicians from different parts of India who joined the UGC committees.

Adjourned Admission

A teacher from Shivaji College came to my office in the University one day He was feeling a little odd because as I later came to know he had initially hesitated to approach me for the required help. I could well understand his dilemma in approaching me, his former Principal of whom he had been a constant critic. He came with the complaint that the Delhi College of Engineering had cancelled the admission of his son on his being absent consecutively for the first seven days of the starting of the classes in accordance with some college norm. I later discovered that the practice had been introduced under pressure of the candidates on the waiting list. I immediately got in touch with the college Principal. He told me that the college had made the norm in order to discourage students who continued to scout for better pastures elsewhere without withdrawing their admission in Delhi College of Engineering.

I pointed out that the relevant Ordinance concerning attendance requirement did not stipulate compulsory attendance during the first seven days of the starting of the course. I further pointed out that the college practice was not maintainable under legal scrutiny. The Principal agreed with me and promised to do the needful. The teacher felt quite relieved of his worry. Before leaving he suggested that that the University should have a system to take care of grievances like the one he had. To this I replied saying that the relief he had got in his case is under a system and that the University administration functioned as a unit. If any body feels disappointed he should at least meet the Dean of Colleges before finally giving up. The teacher agreed with me and confessed that he had reached me as the last resort after being advised by a staff member who was witness to his frustration and helplessness. I assured him of my positive attitude in all circumstances and told him to trust me for any help in future too. He had never been disrespectful to me in the past but turned affectionate to me after the above episode. I equally reciprocate his sentiment.

University of Diversity

Delhi University has more than three lakh students, nearly eight thousand teachers and an equal number of non-teaching staff in over eighty odd colleges, and nearly ninety departments, is largely confined to the urban areas of the National Capital Territory, Delhi. What started as a measure for the de-congestion of the Calcutta University following Sadler Commission recommendations in the form of a small University catering to the needs of the then imperial capital population has grown into a favourite destination for students from all parts of India and abroad. It is a national institution in the true sense of the word. Its educational standards and excellence in extra curricular activities and sports has earned for it a high niche on the educational pedestal. The courses range from the time tested B.A (Hons) to the latest in the field of Bio-medical Science. It has colleges which rank among the top ten in the country, and at the same time it has continued to be plagued by one or the other sick college over the years. The diversity in college managements makes it a true replica of India. IT has colleges run by religious minorities, private trusts, the Delhi government, the central government and last but not the least by the University itself.

The University has a strong teachers' organization (DUTA) which has been on the fore front for fighting for the cause of the teachers of not only the University but also of the country as a whole. But the teachers have always risen to the occasion when it came to maintaining the academic calendar, timely holding of the examinations and declaration of results. Admissions to all professional and a few other prestigious courses are made through central entrance tests conducted by the University and in some cases by the concerned colleges themselves under the guide lines approved by the University. Where there are no entrance tests, admissions are made on the basis of merit determined on criteria decided upon in accordance with the guidelines set out by the University and as per a centrally prescribed schedule. St. Stephen's College has its own modalities including a component of interview for selection of candidates. The College had to slog it out in the court to retain its right to interview the candidates for admission. The court allowed weightage to interview up to a quantum of 15 % of the marks. Though the tuition fee and development funds are uniform for all the colleges, the other charges differ widely.

By and large the colleges on the campus are leading ones. There is already an informal ranking arrived at by students' preferences for admissions. There are off campus colleges like Lady Shri Ram and Sri Venkateshvara, which are favourite of the students. Jesus and Marry College, Gargi College and Kamla Nehru College, located as they are in posh south Delhi areas, are making rapid strides in stealing a march over many other colleges of their age. The middle level colleges like Rajdhani, Shivaji, SPM, JDM (the acronym remained intact even after replacing 'Mahavidyalaya' with

'College' and adding 'Memorial' at the end). Some reverse sanskritisation this!); , ARSD and PGDAV generally converge on the Ring Road and have maintained a steady position. Dayal Singh College has successfully overcome disadvantages hogging it in its early days. The rural areas are being well served by SSN College, Bhagini (added later) Nivedita College and Aditi Mahavidyalaya. The two Colleges of Applied Sciences in East and west Delhi respectively, though small in age and size have already justified their existence, both poised to take quantum l;eap in their new state of the art prem ises. Vivekanand College (hving dropped the nomenclature Mahila (as if flexing its muscles) has withstood the disadvantage of location in east Delhi and has acquired a name for itself for high standards in undergraduate education. B. R Ambedkar also managed to transcend its geographical location in the east in a short time with the untiring efforts of its founding Principal P.C. Patanjali. The College of Business Studies has emerged as an example of small is beautiful. Sri Aurobindo College has to work hard to realize the potential of location in a posh south Delhi area. The College of Sports Science is doing good work in spite of limitations of space for play grounds. The professional colleges in engineering, medicine, pharmacy, nursing and fine arts enjoy high reputation.

Women s' colleges are generally well managed and have a better academic environment. Till a few years ago Women Principals were unknown to co-educational colleges. However, the male bastion has fallen and there are ladies Principals of several such colleges. The number of women among teachers in these colleges is going up year after year. The facility of Metro Rail has been providential. It has saved the University community from the chaos of collapsing bus transport system. The Metro manners and passenger behaviour norm have not left the students untouched. The stories of daily brawls in buses are stories of the past, more or less. At the same time the Cycle Riksha infested Campus has started looking not only drab but also a cramped place. Swarms of students, walking along the Chhatra Marg almost the whole day is history now.

Teachers All

Ever since the creation of the University Grants Commission the pay scales of teachers in Universities and colleges have continued to improve. In 1961 the ancillary but important cadres of director of physical education and college librarian were given grades equivalent to those for lecturers i.e. Rs.400-800. There was widespread appreciation of the decision. But it did not take long for the library staff to feel left out when they were denied the marginal improvement in the pay scale to make it Rs. 400-950 for lecturers. Failing to get any reddressal they moved the court. The matter dragged on and so did the representations and agitations. Inspired by the perception that their lot would improve only if they were designated as teachers they agitated to achieve the same.DUTA had enrolled them as members for their votes. Some of them made it to the executive committee of DUTA. But they were left out in the elections to the Academic Council and Executive Committee of the University. When I joined Professor Moonis Raza's team as Dean of Colleges I was asked to negotiate with the agitating library staff. It did not take long for me to reach an agreement on giving them parity with teachers rather than changing their designations. Their seniority was clubbed with teachers for the purpose of Study leave, allotment of houses and grants for attending conferences. Suitable amendments were made in the relevant Statutes for giving them representation in the A.C. and E.C.by bunching them with teachers, their designation staying unaltered. The arrangement proved successful and we saw several members of these cadres making it to the A.C .It was hoped that the old itch of getting oneself designated as teacher was cured.

The calm on the front of the library staff turned out to be short lived. Some time during the earlier part of Professor Mehta's tenure the junior library staff led by some ambitious and well qualified Professional Assistants (P A) launched an agitation putting forward a wide gamut of demands including the already settled issue of recognition as teachers, But the entirely new demand was to fill the post of Professional Junior(P J) by promotion from amongst Professional Assistants. There was a paradox in the demands. On the one hand the demand was for teachers' designation which could be at par with lecturer and on the other there was demand for declaring the same as a promotion pos, knowing full well that lecturer's post was not a promotion post. It was not difficult to fathom the reasons. Tshe junior (P A s) aspired to move a ladder up and then get bracketed with teachers to become entitled to benefits in future hitherto not extended in the case of non teaching staff i.g. age of retirement. Fortuitously for the administration the Supreme Court had given its verdict in the writ petition filed by library staff a number of years back that librarians were not entitled to the designation or service conditions including emoluments as given to teachers. A copy of the judgement was procured for the V.C.'s perusal. He firmed up his stand and rejected the demands. The agitation petered out in a couple of days.

Zero Sum

On the basis of the recommendations of the committee headed by Professor Kandaswami, of which iwas also a member the UGC revised the strength of non teaching staff in Delhi colleges receiving grants from it. Along with upward revision of staff strength in various cadres a new post of Administrative Officer in the pay scale admissible to Assistant Registrar was sanctioned with the rider that the minimum qualification for the post shall be a Master's degree in any subject and that it shall be filled up through open advertisement .Further it was to be granted in colleges where student strength exceeded one thousand. I had personally pushed for the creation of this post in the hope that a qualified senior functionary in the non-teaching staff will assist the Principal in taking care of the ever increasing administrative work in colleges where almost 100% internal promotion norms had rendered competence a rare commodity. But this remained only a fond hope as subsequent developments proved. Initially the non- teaching staff at different colleges took a dim view of the open post. There was hardly any senior functionary among them in any college to compete for the same. So the karamchari unions worked concertedly to get the eligibility diluted systematically and the norms of filling up of the post to suit rthe internal candidates even while maintaining the semblance of open advertisement. With the passage of time the post has relapsed virtually to a promotion post, a zero sum without any addition of value.

Right not Wrong

Ordinance XVIII of the Ordinances of the University provides for governance of colleges other than those maintained by the Government (and also those maintained by the University as they have each a separate ordinance for the purpose).Several matters provided for in Ordinance XVIII considered to be applicable also to colleges maintained by the University were listed in Ordinance XVIII-B. The procedure regarding the appointment of principal was not included in the above said list (as there was a self contained provision for the same in the respective ordinance of such colleges). But it is known that the University followed some parts of the ordinance applicable in its case and also went ahead to a part of the procedure provided in Ordinance XVIII reportedly to wade off some perceived wrong doing on the part of the chairman of the governing body of the college. No eye brows were raised on the issue as the person appointed was known to be most competent and deserving. The right choice had been made. Right could not be wrong, perhaps.

Vice Dropped

With the closure of Punjab University Camp College in Delhi two developments took place, first was the opening of Dayal Singh College as a Delhi University affiliated college, and the second was the opening of evening classes as independent units in some colleges with a Vice-Principal in-charge to look after the work of the unit under the over all supervision of the Principal.

Accepting to the recommendations of the committee chaired by me the University re-designated the post as Additional Principal with a pay scale higher than that of Vice-Principal and lower than that of the Principal.. The UGC was accordingly informed and an understanding was reached to implement the decision. .Justice was not fully done to the incumbents, but there was progress. Things moved on. The matter regarding raising the pay scale of the incumbents to be at par with that for Principals was again taken up during the tenure of Professor Mehta. On his directions I took up the matter with Mr.. Mukhopadhyaya, Additional Secretary, in-charge higher education. He patiently heard the matter and assured me that if the University could show that the Evening Classes were independent units in all respects he would take a sympathetic view in deciding the case. The University promptly replied supplying the required information. It did not take long for the Ministry to convey its concurrence to the proposal of the University. There was great sense of relief among the concerned persons. I had the satisfaction of acting mid-wife in delivery of a sort where gestation period had extended to rather long years.

College Course

The University had appointed a committee in 1973 with Professor U.N, Singh as chairman to consider the proposal of the Director South Campus, Professor Amrik Singh for enrolling students in post graduate courses in some more colleges to add to the viability of the Campus. The head of the department of Sanskrit deputed me to attend the meeting .Initially most of those present did not favour the proposal. Taking my turn pleaded for a positive consideration of the issue. I submitted that introduction of post graduate classes, though only formal, in the upcoming colleges of south Delhi would serve as a catalytic for improving their academic health at almost no cost to them. The book grants received from the UGC would enrich their libraries. I also emphasized that the expanding opportunities, this would be made available to college teachers in the co-operative system of teaching would enthuse them for academic upgradation leading to some kind of ripple effect. My fervent appeal did not fall on deaf years. There were more supporters of the proposal now. Even the doubting Thomas had relented.

The discussion did not prolong any more. The chairman summed up the discussion and ruled that the committee favoured the introduction of post graduate courses in as many colleges as the concerned departments thought fit. Professor U.N. Singh, who himself had revised his opinion in the matter during the discussions profusely complemented me for my stout stand supporting colleges. Moving out of the meeting hall, with his right hand placed across my shoulders, he observed that no better advocacy of the case of colleges could have come from the quarters of some body working in a department. Upon this I offered the explanation that before joining the department of Sanskrit as reader I had served as a college teacher for over fifteen years. Then on he kept a kind eye on me and always encouraged me for doing good work.

Turf Talk

Ordinance XV-B clearly spells out the authorities responsible for maintenance of discipline among students of the University. In general as per clause 1., all powers relating to discipline and disciplinary action are vested in the Vice-Chancellor, clause 5.inter alia states that the Principals of the colleges shall have the authority to exercise all such disciplinary powers over students in their respective colleges. According to clause 2.The Vice-Chancellor may delegate all or such powers to the Proctor as he deems necessary.

A certain year the Proctor landed at Hans Raj College and started handling a case of some students, led by the secretary of the Delhi University Students' Union. sitting on Dharna. They demanded action against a teacher amid allegations of sexual harassment of a couple of students even as the acting Principal, Shri J. P. Vidyalankar was seized of the matter. The acting Principal, feeling annoyed talked to me on phone and asked for my advice. .I suggested that the Proctor be informed that the the College was looking into the matter and the University would be informed after appropriate action had been taken. Showing impatience the Proctor approached the Vice-Chancellor for intervention. The V.C. instead asked me for my advice. My view was that the Proctor at that stage had walked on the acting actin Principal's turf and that if after the action taken by the College was found not to the satisfaction of the V.C., he had the power to act under clause 1. The V.C. agreed with me and advised the Proctor to hold his horses. The acting Principal of course, settled the matter efficiently and justly in no time.

Leave Relief

Till the late eighties there was no provision in the rules of Delhi University lo deal with the question whether teachers of the

University elected//nominated to Parliament or state legislatures could continuė doing both the assignments without taking leave from their parent post. Professor V.P. Dutt on being nominated as ember of the Rajya Sabha continued to function as Pro-Vice-Chancellor. Earlier Dr. Vijay Kumar Malhotra had proceeded on leave to function as Chief Executive Councillor of Delhi, .Professor C.P. Thakur of the Management Studies chose not to proceed on leave when elected to the Rajya Sabha whereas Dr. Ratnakar Pandey, Principal of Moti Lal Nehru College on becoming member of the same house preferred to take leave from the College. Taking note of the phenomena in Delhi University and elsewhere the University Grants Commission put in place a regime of comprehensive rules regarding the issue. Now teachers nominated/ elected to the legislative bodies were to compulsorily proceed on leave which would be for the entire period of their membership of such bodies and the leave period would count as authorised service for the purpose of annual increments and pension etc. Dr. O.P. Kohli of Deshbandhu College on becoming member of the Rajya Sabha proceeded on leave but some time after taking advice from me chose voluntary retirement with pension.

The diarchy regime did leave some amusing and not so amusing situations.Professor V.P.Dutt could not imagine that the sticklers for rules would emerge to point out that he had committed a kind of theft by ordering a cartload of garden manure for his official house allotted to him as Rajya Sabha member. Had he lived in the University house his garden would have been maintained free of charge (he perhaps had thought!). Dr. Pandey put himself to an avoidable embarrassment by joining his position as Principal after the UGC regime on compulsorily proceeding on leave had been implemented, even while he continued to be member of the Rajya Sabha. He perhaps did it simply to serve as a cog in the succession plan for Officiating Principal during his absence on leave.

Epilogue

If I live on I would be 80 years old on 2nd April 2016 as per official records. However, I crossed this stage on 16 August 2015, the actual date of my birth. This is a sufficiently long span to have been lived irrespective of any quality that I might have been able to bring into it by my own exertions. Personally, I would like to attribute the good things happening in my life to the hand of God and to the heaps of humaneness and kindness showered upon me by a multitude of humans, both men and women at times when I needed these most. At certain times I did, indeed, feel overwhelmed at the turn of events as they did. But it does not mean that I simply remained a complacent, pampered or favourite child of fortune or that I failed to learn lessons from the tide of time or that I ever lost sight of the ground on which I essentially stood or that I, at any time, became oblivious of the common belief that there was no alternative to hard work and sincerity of purpose for success in life.

Without trying to enter the domain of philosophy or spirituality I would like to say that a good turn is sure to revisit on one or the other day in this very life. It is a different matter that one may miss to notice it when it comes. Several things and happenings in our lives are likely to remain unexplained and not understood fully. It has happened to me several times in my life. I believe that prayer has not only its sound value, but has also proved to be a sound medium of achieving calmness, so very essential for attaining balance in our thoughts and deeds. I do not remember to have ever forgotten to pray, formally or informally, aloud or in silence. In other words prayer is a user friendly device.

Ever since my student days, when I read the edicts of king Ashoka for the first time, I have been fully convinced of, and have been following, the adage postulated by that great monarch of ancient times, that administration is best done when it guarantees accessibility and availability to people. As a teacher I taught these principles to my students and followed them in my working as an administrator with a reasonable degree of success and satisfaction. And I have no amount of hesitation in commending the same to the younger generations.

I always wondered at the philosophical formulation of Shankaracharya- *Brahma satyam jagat mithya*- Brahma alone is true, the phenomenal universe is unreal (made up). It dawned on me very late in life that all made up things can be unmade and reduced to atoms by one or the other process. Shankara's formulation became clear when the scientific fact that every thing in this universe is constituted of atoms was found explained in Bill Bryson's book *A Short History of Nearly Every thing*. Similarly the import of *gnanam anantam Brahma* bared it self to me in the light of the narration of Bryson regarding the evolution of the universe as discovered by the galaxy of researchers in the world of Science.

The common belief that a good turn or good work done by a person never goes unrewarded got strengthened in my case on a number of occasions. *Shrimadbhagavdgita* had millenniums of years ago said - *na hi kalyanakrit kashchid durgatim tata gacchati* – verily my dear, a person of noble deeds never falls to bad days. And again in the manner of the teaching of the same book I considered my enjoined duty as the most important thing. And in the course of doing the same I never got deterred by extraneous considerations. Praise or criticism hardly mattered to me. Had not the celebrated Sanskrit poet Bhavabhuti, thousands of years ago declared? – *sarvatha vyavahartavyam kuto hi avachaniyata* – One should by all means do what was right, how can one be free from criticism or verbal censure of others.

I have learnt the hard way that patience is its own reward. Nature amply demonstrates it daily in its ways. The sun traverses (appears) across the horizon, patiently providing us with several of its hues and giving us clues of when and where to go to get our dues. The wind blows incessantly day and night wiping sweat from the brow of a weary traveler or producing musical sounds in a desolate forest. And if lessons in fortitude were to be learnt the good earth was there bearing the burden of animates and unanimated even as it was busy endlessly in the business of encircling the sun for much higher mission. The all-cleansing water is present there ever since before the emergence of this universe to teach us continuity and adaptability. The symbol of life and energy, the element Fire teaches us how one can always continue to be sought and yet remain unassailable. In fact these very elements of nature combined with the receptacle element of Space constitute the very essence of our being. As I advance in years these aspects offer a rich source of inspiration and key for understanding the secrets of life and its purpose. The Bible fascinated me as a young man and continues to fascinate today for its simple and yet shuttle language and pious thoughts contained therein. The Japuji Sahib resonated the wisdom of the Upanishads,

I find myself privileged to have continued access to good books through the libraries of Delhi University, Shivaji College and Maharaja Surajmal Institute. Of late I have developed interest in issues of history and sociology of the Jats. This new interest is a by product of my playing active role in the proceedings of the annual seminars on Jat history and sociology so ably organized by the Research and Publication Center of the Surajmal Memorial Education Society through the untiring efforts of its founder Director, the late Dr. Vir Singh. During these years I had occasions to critically go through the writings on the subject like K.R. Kanungo's '*History of the Jats*' (incidentally the pioneer authentic work on the subject), and Deshraj Thakur's Hindi book '*Jaton ka Itihas*'. I was left curious on the issue of the origin of the Jats. Later when I read B.S. Dahiya's '*Jats :The Ancient Rulers*' and Hukam Singh Panwar's *The 'Jats: Their Origin, Antiquity and Migrations*' I felt myself trapped as it were in a jungle of words weaved craftily in a rather arbitrary manner. Apparently both being Jats themselves, have played to the galleries, so to say, and with no holds barred as far as assumptions go. While the antiquity spade of Hukam Singh would dig in any where to find the Jats, no matter what perambulatory course his arguments take, Dahiya has an obsession with the letter 'J'(or any transformation) which is enough to lead him to find his subject any where and in any form, linguistic principles and etymological rules not being his problem. It took me several readings of both the above works over a number of years before calling it quits. While I value the hard work and sincerity of both the above authors in writing on Jats most sympathetically, I now find it difficult to go along with them in many propositions they have feigned to put forward.

The researches of the German Couple, Sigrid WestPhal-Heilbusch and Heinz Westphal published in their English monograph, *The 'Jats of Pakistan'* and the German work *'Zur Geschiste und Kultur der Jat'* nearly four decades ago gave me new insights on the subject, especially the identity of the Jats. Equally thoughtful and informative were the contributions being the outcome of the extensive field studies in Haryana by another German scholar, G.A. Tiemannm, published in reputed international journals. The incisive observations of Herbert Risley in his *People of India* and W. Crooke in his *Tribes and Castes of the North-Western Provinces* helped a good deal in making things clear on the subject of Jat identity. For the record I have put my findings in my recent book, *Jat, the Label and the People*.

The *Argumentative Indian*; and *Violence* and *Identities* the two recent titles penned by the Nobel Laureate, Amartya Sen have impressed me a great lot. While the former brings out different aspects of the great Indian intellectual tradition, the latter is a dispassionate exposition of the question of communal identities in the context of conflict. Sen vehemently rejects Huttington's theory of 'civilisational conflict' as the root cause of most terrorists coming from the Muslim world. Obviously Sen's world view is that of a humanist, a cut above the average thinker. He firmly holds that religious identity is just one of the many identities every human being has inherited and acquired. Sen's new book '*The Idea of Justice*' is another thoughtful title that has caught my imagination. To me it appears to be a philosophy of philosophies of justice.

I would like to mention here some of the other good books of general interest that I have had in my reading list, apart from the books on my subject of teaching and research (Sanskrit). Even a representative number is likely to be rather large and yet inadeqo choose to mention a few titles at random. Lala Hardayal's book,

Hints for Self Culture proved literally true to its title when I read it first during my formative years. I recommended it to all young men and women who would come into contact with me for gui dance. Equally rewarding was reading Ramdhari Singh Dinkar's compendium in Hindi on Indian culture, viz. *Sanskriti Ke Char Adhyaya. Thus Spake Zarathuthsara* impressed me in my youth so did the Reconstruction of Humanity by P. Shorokin. *The Second Sex* contained material on understanding the man woman relationship, together with a full discourse on the psychology of the two sexes.

Jordan's book on Rishi Dayananda, *The Tritavada of Rishi Dayananda* not only offered an authentic biography of the great Rishi but also brought out his philosophy in a succinct manner. I found *The Continent of Circe*, an authentic and lucid exposition of the course and result of the 'east ward migration of the Aryans'. I found V.S. Naipaul's, *Among the Believers;* and *India: A Million Mutinies Now*, both informative and engaging reading, the former a journey through the contemporary Muslim world and the latter a candid description of the twentieth century India marching ahead with all its turmoil and tribulations. Here, Naipaul, earlier a curt critic of India comes a clear pro. Naka Mora's *A Comparative History of Ideas* has continued to be on the top of my reading desk for many years now. *Tao of Physics* and *Hidden Connections* by Fritz of Capra have added to my understanding of the relationship (or connection) between Science and Mysticism. Reading biographies of Mahatma Gandhi, Jawaharlal Nehru, Sardar Vallabhbhai Patel, Babu Rajendra Prasad, Maulana Azad were a sort of Safari through the era of struggle for India's freedom. But Jawahar Lal Nehru's *Discovery of India* and *Glimpses of World History* turned out to be unique duo for a whole generation of young people wishing to understand India and also the world, at least up to better part of the first half of the twentieth century.

Among books of fiction in Hindi I would like to make a special mention of Agyeya's *Shekhar ek Jivani* and *Apne Apne Ajanabi*; Ilachand Joshi's *Sanyasi*; Shri Lal Shula's *Ragdarbari*; Hindi versions of Sharat Chandra's *Devdas*; Pratibha Rai's *Draupadi* (original *Yajnaseni* in Oriya); Premchamd's classics like *Godan* and *Nirmala*. It was quite an experience to read Hindi translation of Rabindra Nath Tagore's

Gitanjali. Going through parts of Yuan Chwang's account of India, and Al-Beruni's *Indika* in recent years has been helpful in placing in perspective several issues of Indian history which subject, in spite of losing its pride of place in the choices of the modern day students, has continued to fascinate me. The new book on Indian history that has caught my imagination is John Keay's *India, a History* published in U.S.A .in 2003 (revised in 2010). In this single well researched volume Keay has presented an objective and engaging narrative of India through the centuries which he rightly calls a history of histories. Lesley Hazeltene's recent book, the First Muslim has proved to be the most informative, educative and enlightening work that I ever read about Islam and its early history. The writer is a Jew lady and has done full justice to the delineation of life of Prophet Mohammad as a protagonist.

I wish to conclude with the vedic prayer:

Sarve bhavantu sukhinah, sarve santu niramayah /

Sarve bhadrani pashyantu, ma kashchid duhkhabhag bhavet //

Let all be happy, let all be healthy /

Let all see good things, let no one suffer //